EDUCATING
CITIZEN DESIGNERS
IN SOUTH AFRICA

Elmarie Costandius
Herman botes

SUN PRESS

Educating Citizen Designers in South Africa

Published by AFRICAN SUN MeDIA under the SUN PReSS imprint

This publication was subjected to an independent double-blind peer evaluation by the publisher.

The editors and the publisher have made every effort to obtain permission for and acknowledge the use of copyrighted material. Refer all enquiries to the publisher.

Views reflected in this publication are not necessarily those of the publisher.

First edition, first print 2018

ISBN 978-1-928357-72-8
ISBN 978-1-928357-73-5 (e-book)
DOI: 10.18820/9781928357735

Set in Gill Sans MT Light 9.5/13
Cover image: Artwork by Marthie Kaden and photograph by Ashley Walters.

SUN PReSS is a licensed imprint of AFRICAN SUN MeDIA. Scholarly, professional and reference works are published in print and electronic format under this imprint.

This publication can be ordered directly from:
www.sun-e-shop.co.za
africansunmedia.snapplify.com (e-books)
www.africansunmedia.co.za

Table of Contents

Preface

In an era of globalisation, design educators need to be fully engaged in order to restructure curricula so that they reflect the current needs of our societies. The creative and critical practice of teaching and generating design is instrumental in the creation of an imaginative and socially conscious citizenry. Moreover, it takes as a starting point the unequal social relations that characterise South African society and, within the educational context, the dominance of particular theoretical and intellectual paradigms that perpetuate inequality. The field of design is a fertile ground upon which to contest boundaries of social inclusion. Social and racial divisions speak through various layers of South African reality. This can be from the turmoil in the country's political realm, to its fragmented social geography and the lived experience and internal consciousness of its citizens. Education in general, and design in particular, should be sensitive to these tensions and facilitate their articulation in order to open them to transformation and thereby strengthen the social fabric. As is the case in many developing economies, the hard sciences and disciplines related to finance and economics take precedence over the social sciences in general, and the arts in particular. The instrumental value of the former disciplines and the professions they generate falls in line with the logic of capitalist development and national growth. However, strong arguments have been made for the importance of the 'softer' sciences, particularly in a country as culturally diverse, rapidly developing and challenged by its past as South Africa. *Educating citizen designers in South Africa* aims to share critical citizenship design teaching and learning pedagogies from a range of authors.

Elmarie Costandius and Neeske Alexander write from Stellenbosch University, giving an account of research on critical citizenship education since 2010. The aim of critical citizenship education is to promote social justice, shared values and critical thinking, which could lead to harmony in society. Costandius researched critical citizenship education in a practical way by applying it to the first- and third-year Visual Communication and Design curriculum at the Department of Visual Arts at Stellenbosch University. Power relations and structures, stereotyping and prejudice, and whiteness have surfaced as barriers to critical citizenship education. The strategies proposed for addressing these barriers include dialogue, community interaction, reflection and design as a medium of learning. Students', lecturers' and community members' reactions to these barriers and strategies are investigated.

Herman Botes, from the Tshwane University of Technology, applies a critical citizenship lens to the Graphic Design curriculum. A thorough explication of a proposed critical citizenship framework is investigated. The analytical critical citizenship framework as developed by Johnson and Morris (2010) is used as a theoretical framework for this investigation. Praxis/engagement with critical citizenship education, including skills from the political/ideological conception of critical citizenship education, is emphasised. In his chapter he maintains that the transformation of South African society will be advanced if design educators can capacitate design students with skills of critical and structural social analysis. Botes argues that students should investigate deeper causalities within society and experience academic freedom and that this freedom should accommodate the ability to politicise notions of culture, knowledge and power.

Rudolf Perold and Hermie Delport share and reflect on their experiences in live and design-build projects at the Design Build Research Studio, situated within the Department of Architectural Technology and Interior Design at the Cape Peninsula University of Technology. Since 2011, their work at the studio has supported both authors' doctoral research and continues to foster a space for architectural innovation, education and research. Design-build projects are educational spaces that enable the development of critical citizenship, with learning opportunities that challenge the existing notions of architectural (design) education and practice. These projects refocus the discipline of architecture from serving an elite minority to improving the quality of life of the majority with architectural design interventions and solutions. Perold and Delport present five community-situated live and design-build projects, all of which aim to make a positive difference in the lives of people through an architectural intervention based on collaborative practice. live and design-build projects are uniquely situated in architectural education, allowing them to cross several boundaries in the landscape of architectural practices. In crossing these boundaries, they are engaging in an emergent, more grounded architectural practice, which supports the principles of critical citizenship.

Amira Osman, currently with the Tshwane University of Technology, lectures in housing and urban policy. She writes from the context of South African university turmoil around the #FeesMustFall campaign and the demands for free decolonised education. Her teaching has revolved around the themes of housing and urban environments. She focuses on instilling the values of citizenship and design activism by emphasising the belief that design can make a difference in society. Architectural skills and a multidisciplinary approach are useful in this regard. Innovation is not necessarily embedded in the narrow confines of a single discipline, and mostly exists at the interface between disciplines. Osman presents architecture as a social act, based on social agreements, serving the needs of 'the individual' as well as 'the collective'. She combines learning goals and community service in a manner that aims towards knowledge exchange as opposed to knowledge transfer. Osman encourages a search for design and technical solutions through a deeper understanding of people, place and context, rather than deriving solutions in isolation, using abstract theories that may not have relevance to partner communities. In order to appreciate the unique characteristics of inner city and township settings, it is important to understand the inherited realities of post-apartheid South African cities.

Angus Donald Campbell and Ivan Leroy Brown write from the University of Johannesburg in the field of industrial design. They argue that the context of South Africa provides a multitude of opportunities for student designers to use their expertise to bring about change. However, to encourage positive outcomes, an appropriate pedagogy, strengthened through praxis and grounded in economic, social and environmental realities, is required to prepare students for critical and sustainable change making. Campbell and Brown explore the education of industrial designers in South Africa, utilising a 'potential difference' model for critical citizen design. This model considers stakeholder relationships as key to increasing people's capabilities through appropriate technology. This is contextualised through a case study of an appropriate technology beekeeping system for urban farmers in Johannesburg.

Brenden Gray critiques the neoliberal advancement of entrepreneurship as an application to design citizenship education. Specifically, he argues that the curricular activation of design students as 'creatives' creates a habitus resistant to critical citizenship and that the over-determination of the 'preneurial' habitus averts attention away from the causes of community problems, which necessarily stem directly and indirectly from capitalist domination. Gray reflects on the implications of entrepreneurship ideology in education regarding his experience of the undergraduate design project "Design for and with local communities" (at the University of Johannesburg). He maintains in his chapter that design educators who advocate critical citizenship must directly challenge the assumptions upon which neoliberalism is based, and that they should develop approaches in which students are encouraged to be activists working in partnership with communities to affect social change.

Fatima Cassim, from the University of Pretoria, focuses her research on experiential learning. She argues that design thinking has gained prominence within a widening domain today and is viewed as an alternate mode of enquiry to complement more traditional, analytical ways of thinking. Using Kees Dorst's argument on the core of design thinking as a point of departure, the nurturing of design thinking skills and practices in students, namely abductive thinking and framing, is considered. Cassim argues that experiential learning can facilitate design thinking in order to teach design students the importance of imbuing their work not only with good design values, but more significantly, with critical citizenship values. To this end, the chapter presents a theoretical argument from a design educator's vantage point for nurturing design thinking skills in students using a curriculum-related design-for-development project. The discussion is guided by the education philosophy of both John Dewey and Paulo Freire: the real world as the context of experience, the relationship between teachers and students and the experiential learning process (praxis).

Terence Fenn and Jason Hobbs from the University of Johannesburg state that the role of the designer as an intermediary between forces that affect design problems and the subsequent solutions is well established. When designers engage with complex problems, which are often illusive and subjectively indeterminate, this intermediary position can become fraught with the repercussions of decision making. A brief theoretical argument is provided for how criticality can be applied in the context of the changing nature of contemporary design. This theoretical position provides a background to the introduction and discussion of two novel design tools, the Firma Model and Experience-led Relationship Models. These models were designed by Fenn and Hobbs and were effectively applied in the work of third- and fourth-year Interaction Design students. Both the models and the theoretical discussion aim to aid design students in understanding the role and value of critical citizenship and human-centred design thinking in contemporary design practice.

Anika van den Berg, lecturing at VEGA School, a private higher education institution, posits that critical citizenship education inspires both educator and student to act on their courageous convictions. This complex theoretical landscape reaches beyond the norms of academic enquiry. While the affairs of state, of technology and of inequality set many South Africans on the course of collective victimhood, critical citizenship education leads young citizens towards collective hope. Students are seen as social beings designed to function interdependently in the community. Kinship and collaboration are cultivated through social learning, where students employ realistic ideation as they unravel authentic multi-layered problems. This bridges the gap between theoretical insight and practical implementation. Van den Berg posits in her chapter that a reliable academic foundation will steer students beyond generalised opinions towards the unexpected territory of empathy and active problem solving. This academic application is based on theories that unpack representation, cultural imperialism and post-modernisation. Power embedded in the media, ethnic stereotypes, the internet and imperial ideologies are considered within the context of citizenship.

Amollo Ambole offers a critical introspection of her PhD research experience as a designer in the South African context. What is unique about her experience is her dual identification as both an outsider and an insider in a complex multidisciplinary research process fraught with conflict. Ambole looks at her 'outsiderness' as a foreign student from Kenya, which she contrasts with her 'insiderness' when she, albeit in limited ways, was able to identify with the black consciousness of a post-apartheid South Africa. In her attempt to navigate this complexity, she inadvertently became a critical citizen designer. She sought emancipation and resolution, not just for herself, but also for the South African condition. In the end, she did not find a perfect resolution, but was able to articulate her research journey in a way that is theoretically significant. She offers key concepts of co-production, voice and reflection as considerations for critical citizenship learning practice. Ambole uses a highly subjective approach that she states may seem self-indulgent at first, but is a useful self-reflexive approach that contributes to the growing call for critical global citizenship.

The final chapter by Karolien Perold-Bull aims to provide a theoretical exploration of the notion of design and its concomitant education from posthuman perspectives. During the aftermath of apartheid, transformation has come to signify the change necessary to right the wrongs of the past. Perold-Bull argues that despite the extreme complexity involved in the negotiation of this kind of change, the dominant transformation discourse seems to rely on dualistic logic. Within this ideological frame of reference, the notion of critical citizenship has gained strength, and education considered as a process of emancipation driven by humans has been dominantly regarded as an effective medium to help drive the realisation of democratic ideals. In contrast to such a teleological interpretation of transformation, Perold-Bull holds that acknowledgement of our posthuman condition can facilitate productive change. She consequently argues for an ontological shift in terms of how we think about design, how we do design, and how we ultimately negotiate design in the realm of education. Instead of asking how to educate *for* citizenship, she believes the central question should be how we can harness the productive power of ontological design *within* the context of South Africa through its education. Such a shift can challenge and extend the anthropocentric tendencies within the notion of critical citizenship education and provide a possible way forward in the field of South African design education.

The aim of this book is to contribute to the critical citizenship discourse by offering a South African perspective. It is not a fully representative account of the South African context, but serves as a point of departure for the promotion of critical citizenship design education and beyond in South African institutions.

Exploring Barriers and Strategies for Critical Citizenship Education: A Reflection on Practice

ELMARIE COSTANDIUS AND NEESKE ALEXANDER[1]

Introduction

Engaging critical citizenship education requires an involved perspective. Boland and McIlrath (2007: 84–85) describe the action of engaged teaching, learning and curricula development as follows:

> Engagement infers mutual listening, reciprocity and dialogue which is focused on something beyond the self. It comprehends both a promise of action and the outcome of action. ... Engagement is full of potential, promise, risk and uncertainty, often because it entails a willingness to change. It entails accommodating the other and preparedness to be transformed in the process.

Barnett and Coate (2005) stress that, even though a curriculum can be considered as engaged, it is only via 'pedagogies of engagement', through teaching strategies and pedagogical relationships between students and lecturers, that critical citizenship education can be realised. There is a relationship between knowing and being, and Barnett, Parry and Coate (2001) argue that, apart from the knowledge and skills that are developed in education, one should also look at the person of the student and the lecturer. Barnett and Coate (2005) propose the idea of a curriculum as engagement and use the three building blocks of knowing, acting and being. They argue that "an act of knowing is a positional and personal act" and "an act of knowledge calls for a public act in which the individual shows herself, proclaims herself" (Barnett & Coate, 2005: 60). Knowledge therefore involves the personal and the social. The concept of the self, being or becoming, is emphasised, which relates to self-realisation, self-confidence and self-understanding (Barnett & Coate, 2005). Critical citizenship education cannot be developed without considering the diversity of the inner lives of students and lecturers, even more so because of the traumatic past in South Africa. Barnett and Coate (2005) stress that the forms of life that are encouraged these days are much more 'being-in-the-world', rather than 'being-in-knowledge'. Being resilient and emotionally sustaining in the world becomes

---

[1] Elmarie Costandius facilitated the critical citizenship projects. Neeske Alexander is a former master's student who assisted in writing the chapter.

more and more important and this calls for not only content and field-specific knowledge, but also more of a "curriculum of life" (Barnett & Coate, 2005: 119) that prepares students academically, socially and emotionally.

According to Johnson and Morris (2010: 77–78), citizenship education is based on the promotion of a "common set of shared values (e.g. tolerance, human rights and democracy), which prepare young people to live together in diverse societies and which reject the divisive nature of national identities". Citizenship education "contributes to the promotion of social justice, social reconstruction and democracy" (Johnson & Morris, 2010: 78). However, what is lacking in this definition is a critical perspective. The word 'critical' is added to citizenship education and therefore includes critical thinking and critical pedagogy (Johnson & Morris, 2010). Apart from critical citizenship education, a variety of other conceptual formations exists, for instance multicultural, democratic, political, pacifist, global, moral, anti-racist, humanising and reconciliatory education. Multicultural, intercultural, political or democratic citizenship education is often closely related to critical citizenship (Keet, Zinn & Porteus, 2009; Nussbaum, 2006; Waghid, 2010).

Critical citizenship projects were introduced and implemented from February 2010 to November 2015 for first- to third-year Visual Communication Design students at the Department of Visual Arts at Stellenbosch University. Before the introduction of the critical citizenship components, social transformation issues were often mentioned, but they were implicit and never directly addressed in my modules of the Visual Communication Design curriculum.[2] Action learning and action research (ALAR) was used as the teaching and learning methodology for the critical citizenship projects, thereby enabling students, lecturers and community members to actively participate. The theoretical framework or lens that guides the ALAR process entails grounded theory (raw data and contextual knowledge), personal construct theory (active constructors of knowledge), critical theory (self-critical attitudes) and systems theory (holistic resolutions to complex problems) (Zuber-Skerritt, 2001). The aim was not to arrive at generalisations, but to get to know, understand and enhance social transformation for the benefit of all participants. My critical citizenship projects consisted of readings, conversations with community members outside the university environment, group work, structured reflections and the use of the content of conversations as inspiration for design layouts. These strategies are discussed in this chapter. However, before strategies are discussed, the barriers to critical citizenship teaching and learning need to be explored. The specific barriers and strategies were chosen because they were used and presented while facilitating the critical citizenship projects. They were identified as the most crucial barriers and strategies in the critical citizenship educational learning context, although other barriers might exist that have not been identified and considered yet. Three barriers and five strategies will be discussed in the following section.

---

[2]   Several lecturers teach in the Visual Communication Design curriculum and I cannot comment on the modules taught by the other lecturers. I therefore specifically state that I am referring to the modules taught by me.

Barriers to critical citizenship education

Power relations and structures

Foucault (1998: 93) remarks that "power is everywhere, not because it embraces everything, but because it comes from everywhere". He argues that each discourse, at base, is structured on power relations. We cannot escape power relations. "[P]ower is not an institution, and not a structure; neither is it a certain strength we are endowed with; it is the name that one attributes to a complex strategical situation in a particular society" (Foucault, 1978: 93). Power often comes in a subtle form; one that is mobile and transitory and that forms a dense web with the potential to shift society, fracturing unities physically and mentally. Foucault (1998) proposes that people are regulated by socio-cultural processes that make them knowable and therefore controllable, and warns that people start to regulate their behaviour to conform to pre-established ideas. Such regulated behaviour then becomes the norm.

The identity constructions of the colonised in Africa were adjusted and manipulated by the colonisers, and the same situation manifested during apartheid. The identities of both colonised/oppressed and the coloniser/oppressor were formed in the process (Fanon, 2006). Identity transformation always involves processes of power. The individual has the power to define him-/herself, to form identity stereotypes of others, to contest power domination, to resist stereotypes and to refuse to accept social conceptions (Ratele & Duncan, 2007). However, despite the power of the individual, it is in the interest of a dominant group to keep social hierarchies in place. Hegemony, as described by Gramsci (1971, cited in Macey, 2000), occurs where power and control are achieved through consensus and not force.

Kumashiro (2000: 32) also suggests that the "knowledge many students have about the Other is … incomplete because of exclusion, invisibility, and silence". What makes these partial knowledges so problematic is that they are often taught through the informal or 'hidden' curriculum (Jackson, Boostrom & Hanson, 1993), which means that they carry more educational significance than the official curriculum because they are taught indirectly, pervasively and often unintentionally (Jackson et al., 1993). By not considering the hidden curriculum, we could maintain current power structures.

Jansen (2009) emphasises the pervasive ignorance of and silence about the past, especially referring to his experience as dean of Education at the University of Pretoria. Giddens (1984) differentiates between discursive consciousness (what we can talk about) and practical consciousness (actions that are subconsciously carried out and not verbalised because they are 'hidden' in the subconscious). Jansen (2009: 171) also refers to the hidden information as the "knowledge in the blood" or "indirect knowledge". This hidden information could also be suppressed information that a person hides because of fear of the emotions that accompany this information. These sensitive issues could be volatile. Our critical citizen projects, and specifically the community interactions, were aimed at breaking the silence on such sensitive issues by obtaining more perspectives. It would be beneficial for all people to open up sensitive issues; Freire and Shor (1987: 123), for example, describe the phrase "culture of silence" as "passive tolerance of domination".

A problem-posing educational approach was suggested by Freire (1975), in which students become active participants in creating and negotiating knowledge, and are not relegated to a position of only receiving knowledge. Freire (1975: 143) referred to the negative effects of "banking education", where students become the containers and therefore "adapt to the world of oppression". Giroux (1985) argues that the new sociology of education challenges the claim that knowledge is objective. He states that knowledge is a "particular representation of the dominant culture, one that was constructed through a selective process of emphasis and exclusions" (Giroux, 1985: xv). In the same vein, Apple (1979) argues that texts for educational purposes are shaped to be politically acceptable – for instance, in terms of meeting the demands of the economy. He states that texts have multiple interpretations, but some are more preferred or have greater influence. According to Weedon (1987), education is geared towards the requirements of a specific educational institution, informed by the values, modes and preferences of the dominant group. Weedon (1987) remarks in this respect that at the centre of the apparatus of power lies the education system.

Stereotyping and prejudice

Stereotyping can be described as a conservative, fixed and oversimplified perception of an individual or group. In daily social interaction, our acts of cooperation, competition, helping or aggression (Trope & Gaunt, 2003) mainly depend on our perceptions or impressions of others. We constantly assess a person in our mind and subconsciously categorise the person in groupings with which we are familiar. Devine (1989) argues that we automatically categorise other people, but with different outcomes depending on whether we are aware of the action and whether self-reflection occurs when categorising. Devine's (1989) research also shows how people unconsciously categorise and stereotype other people, even if they do not believe in stereotypes, and to what extent this still affects their perceptions. The categories could be of race, class, gender or language, among others. In a South African context, racial prejudice is specifically prominent because of the apartheid classification of race according to skin colour. The categories that we have in our minds, according to Trope and Gaunt (2003), are socially constructed and pre-existing, and the result of the categorisation could determine our actions, emotions, motivations or behaviour.

Categorising could be of either the out-group or the in-group. The latter behaviour is also called self-stereotyping (Wright & Taylor, 2003). Self-stereotyping occurs when members of a group assign categories to themselves that distinguish them from others. This is often used as justification for their particular behaviour. A study by Clark (2001) of the relationship between racial and gender stereotypes and self-concept found that black and white students expressed an ethnocentric bias towards their own racial group. The views of the out-group can be adopted, but such adoption does not necessarily lead to self-rejection of the in-group. Negative stereotypes of, for example, students' own in-group could be expressed when evaluating the group, but when evaluating themselves as individuals, these are overlooked.

Leibowitz, Booi, Daniels, Loots, Richards and Van Deventer (2005) analysed the biographies of lecturers to explore the concept of an African university. The main argument in their study focused on the recognition of difference, and stressed the need to guard against stereotyping people according to race and gender. This exploration of lecturers' biographies forced the lecturers to reflect on their own expectations and their own stereotyping of students and of themselves.

Perceptions influence expectations of others and ourselves. The expectations or beliefs that lecturers have about students could influence classroom practices. If a lecturer has low expectations of a student from a certain class, race or gender, it would influence the actions of both lecturer and student. Studies by Clifford and Walster (1973) and Kuh (2003) point out that high expectations of a student could influence the academic success of that student. Jamar and Pitts (2005) stress that lecturers' perceptions of students' abilities are not changed by merely implementing policies regarding multiculturalism and equality. It is the fundamental belief system of the lecturer that forms the basis of expectations of students, regardless of the policies or regulations that are in place (Jamar & Pitts, 2005). Stereotyping is often ingrained in one's mind and does not suddenly change when a government system changes. Ingrained stereotypical perceptions are often subconscious and therefore could influence the teaching, learning and construction of a curriculum in subtle and complex ways.

Reflection on whiteness

Whiteness as a field of study has only recently been established explicitly in post-colonial studies. Lopez (2005) refers to Fanon and Bhabha, who explicitly discuss the relationship between race and white power. He also highlights the status of whiteness and the persistence and transformation in the contemporary post-colonial world – also in places such as South Africa. Lopez (2005: 4) for instance asks "what happens to whiteness … after it loses its colonial privileges?" In a South African context, Steyn (2005: 133) reflects on whiteness as a complex hybrid identity and urges a "continuing need to build self-reflexivity amongst white people". The influence of whiteness on the teaching and learning environment could still be prevalent in subtle ways.

Vice (2010) wrote a self-reflection on whiteness from a white perspective, urging white people in South Africa to be humble and not to perpetuate whiteness. Snyman (2008) remarks that what makes white identity problematic is that it is taken as the norm and black as the other. He also remarks that this perception will not change before whiteness is not critically analysed within whiteness itself. Dowdy, Givens, Murillo, Shenoy and Villenas (2000) point out that white Western educational privilege is often disguised as the 'norm'. Coming to terms with whiteness is one of the aspects that require closer consideration, specifically within the context of learning and teaching in higher education.

Leonardo (2004) advocates neo-abolitionist pedagogy, which suggests that lecturers and students work together to name, as well as to reflect on, historical and current contexts and to dismantle supremacy discourses of whiteness. Neo-abolitionism does not entail denying whiteness (Leonardo, 2004), but lecturers and students of all races have to work together actively to unpack multiculturalism. Leonardo (2004: 132) emphasises that global pedagogy and neo-abolitionism "are not only acts of free speech but of praxis".

According to Santas (2000), many white educators fail when teaching about racism, blackness and whiteness because of their paternalistic impulses. Santas (2000) maintains that there is a built-in assumption in some white people that black people need to be cared for and treated like children. They are "perceived as inferior, epistemically, organizationally, and even morally, to their would-be saviors" (Santas, 2000: 349). This internalised sense of superiority is strengthened if not critically analysed and questioned by people and institutions. Teaching about racism is then "doubly prone to failure because the internalised superiority of the teacher as 'all-knowing teacher' is most often coupled with that of 'well meaning white person'" (Santas, 2000: 349–350).

In facilitating critical citizenship, the assumption is that the facilitator is emotionally ready and able to handle sensitive discussions of issues such as whiteness. For a lecturer of any race, reflecting on and learning about the self are vital for facilitating transformative learning in students.

Strategies for critical citizenship education

Dialogue and discussion

Socratic discussions are based on questions that create a space for the discussion partners to see the truth for themselves (Rowe, 2005). Socrates was aware of his own lack and therefore searched for others who might possess the knowledge. He was searching for essence and not examples, and used the method of refutation where his discussions ended in *aporie* (insoluble contradiction) that should encourage further philosophising (Sluiter, 2007). In an educational sense it refers to "learning as searching ... that there are truths out there, as it were, waiting to be discovered, deciphered and interpreted" (Rowe, 2005: 6). Although Socrates could be considered the father of Western moral philosophy, similar methods were utilised in many other parts of the world. The Indian concept of Samvad, which means dialogue or reasoning, for instance, refers to the long "argumentative and dialogic tradition transgressing gender, caste, economic, political and religious divides" (Samvad Dialogue, 2011: n.p.). This type of dialogue process enables many layers of complexity and richness that can function at the same time. The dialogic method can be successfully used when many voices and a variety of opinions need to be heard. Dialogues are used in negotiating boundaries but also "to resolve conflicts, to build consensus, to elevate understanding, to consolidate different perspectives, to push accepted boundaries, to interrogate, to introspect, to inquire" (Samvad Dialogue, 2011: n.p.).

Schuitema, Ten Dam and Veugelers (2008), in their review of various moral educational programmes, found that the Socratic method of discussing was used in most programmes/projects. Leading the students through questions to a 'right answer' could be considered as not very student-centred because the educator could enforce his/her own views by deciding what is right and wrong. "It is plausible that they [the students] will quickly understand what the 'right' and 'wrong' answers are, without learning to form, evaluate and discuss their own opinions" (Schuitema et al., 2008: 77). An alternative would be to encourage diversity in answers and conclusions and use the Socratic method for scaffolding (Frick, Albertyn & Rutgers, 2010). Saye (1998) and Tredway (1995) use an 'indirect approach' where one is not committed to one answer. Tredway (1995) argues that, by using the indirect approach, students develop critical thinking skills, but also cultivate respectful, tactful and caring attitudes and behaviour. Students should be enabled to do their own learning and be involved in knowledge building.

Three important stages in undoing unequal power relations and racism are suggested by Santas (2000: 359), namely "de-centering dialogue, building classroom community, and institutionalizing peer accountability". According to Santas (2000: 359), real dialogue "requires radical equality, a breaking down of barriers in such a way that painful truth will invariably come out. Yet truth rarely flows freely in settings in which a single power controls the discourse". Often in classrooms "dialogue … almost always centres on the teacher, who wields power by virtue of grades, authority and eloquence, and who is trained to keep things under control" (Santas, 2000: 358). However, even in small-group discussions where the lecturer is not present, there will always be some hierarchies of, for instance, race and gender, but at least it could be more personal and students' own voices could be heard. Building trust in these groups is crucial (Santas, 2000).

Tappan (1998) argues that students should learn about morality as a cultural practice of participation, and not only learn how to reason about morality. In discussions aimed at transformative learning, students and educators should negotiate and compromise. To compromise is not to obey and conform, but to realise that solutions need to be found for the benefit of all; this could mean giving up something that is important to yourself because you realise that it only benefits a small minority. Students and lecturers are encouraged to listen carefully to different voices and to learn how to feel empathy for others. Consensus regarding the content of social responsibility and citizenship might not be reached, but the aim of the conversations is to open up social issues that are normally silenced (Jansen, 2009).

The risk of perpetuating issues such as power relations and skewed perceptions in these conversations is an aspect that one should be aware of all the time. Taylor (2007) stresses that if issues such as authority, role, gender, power, influence, status and levels of collaboration are not open for discussion in class, the chance of what he calls 'whole-person learning' taking place is very small. Kumashiro (2000: 34) argues that "[l]earning about and hearing the Other should be done not to fill a gap in knowledge … but to disrupt the [harmful/partial] knowledge that is already there".

For discussion of sensitive social issues to take place, a safe space where participants can communicate freely without being labelled needs to be agreed on and created. A safe space for students means a space where what is said in conversations will not be held against them and will not affect their marks. Waghid (2010) refers to safe speech that does not enhance growth; a safe space should not mean safe speech. The safe space is necessary because our ability to self-reflect is vulnerable to influences such as ideology, tradition, habit, authority and institutionally imposed structures.

Community interaction

Community interaction as a teaching methodology is associated with the philosophy of experiential learning (Dewey, 1951) or learning through experience. Dewey (1951) refers in this regard to activities that involve the mind and the hands as reflective activities. Gitterman (1988: 33) makes a distinction between students "knowing that" and "knowing how", and also emphasises encouraging students to find the fleeting connections between the abstract and the real world. Morgan and

Streb (2001: 167) argue that community interaction can indeed build better citizens when people have "authentic experiences that can break down barriers as opposed to artificial experiences that are often brief in duration and lack intensity and personal contact".

Community interaction is not a mental experience only, but also a bodily experience, and attempts to deal with issues such as racism that could benefit from addressing them in a mental, bodily and symbolic manner (Hook, 2004). Bickmore (2001: 159–160) stresses that "critical thinking and participatory problem solving simply cannot be learned without opportunities to practice – to critique and address meaningful problems, such as the reasons for violence and the system of justice for handling it". Experiencing mental and bodily discomfort when dealing with sensitive issues such as racism is a good space for starting critical self-reflection and change. Leibowitz, Bozalek, Rohleder, Carolissen and Swartz (2010) argue that discomfort can serve as pedagogy for change.

Because experiential learning in the form of community interaction could be a very powerful learning experience, it is crucial to critically assess what is happening in the interactions. Some perceptions and attitudes could be confirmed and perpetuated in the interactions and conversations, instead of shifted. By taking community interaction simplistically or as an action without critically reflecting on it, interactions would remain at the superficial level. Community interaction in itself might not change perceptions positively, because the objectives can vary from political engagement or critical thinking to fostering respect for social differences or fostering caring attributes (Schuitema et al., 2008). Morgan and Streb (2001: 166) argue that there could be cases in which a community interaction or service-learning approach "does not help everyone equally; perhaps it increases the gaps in citizenship that may exist already based on race, gender, academic performance, or engagement in school".

The way in which community interactions are structured is important: It should not be a situation that includes givers and receivers only, but should aim at a mutual exchange of giving and receiving. Community interaction is often connected with the ideas of helping behaviour. Bhattacharyya (2004) argues that helping behaviour could perpetuate relations of dependency, therefore the concept of working with and not for communities should be followed. Gibbons (2005) similarly refers to a new type of contract between society and science where society has a voice and can speak back.

Unfacilitated learning groups, where students and community members self-manage their group process and undertake collaborative learning tasks, are increasingly being used in service-learning curricula in higher education (Lizzio & Wilson, 2005). Although the success of student and community learning groups varies considerably in terms of member satisfaction and quality of educational outcomes (Lizzio & Wilson, 2005), there are many advantages to group work as a teaching and learning strategy. According to Bourner, Hughes and Bourner (2001), group work may positively influence skills development through experience and more effective, in-depth knowledge acquirement. This is achieved by students taking some of the responsibility of learning upon themselves and becoming active rather than passive learners (Bourner et al., 2001). Group work further provides an opportunity for students to develop skills needed for lifelong learning (Bourner et al., 2001), such as teamwork, communication, leadership and project management (Davies, 2009).

Reflection

For Jaspers (1963), self-reflection includes self-observation, self-revelation and self-understanding and Habermas (1978) defines reflection as practising critical self-determination. Mezirow (1998), on the other hand, suggests that meaningful personal and social transformation may result from self-reflection to benefit ethical and moral development and Schön (1987: 21) maintains that reflection is a consistent process of self-involvement in what he calls "reflection in action".

The value and function of the process of self-reflection are described extensively in literature, but the actual process that takes place in one's mind when reflecting is still underexplored in the field of teaching and learning, although it is currently being explored with new technology within the field of neurology. The relationship between a person's conscious and unconscious mind is still being researched (Jarvis, 2006; Schön, 1987), and has been shown to be a closer relationship than has been realised. Massumi (1995) argues that affect is when our bodies react spontaneously and unconsciously on an impulse before our thinking brain can make sense of that reaction, and the emotion comes after that. Massumi (1995) says that affect is a matter of autonomic responses that are occurring below the threshold of consciousness and cognition and are rooted in the body. Snaza and Weaver (2014) even propose embodiment as more important than consciousness and embodied learning as effective as cognitive learning. Consciousness that was associated with primarily the brain is now considered as embodied or distributed (Nayar, 2013). Yip (2007: 294) argues that "[t]he gap between the intended mindfulness and unintended unconscious is lessened by a spontaneous self-reflection".

Dewey (1910, cited in Bringle & Hatcher, 1999) points out that a place of discomfort is the point where reflection starts. Kolb (1984) believes in integrating emotional experience with reflection, and explains that experience alone does not teach. Mezirow's (1991: 29) theory of transformative learning puts critical reflection at its core, as it brings "assumptions, premises and criteria into consciousness". Kayes (2002: 5, 6) describes the cognitive approach to learning as leading towards simplification, but maintains that the reflective approach to learning "leads towards complicatedness". Self-reflection is also a "self-constructed process that is influenced by social, cultural, political and organizational contexts" (Yip, 2007: 296) and therefore it is an important practice for both students and lecturers.

Design as medium for learning

Wesley (2007: 13) contends that art could generate a special "sacred learning space" that is conducive to emotional growth and creates multiple ways of learning and knowing. She adds that arts participation is an "underused way of coming to know and value the diversity in our complex, interrelated, and changing world" (Wesley, 2007: 13). Gibbons (2005: 8) refers to a "boundary object" – neutral objects that serve as a temporary medium to create the conditions that open up the space for deeper emotions. In the same way that technology can be a boundary object, art practice could also be used as a boundary object, as it can serve as a medium to express feelings and in that way helps a person to come to terms with real and hidden emotions

Dewey (1958) highlights the critical and social function of art and argues that the process of design or creativity is found in all human actions. Theory and practice are integrated in praxis, where praxis refers to learning by doing, reflection-in-action or reflective practice (Schön, 1987). Praxis in our critical citizenship projects includes creative practical activities such as drawings and photo documentations. The creative process of compiling data randomly and forcing new meanings by putting sensory and visual imagery together is a way of finding alternative or unexpected solutions and creating new meanings. In this creative process of making variations of meanings it is pointed out that there could be a variety of solutions, but all the variations could be valid. Students could be more emotionally involved in their assignments because activities such as drawing and acting involve them physically as well as mentally; this acts as an embodied experience, and learning involving the body and the mind has the potential to be more effective than cognitive learning alone.

Methodology

For this study I worked with an interpretative lens (cf. Klein & Meyers, 1999). An interpretive lens on knowledge requires reflection on how data are socially constructed and a sensitivity to contradictions, interpretations, distortions and biases of the narratives generated (Klein & Meyers, 1999). I used a case study research design (cf. Creswell, 2003) that was aimed at exploring and providing an in-depth investigation of the critical citizenship projects. A case study allows the researcher to work out why events or phenomena occur the way they do, so that changes that are grounded in past instances and experiences can be made. To enable this, a detailed investigation was necessary to understand the particulars of the case within the South African, Stellenbosch University and Visual Communication Design curriculum contexts.

Written reflections were used as the main source of data, while semi-structured interviews were conducted with students, lecturers and community members. The reflective writing that students, lecturers and community members undertook followed the affective-cognitive model (Du Plessis & Smith-Tolken, 2009), a model that was developed and used at the Department of Sociology of Stellenbosch University. It involves describing emotions within a theoretical context (connected to library research). Inductive content analysis was utilised to analyse the data. The research sample consisted of all the students, lecturers and community members involved in the critical citizenship projects: seven black students, ten coloured students, one Indian student, eighty-one white students, thirty-five community members and one lecturer, besides me. The aim of the study inevitably was not to generalise, but to provide an in-depth exploration of the phenomena that became visible during the investigation. Ethical clearance for this research project was obtained from the Research Ethics Committee: Human Research (Humanities) of Stellenbosch University.

The critical citizenship projects required students to use action learning (cf. Zuber-Skerritt, 2001) to collect data from community members in Kayamandi, Idas Valley and Cloetesville. The projects were structured so that the students would have discussions with community members about certain topics such as power relations, stereotyping and gender, or about their lives, such as in the "See Kayamandi, see yourself", "Action research: Learning life skills in Kayamandi" and "Die Vlakte" projects, to enable students to 'put themselves in the shoes of others' – Nussbaum's 'narrative imagination' (2002). The reactions of different students and community members often varied, in that one felt positive and another negative about the same experience, for example. This variety is not fully reflected in this chapter because of the word limitation.

Engaging in research is a constructivist process. While I was doing the research, I realised that I was constructing a 'reality' that could be different from someone else's reality. It is the nature of interpretative studies that the researcher's ontology and epistemology play a crucial role in the interpretation of the data (Henning, 2004). I am politically, socially and emotionally involved in this research and it often makes me uncomfortable. It is also my own journey and I could possibly be exposing my own subjectivity and naivety in this process. According to McIlrath and MacLabhrainn (2007: 84–85), engaging in teaching and curricula is "full of potential, promise, risk and uncertainty, often because it entails a willingness to change … and preparedness to be transformed in the process".

Data and discussion

In this section we present and discuss the data collected from the critical citizenship projects, aiming to reflect on the barriers of critical citizenship education and strategies used in the teaching and learning process. I chose the data excerpts that were the most prominent and that I considered relevant to the teaching of critical citizenship education in the curriculum. The barriers resulting from power relations and structures, stereotyping and prejudice, and whiteness are addressed by the proposed strategies, namely dialogue, community interaction, reflection and design as medium for learning.

Dialogue

Dialogue and discussion are affected by power relations and structures when there is an imbalance in power between those involved in the dialogue. Allowing open dialogue and discussion gives power to participants because their voices are heard. Dialogue and discussion can reveal stereotypes and prejudice and can address these issues. Related to both power and stereotypes is the presence of whiteness in dialogue. White people may feel very uncomfortable when discussing apartheid or related issues due to feelings of guilt. Below are some examples where participants felt that dialogue was uncomfortable, but necessary for understanding. Participants also noted how language and phrases can hinder dialogue.

Student 2 found dialogue challenging, but powerful:

> I personally struggled a lot with engaging in conversation with people about the history of [apartheid], for it made me extremely uncomfortable and self-conscious, but after conversation, interviews, presentations and a lot of writing, I now acknowledge and realise the power of confronting and really dealing with an uncomfortable situation ...

Participants felt that dialogue 'opened their eyes' to the reality of the topic at hand. Student 31 said: "I am guilty of living in a bubble. A bubble of safeness against the harsh reality of the world." Many students, through discussions, described how they can now see the topic and its underlying issue much more clearly after opening up through dialogue with the community involved:

> For the first time I could really speak out and give my opinion and I am grateful for the opportunity. Because it is not easy to talk about lasting issues like the shadow of apartheid or skeletons in the closet, my eyes where opened to my responsibility for the future. (S7)

Through dialogue, students discovered stereotyping in the community members' lives. Student 4, for instance, stated as follows:

> The topic of racial stereotypes is still evident in Kayamandi. He admits that the Kayamandi community associates white people with wealth, whereas they associate the black community with danger, bad psyches and immoral people. [Name of person] is also stereotyped according to his race as he feels that "the black person is always a suspect".

Language and the use of certain phrases can hinder dialogue and discussion. Student 5 said the following:

> Well, the thing is … I know it's an Afrikaans university … but then again the language thing, sometimes I feel like excluded and … I know okay, they [are] also supposed to speak their language, Afrikaans and stuff, but then … let's say you are working in a group and then you have someone that does not understand Afrikaans, I think they should also be considerate. I'm not saying don't speak Afrikaans, I'm just saying try to make that person feel … welcome and stuff. I feel excluded … I'd have to ask someone to translate for me … then I don't feel a part of the group.

Student 33 remarked as follows:

> Take out words like tolerance and human rights, and all those things which have old South Africa connotations. And we are 17 years on now, and we have to look for new words to describe what we [are] actually trying to move towards.

Community interaction

The community interactions comprised actual and active exposure for students, lecturers and community members, compared to studying in the library, which does not necessarily produce the same emotional response. Student 49 said: "It dawned on us as a group that we were not working with a usual source like Google for our research, but with human beings, who have feelings, perceptions and sensitive histories of their own." Community interaction allowed the students to fully appreciate the topic of the project beyond its academic significance:

> It is now that I understand the profundity in the simple research conducted at Kayamandi; it allows for an internal inspection of your own situation through others, the people you thought were so different from you. The knowledge shared and gained goes beyond the simple bounds of a project or a mark … (S28)

The barriers of power relations, stereotyping and whiteness can be addressed through community interaction. An imbalance in power could be perpetuated through community interaction when notions of superiority and charity are present. Community interaction can also dissolve power differences when all involved are equal partners in a project. Student 71 felt that critical citizenship education is associated with charity. Student 34 noticed a shift in power when participants from the township community were allowed to contribute (and not only 'receive').

> [Critical citizenship education] is the typical definition of something that is associated with community work and social work and charity. (S71)

> One has to guard against … viewing the white person as the 'saviour' figure, and the black students as those in need of saving – especially when the scene playing out in front of you seems to reinforce those exact stereotypes. The interview with my project partners served in flipping this relationship, though. By

asking them the research question of the day ("What skill can you teach me?"), the power to give was placed in their hands. And they grabbed it with both hands. (S34)

The issue of stereotyping surfaced and was addressed during community interaction. When reading an article about the damaging effects of stereotyping in class or at home, it is easy to agree that stereotyping is bad. It is a different experience, however, when faced with one's own stereotypical ideas within a community interaction context. Devein (1989) argues that although we might not believe in stereotyping, we spontaneously categorise people, but that the important issue is whether we become aware of and reflect on the action. During the critical citizenship project, Student 6 remarked: "A reason for visiting this area has never revealed itself to me and to be honest my own internal fears and stereotypical attitude towards Kayamandi are to blame." Student 68 commented:

> In all honesty I can say that I was very sceptical when we received our design brief at first. But I was pleasantly surprised by our visit to the Kayamandi township. This helped me break down my own preconceived idea of the township and its way of functioning.

Whiteness and race were evident as barriers to critical citizenship education during community interaction. Many white students had never been to a township before and they felt like tourists. Black students who grew up in a township struggled with simultaneously feeling like an outsider and an insider.

> It felt as if we were tourists exploring a foreign country on our first touring of the Kayamandi area. I found that the conditions within which they live are so different to my own, although I live a mere 10 km away. (S27)

> It was a bit difficult for me to spot things in Kayamandi that some people might find strange, because I grew up in the township. Once in a while I had to try to step outside myself, and view Kayamandi like a tourist or someone who grew up in suburbs. I started appreciating the little things about the place, like how the people built their shacks, because it shows creativity and it is only they that can build shacks [on] a small piece of land … (S26)

The feeling of being a tourist or foreigner and the curiosity that was evoked when visiting a new place can be understood because of our divided past and the current status quo, which has not changed much. However, it could border on the concept of the 'exotic tourist' or the 'exotic gaze' (Urry, 2001). Fanon (1952) also refers to the 'white gaze' and the 'fascination with the poor or exotic'. If the interaction remains on the level of fascination, actual reflective learning could be hampered. Feelings of distance and fear also surfaced.

Student 77 remarked as follows:

> It is hard to navigate my way through a relationship that is 'work' and 'academic', but wanting to be sincere about my enquiries and wanting to be his friend. At the same time I am uncertain about w[h]ether it is appropriate for him to SMS/call me, and that makes me feel like I AM not really his friend, I am actually just a strange, white student who doesn't want to get too close?

Another student, S55, said: "It occurred to me that everyone seems to be boxed into their own communities and have a fear [of] getting involved with others." Student 41 remarked: "My classmates are too scared to go to the township."

Community interaction can be an effective strategy for addressing the barriers inherent in critical citizenship education, but care has to be taken. Participants should guard against superiority and a charity mindset. Within community interaction the different identities and racial contexts of participants should be respectfully considered. When participants feel excluded, afraid or uncertain they should have the opportunity to voice these feelings. Spaces for confronting own stereotyping thoughts and actions should be created (here reflection can be effective).

Reflection

The practice of reflection allows participants to recognise barriers such as power relations, stereotyping and prejudice, and whiteness. Students often found the process challenging, but also very useful for observing changes and gathering ideas and solutions.

Reflection uncovered hidden prejudices and stereotypes. Practically, the process of reflection allows students to first experience the negative affective response, and then to rework it in a way that offers resolution without denial. As a process, reflection is invaluable in teaching critical thinking. It is certainly not a pleasant experience for students, lecturers and community members to reflect on and become aware of their own biased views. For me, being directly involved with these projects, it is not always pleasant either. One realises one's own limitations, but one also reflects on things such as "Maybe I can teach Visual Communication Design without these uncomfortable moments" and "Should I put myself through this?" Student 11 noticed how reflection helped to change her perceptions of the apartheid past:

> The majority of people, when I asked how they felt about these unjust evictions [in Die Vlakte], said that it did not bother them, as it was "not [their] people". They felt that this issue was irrelevant to them because it had not affected them directly. These words were terrible for me to hear, but at the same time I could understand their disinterest, which I too had felt at the beginning of this project. Only after a period of serious reflection and repositioning of myself in a similar context could I fully sympathise with their past.

Reflection allows individuals to understand their own context as well as their broader context of post-apartheid South Africa. All races can benefit from reflection, but in the specific context of Stellenbosch it is vital that white people reflect on the past, present and future ways in which oppression was, is and can be created. It is also necessary to process feelings of white guilt, fear and uncertainty. Student 39 commented on this:

> It was after these meetings that I changed my outlook on life. I realised that we lived in a country that had faults, and that South Africa was still recovering from the awful period of apartheid. But it was also evident that there was a desire to overcome these hardships and aspire to a future where everyone was equal. I therefore walk away from this experience with a renewed understanding of my position in society as a white person, and a profound respect for those less fortunate than I am. Thus, my feelings regarding this project are now feelings of deep appreciation and respect, and no longer fear and uncertainty.

Students acknowledged the realisation of being part of something 'bigger than themselves'. Reflection allowed them to look past the academic requirements of the project and to appreciate the practical application and significance of their work. Reflection also built up new sources of knowledge and ideas, as described below:

> The reflection was incredibly difficult, but it played a large role in formulating our final concept. As designers, it motivated us to sit and think and debate about the information that we received in the first week. The reflection ensured that we built a basis for ourselves to work and design from. It also provided an information source on which we could fall back if needed. It is always good to first think and then do ... We were thrown into the deep end, but it taught us patience, raised our personal standards and developed our skills. As designers, we grew ... (S24)

Design as a medium for learning

Using design for learning can be an effective means of addressing barriers to critical citizenship education because it allows participants to think critically and to see the 'multi-faceted' nature of an issue. Some participants felt that, as artists and designers, they are not equipped to address social issues such as the effects of apartheid. Others felt that the combination of critical citizenship education with design as a medium for learning finally allowed them to grasp the social responsibility of designers in a practical way.

By posing the project in terms of socially significant events, critical citizenship may be taught through the use of art. Students found ways of expressing the 'multi-layered' aspects of the topic, while maintaining the significance of the community it touched.

> It has been a roller-coaster of emotions engaging and executing this project ... Something that needs to be designed well, but at the same time has lots of sensitive issues that need to be dealt with before the design principles can be engaged in. (S22)

> Being a design project ... these conversations were also really refreshing to me since, in the past, I struggled to link these two things that I love. The project really brought worlds together for me, and I am really happy I got to experience that. (S36)

> We also realised that the community's emotions were still understandably extremely raw ... The community's participation and involvement in this project [were] of the utmost importance to us and therefore we felt [that] a newspaper filled with poetry, short stories and articles composed by students and community members would best capture the emotions ... (S19)

Student 76 felt ill-equipped to deal with sensitive social issues:

> I certainly believe that the intentions of this project and others like it are good, but the greater issue of 'us' and 'them' seems to me to be too sensitive for us as graphics students, with no psychological sort of training, to attempt to bridge the gap.

Students 2 and 35 realised the need for responsible design.

> Although I was negative about the project at first and mainly negative about the theme of the brief, I am glad that I was exposed to it; it is not really the type of project I would prefer but I liked how it challenged me as designer to make the best out of the situation. This project also made me aware of and got me to question the responsibility of the artist, the responsibility to stay objective, to not move into a propagandistic direction and to include and keep different groups of people directly affected and not so directly affected by this historical event in mind. (S2)

> The social responsibility of being a designer is a fact that our course has emphasised to us from the very beginning of [the] first year of our studies. However, I have always battled to comprehend exactly why it is stressed so much. It was only during this project that I have begun to understand this role. (S35)

Students are able to use design as a way to not only learn, but also to teach all who view their work. As a strategy it raises awareness from knowing the particulars of an event to knowing how it felt and how it must now be remembered. It offers students the skills needed to formulate complex answers to questions that carry deep significance, and allows for resolution without denial as the questions are worked through thoroughly. One student voiced this as follows:

> Creativity can be a powerful outlet for our troubles. By drawing, making something by hand, painting or reflecting, both visually and typographically, we can help others, especially our society's youth, by helping ourselves in the first instance. Art and creativity [have] always played an important role when conveying human emotions. That is also true in this project. (S37)

Conclusion

Power relations and structures, stereotyping and prejudice, and whiteness can all hinder critical citizenship education. Strategies of dialogue, community interaction, reflection and design as medium for learning can address these barriers in overlapping ways.

Ingrained stereotypical perceptions are often subconscious. Stereotyping and prejudice surfaced in the critical citizenship projects. This influences the teaching, learning and construction of a curriculum in subtle and complex ways. Dialogue in a safe space with others can help to overcome prejudices and community interaction and reflection can help participants process their own biases, fears and uncertainties. According to Morgan and Streb (2001: 167), community interaction can indeed build better citizens when people have "authentic experiences that can break down barriers". Student S68 said of the community interaction in Khayamandi: "This helped me break down my own preconceived idea of the township and its way of functioning".

When white identity and Western educational privilege are regarded as the norm, it could create unequal power structures. Critical citizenship education promotes democracy and social justice and therefore unequal power structures should be discussed and reflected upon. We should be wary of privileging dominant narratives above narratives of the oppressed (Donaldson & Daughtery, 2011). According to Santas (2000: 359), real dialogue "requires radical equality, a breaking down of barriers in such a way that painful truth will invariably come out". During community interaction, critical citizenship educators should be especially aware of this and "guard against ... viewing the white person as the 'saviour' figure, and the black students as those in need of saving." (S34)

In order to dismantle supremacy discourses of whiteness, lecturers and students need to work together to name and reflect on historical and current contexts (Leonardo, 2004). This involves open and safe dialogue, reflection and action. Issues surrounding whiteness are relevant in the South African context. Critical citizenship education should foster diversity, tolerance and a critical reflection on the past. All races in South Africa are affected by whiteness. Some white students feel guilty, afraid and uncertain, while some black students feel excluded, oppressed and unwelcome.

Community interaction and reflection can help to process these feelings: "I therefore walk away from this experience with a renewed understanding of my position in society as a white person" (S39). A black student from the township mentioned: "I started appreciating the little things about the place, like how the people built their shacks, because it shows creativity" (S26).

The use of design as medium for learning also allowed students to reflect on sensitive issues such as apartheid. Student 11 mentioned how she was now able to 'put herself in another's shoes' after the design project with community members: "Only after a period of serious reflection and repositioning of myself in a similar context could I fully sympathise with their past." Design practice can serve as a medium to express feelings and can help a person come to terms with real and hidden emotions. The critical citizenship education aim of preparing students to live together in harmony in diverse societies (Johnson & Morris, 2010) requires a critical confrontation with stereotypes and prejudice.

Changes in perception and attitudes, one can argue, can only be measured over a longer period. I specifically tried to spread the interviews and reflections over a couple of years, from 2010 to 2015, but even such a period was not sufficient to measure lasting changes in perceptions. Seeing students for six weeks per year may not be enough to make a permanent difference in their lives. Parker (2001:6) argues that citizenship education is a remarkable and daring undertaking, and it does not "suddenly emerge fully realised on one's 18th (or 80th) birthday".

The investigations in this research aimed to explore barriers to and strategies for critical citizenship education. Personal perceptions and attitudes of students, lecturers and community members were influenced in various ways by the critical citizenship projects. These reactions revealed various aspects of their immediate teaching and learning context, but also of the broader context in which students, lecturers and community members found themselves. This research contributes to the field of critical citizenship education in visual communication design in the South African context of a postcolonial, post-apartheid and previously white Afrikaans university.

References

Apple, M.W. 1979. *Ideology and curriculum.* London: Routledge
https://doi.org/10.4324/9780203241219

Barnett, R. & Coate, K. 2005. *Engaging the curriculum in higher education.* New York, NY:
Open University Press.

Barnett, R., Parry, G. & Coate, K. 2001. Conceptualizing curriculum change. *Teaching in Higher
Education,* 6(4), 435–449. https://doi.org/10.1080/13562510120078009

Bhattacharyya, J. 2004. Theorizing community development. *Journal of Community Development
Society,* 34(2), 5–34. https://doi.org/10.1080/15575330409490110

Bickmore, K. 2001. Student conflict resolution, power "sharing" in schools, and citizenship education.
Curriculum Inquiry, 31(2), 137–162. https://doi.org/10.1111/0362-6784.00189

Boland, J.A. & McIlrath, L. 2007. The process of locating pedagogies for civic engagement in Ireland:
The significance of conception, culture and context. In: L. McIlrath & I. MacLabhrainn
(Eds.). *Higher education and civic engagement: International perspectives.* Burlington:
Ashgate, 83–97.

Bourner M., Hughes, M. & Bourner, T. 2001. First-year undergraduate experiences of group project
work. *Assessment & Evaluation in Higher Education,* 26(1), 19–39.
https://doi.org/10.1080/02602930020022264

Bringle, R.G. & Hatcher, J.A. 1999. Reflection in service learning: Making meaning of experience.
Educational Horizons, 77(4), 179–185.

Clark, M.L. 2001. Social stereotypes and self-concept in black and white college students.
The Journal of Social Psychology, 125(6), 753–760. https://doi.org/10.1080/00224545.1985.9713549

Clifford, M.M. & Walster, E. 1973. The effect of physical attractiveness on teacher expectations.
Sociology of Education, 46(2), 248–258. https://doi.org/10.2307/2112099

Creswell, J.W. 2003. *Research design: Qualitative, quantitative and mixed methods approaches.*
London: Sage.

Davies, W.M. 2009. Groupwork as a form of assessment: Common problems and recommended
solutions. *Higher Education,* 58(4), 563–584. https://doi.org/10.1007/s10734-009-9216-y

Devine, P.G. 1989. Stereotypes and prejudice: Their automatic and controlled components. *Journal
of Personality and Social Psychology,* 56, 5–18. https://doi.org/10.1037/0022-3514.56.1.5

Dewey, J. 1951. *Experience and education.* New York, NY: Macmillan.

Dewey, J. 1958. *Art as experience.* New York, NY: Capricorn Books.

Donaldson, L.P. & Daughtery, L. 2011. Introducing asset-based models of social justice into service
learning: A social work approach. *Journal of Community Practice,* 19(1), 80–99.
https://doi.org/10.1080/10705422.2011.550262

Dowdy, J.K., Givens, G., Murillo, E.G., Shenoy, D. & Villenas, S. 2000. Noises in the attic: The legacy of
expectations in the academy. *International Journal of Qualitative Studies in Education,* 13(5),
492–446. https://doi.org/10.1080/09518390050156396

Du Plessis, J. & Smith-Tolken, A. 2009. The significance of emotions in enhancing effective learning through reflection in service-learning. Unpublished paper delivered at the Third International Symposium on Service-Learning, 23–24 November, University of Indianapolis.

Fanon, F. 1952. *Black skin, white masks*. London: Pluto Press.

Fanon, F. 2006. The man of colour and the white woman. In: A. Haddour (Ed.). *The Fanon reader*. London: Pluto, 46–58.

Foucault, M. 1978. *History of sexuality: An introduction*. Volume 1. New York, NY: Vintage.

Foucault, M. 1998. *The history of sexuality: The will to knowledge*. Volume 1. London: Penguin Group.

Freire, P. 1975. Pedagogy of the oppressed. In: M. Golby, J. Greenwald & R. West (Eds.). *Curriculum design*. London: Open University Press, 138–149.

Freire, P. & Shor, I. 1987. *A pedagogy for liberation: Dialogues on transforming education*. Hampshire: MacMillan. https://doi.org/10.1007/978-1-349-18574-0

Frick, L., Albertyn, R.M. & Rutgers, L. 2010. The Socratic method: Adult education theories. *Acta Academica*, Suppl. 1, 75–102.

Gibbons, M. 2005. Engagement with the community: The emergence of a new social contract between society and science. Paper presented at the Griffith University Community Engagement Workshop, 4 March, South Bank campus, Queensland.

Giddens, A. 1984. *The constitution of society: Outline of the theory of structuration*. Cambridge: Polity.

Giroux, H.A. 1985. Foreword. In: P. Freire. *The politics of education: Culture, power and liberation*. Westport: Bergin and Garvey, xv–xxiv.

Gitterman, A. 1988. Teaching students to connect theory and practice. *Social Work with Groups*, 11(1/2), 35–39. https://doi.org/10.1300/J009v11n01_03

Gramsci, A. 1971. The intellectuals: The formation of the intellectuals. In: S.P. Hier (Ed.). *Contemporary sociological thought: Themes and theories*. Toronto: Canadian Scholars' Press, 49–57.

Habermas, J. 1978. *Knowledge and human interests*. London: Heinemann.

Henning, E. 2004. *Finding your way in qualitative research*. Pretoria: Van Schaik.

Hook, D. 2004. Racism as abjection: A psychoanalytic conceptualization for a post-apartheid South Africa. *South African Journal of Psychology*, 34(4), 672–703. https://doi.org/10.1177/008124630403400410

Jackson, P.W., Boostrom, R. & Hanson, D. 1993. *The moral life of schools*. San Francisco, CA: Jossey-Bass.

Jamar, I. & Pitts, V.R. 2005. High expectations: A "how" of achieving equitable mathematics classrooms. *The Negro Educational Review*, 56(2/3), 127–134.

Jansen, J.D. 2009. *Knowledge in the blood: Confronting race and the apartheid past*. Stanford, CA: Stanford University Press.

Jarvis, P. 2006. *Towards a comprehensive theory of human learning*. London: Routledge.

Jaspers, K. 1963. *General psychopathology*. Manchester: Manchester University Press.

Johnson, L. & Morris, P. 2010. Towards a framework for critical citizenship education. *The Curriculum Journal*, 21(1), 77–96. https://doi.org/10.1080/09585170903560444

Kayes, D.C. 2002. Experiential learning and its critics: Preserving the role of experience in management learning and education. *Academy of Management Learning and Education*, 1(2), 137–149. https://doi.org/10.5465/AMLE.2002.8509336

Keet, A., Zinn, D. & Porteus, K. 2009. Mutual vulnerability: A key principle in humanising pedagogy in post-conflict societies. *Perspectives in Education*, 27(2), 109–119.

Klein, H.K. & Meyers, .D. 1999. A set of principles for conducting and evaluating interpretive field studies in information systems. *MIS Quarterly*, 23(1), 67–93. https://doi.org/10.2307/249410

Kolb, D.A. 1984. *Experiential learning: Experience as the source of learning and development.* London: Prentice Hall.

Kuh, G.D. 2003. What we're learning about student engagement from NSSE: Benchmarks for effective educational practices. *Change*, 35(2), 24–32. https://doi.org/10.1080/00091380309604090

Kumashiro, K.K. 2000. Towards a theory of anti-oppressive education. *Review of Educational Research*, 70(1), 25–53. https://doi.org/10.3102/00346543070001025

Leibowitz, B.L., Booi, K., Daniels, S., Loots, A., Richards, R. & Van Deventer, I. 2005. The use of educational biographies to inform teaching and learning in an African university. *South African Journal of Higher Education*, 19, Special issue, 1220–1237.

Leibowitz, B., Bozalek, V., Rohleder, P., Carolissen, R. & Swartz, L. 2010. "Whiteys love to talk about themselves": Discomfort as a pedagogy for change. *Race, Ethnicity and Education*, 13(1), 83–100. https://doi.org/10.1080/13613320903364523

Leonardo, Z. 2004. The souls of white folk: Critical pedagogy, whiteness studies and globalisation discourse. In: G. Ladson-Billings & D. Gillborn (Eds.). *The Routledge Falmer reader in multicultural education*. London: Routledge Falmer, 117–136.

Lizzio, A. & Wilson, K. 2005. Self-managed learning groups in higher education: Students' perceptions of process and outcomes. *British Journal of Educational Psychology*, 75, 373–390. https://doi.org/10.1348/000709905X25355

Lopez, A.J. (Ed.). 2005. *Postcolonial whiteness: A critical reader on race and empire*. Albany, NY: State University of New York Press.

Macey, D. 2000. *Dictionary of critical theory*. London: Penguin Group.

Massumi, B. 1995. The autonomy of affect. *Cultural Critique*, 31, *The Politics of Systems and Environments*, Part II, 83–109.

McIlrath, L. & MacLabhrainn, I. (Eds.). 2007. *Higher education and civic engagement: International perspectives*. Burlington: Ashgate.

Mezirow, J. 1991. *Transformative dimensions of adult learning*. San Francisco, CA: Jossey-Bass.

Mezirow, J. 1998. On critical reflection. *Adult Education Quarterly*, 48(3), 185–198. https://doi.org/10.1177/074171369804800305

Morgan, W. & Streb, M. 2001. Building citizenship: How student voice in service-learning develops civic values. *Social Science Quarterly*, 82(1), 155–169. https://doi.org/10.1111/0038-4941.00014

Nayar, K.P. 2013. *Posthumanism.* Cambridge: Polity Press.

Nussbaum, M. 2002. Education for citizenship in an era of global connection. *Studies in Philosophy and Education*, 21(4/5), 289–303. https://doi.org/10.1023/A:1019837105053

Nussbaum, M. 2006. Education and democratic citizenship: Capabilities and quality education. *Journal of Human Development*, 7(3), 385–395. https://doi.org/10.1080/14649880600815974

Parker, W.C. 2001. Educating democratic citizens: A broad view. *Theory into Practice*, 40(1), 6–13. https://doi.org/10.1207/s15430421tip4001_2

Ratele, K. & Duncan, N. 2007. *Social psychology: Identities and relationships.* Lansdowne: UCT Press.

Rowe, C.J. 2005. Socrates 469–399 BCE. In: A. Palmer (Ed.). *Fifty major thinkers on education: From Confucius to Dewey.* Oxon: Routledge, 5–10.

Samvad: Dialogue. 2011. *International seminar, 31.08.2011 – 01.09.2011.* SID research cell, Faculty of Design, Center for Environmental Planning and Technology University. Available at https://sites.google.com/a/cept.ac.in/samvad2011/samvad-dialogue-2011 [Accessed 4 July 2012].

Santas, A. 2000. Teaching anti-racism. *Studies in Philosophy and Education*, 19(1), 349–361. https://doi.org/10.1023/A:1005298916161

Saye, J.W. 1998. Creating time to develop student thinking: Team-teaching with technology. *Social Education*, 62(4), 356–362.

Schön, D.A. 1987. *Educating the reflective practitioner: Toward a new design for teaching and learning in the professions.* San Francisco, CA: Jossey-Bass.

Schuitema, J., Ten Dam, G. & Veugelers, W. 2008. Teaching strategies for moral education: A review. *Journal of Curriculum Studies*, 40(1), 69–89. https://doi.org/10.1080/00220270701294210

Sluiter, I. 2007. *Op zoek naar Socrates.* Studium Generale, Universiteit Leiden. Den Haag: Home Academy.

Snaza, N. & Weaver, J.A. 2015. Education and the posthumanist turn. In: N. Snaza & J.A. Weaver (Eds.). *Posthumanism and educational research.* Routledge International Studies in the Philosophy of Education. New York, NY: Routledge, 1–11.

Snyman, G.F. 2008. 'Is it not sufficient to be a human being?' Memory, Christianity and white identity in Africa. *Religion and Theology*, 15(3/4), 395–426. https://doi.org/10.1163/157430108X376609

Steyn, M. 2005. 'White talk': White South Africans and the management of diasporic whiteness. In: A.J. Lopez (Ed.). *Postcolonial whiteness: A critical reader on race and empire.* Albany, NY: State University of New York Press, 119–136.

Tappan, M.B. 1998. Moral education in the zone of proximal development. *Journal of Moral Education*, 27(2), 141–160. https://doi.org/10.1080/0305724980270202

Taylor, B. 2007. *Learning for tomorrow: Whole person learning for the planetary citizen.* West Yorkshire: Oasis Press.

Tredway, L. 1995. Socratic seminars: Engaging students in intellectual discourse. *Educational Leadership,* 53(1), 26–29.

Trope, Y. & Gaunt, R. 2003. Attribution and person perception. In: M.A. Hogg & J. Cooper (Eds.). *The Sage handbook of social psychology.* London: Sage, 190–208.

Urry, J. 2001. *Globalising the tourist gaze.* Department of Sociology. Lancaster University. Available at http://www.lancaster.ac.uk/fass/resources/sociology-online-papers/papers/urry-globalising-the-tourist-gaze.pdf [Accessed 20 June 2015].

Vice, S. 2010. How do I live in this strange place? *Journal of Social Philosophy,* 41(3), 323–342. https://doi.org/10.1111/j.1467-9833.2010.01496.x

Waghid, Y. 2010. *Education, democracy and citizenship revisited: Pedagogical encounters.* Stellenbosch: AFRICAN SUN MeDIA.

Weedon, C. 1987. *Feminist practice and poststructuralist theory.* Oxford: Basil Blackwell.

Wesley, S. 2007. Multicultural diversity: Learning through the arts. *New Directions for Adult and Continuing Education,* 116, 13–23. https://doi.org/10.1002/ace.273

Wright, S.C. & Taylor, D.M. 2003. The social psychology of cultural diversity: Social stereotyping, prejudice and discrimination. In: M.A. Hoggm & J. Cooper (Eds.). *The Sage handbook of social psychology.* London: Sage, 432–457.

Yip, K. 2007. Self-reflection in reflective practice: A Jaspers orientation. *Reflective Practice,* 8(2), 285–298. https://doi.org/10.1080/14623940701289485

Zuber-Skerritt, O. 2001. Action learning and action research: Paradigm, praxis and programs. In: S. Sankara, B. Dick & R. Passfield (Eds.). *Effective change management through action research and action learning: Concepts, perspectives, processes and applications.* Lismore: Southern Cross University Press, 1–27.

Educating Citizen Designers at South African Universities of Technology

2

HERMAN BOTES

Introduction

In 2015 to 2016 the South African higher education (SAHE) sector experienced levels of disruption last seen during the 1976 Soweto student uprising. Forty years later, the youth of South Africa is still the voice of the nation. As a graphic design educator that lectures a module on citizenship for final-year design students, I realised that the impact of the 2016 protest on students further emphasised the need for them to fully engage with the notion of critical citizenship. My experience as a design educator at a university of technology (UoT) in South Africa has placed me in a position where I am exposed to a diverse cultural, socio-economic and multi-racial student body. Every day I have the proverbial 'slice of South African life' in my classroom. In the SAHE sector, the UoT is a relatively new concept that emerged from transformed institutions that were previously known as technikons, which focused on vocational training. This process of transformation was undertaken by the South African government to address the legacy of apartheid and colonialism within SAHE. This transformation, together with the promulgation of a new Higher Education Qualifications Sub-framework (HEQSF) to replace the technikon qualifications, termed National Accredited Technical Education Diplomas, offered by the previous technikons, created opportunities and threats for critical citizenship theory in design education.

This chapter identifies opportunities for the transformation of Graphic Design curricula from the past technikons to the current UoTs through a critical citizenship lens. The critical citizenship framework developed by Johnson and Morris (2010) was used as a theoretical framework for this investigation. This framework is ideally suited to interrogating critical citizenship education within the Graphic Design diplomas offered by previous technikons, as it can be used to "contrast the existence of, opportunities for and absence of elements of critical citizenship" (Johnson & Morris, 2010: 91). The results of this analysis can be used to enrich curriculum planning for Graphic Design programmes at UoTs, thereby possibly contributing to the differentiation of design programmes offered at UoTs.

Overview of the Johnson and Morris critical citizenship education framework

In simplistic terms, Johnson and Morris developed the critical citizenship education framework by combining theories in critical thinking, critical pedagogy and the notion of an 'ideal citizen'. The critical citizenship education framework, as depicted in Table 1, correlates (on the horizontal axis) different conceptions of critical citizenship with (on the vertical axis) four primary purposes of critical citizenship education. This description of the framework does not do justice to the work done by Johnson and Morris and can be described as an oversimplification. As a pragmatist, it is my aim to focus on the application of this framework within the context of the transformation from technikon to UoT. To fully engage with the framework, it is advisable to read the original article "Towards a framework for critical citizenship education" (Johnson & Morris, 2010). In their application of the critical citizenship education framework in a comparative study of citizenship education in France and England (Johnson & Morris, 2012), the need for thorough contextualisation was clearly demonstrated.

Table 1   A framework for critical citizenship education

	POLITICS / ideology	SOCIAL / collective	SELF / subjectivity	PRAXIS / engagement
KNOWLEDGE	Knowledge and understanding of histories, societies, systems, oppressions and injustices, power structures and macrostructural relationships	Knowledge of interconnections between culture, power and transformation; non-mainstream writings and ideas in addition to dominant discourses	Knowledge of own position, cultures and context; sense of identity	Knowledge of how to collectively effect systematic change; how knowledge itself is power; how behaviour influences society and injustice
SKILLS	Skills of critical and structural social analysis; capacity to politicise notions of culture, knowledge and power; capacity to investigate deeper causalities	Skills in dialogue, cooperation and interaction; skills in critical interpretation of others' viewpoints; capacity to think holistically	Capacity to reflect critically on one's 'status' within communities and society; independent critical thinking; speaking with one's own voice	Skills of critical thinking and active participation; skills in acting collectively to challenge the status quo; ability to imagine a better world
VALUES	Commitment to values against injustice and oppression	Inclusive dialogical relationship with others' identities and values	Concern for social justice and consideration of self-worth	Informed, responsible and ethical action and reflection
DISPOSITIONS	Actively questioning; critical interest in society and public affairs; seeking out and acting against injustice and oppression	Socially aware; cooperative; responsible towards self and others; willing to learn with others	Critical perspective; autonomous; responsible in thought, emotion and action; forward-thinking; in touch with reality	Commitment and motivation to change society; civic courage; responsibility for decisions and actions

(Source: Johnson & Morris, 2010: 90)

To contextualise this application of the Johnson and Morris framework, I will first explicate the term 'transformation' by identifying the assumptions associated with it and outlining the vision that guides transformation in the SAHE context. Second, I will discuss the institutional changes undergone by the SAHE sector since 1994.

Transformation of South African higher education

Transformation in the SAHE context is a process aimed at the social, cultural and economic development of the country by addressing the legacies of apartheid. President Nelson Mandela commenced the process of transformation in 1995 when he established the National Commission on Higher Education (NCHE). The 1996 report (CHE, 1996) drafted by the NCHE forever changed the higher education landscape in South Africa, as it formed the basis for several policies and legislative documents in the years to follow. Two decades later, the efficacy of this transformation process is questioned due to the prevailing incidents of racism, lack or inability of universities to implement policy and barriers to access for disadvantaged students at South African universities.

The meaning of transformation

The Soudien report[1] identified that SAHE institutions had a very narrow policy-driven understanding of what transformation means (Soudien et al., 2008). Several authors who examined the report later highlighted this narrow understanding as a fundamental problem within SAHE (Lewins, 2010; Oloyede, 2009). Another common element was that transformation is understood quite differently by many of the role players in SAHE (Erasmus, 2009; HESA, 2010; Oloyede, 2009). It was, however, agreed that transformation in SAHE is much more than a numbers game or a "condition-change" (Oloyede, 2009: 430), moving from a state of exclusion to a state of inclusion. In response to the Soudien report, SAHE institutions acknowledged that there should be a broader understanding of transformation and that "[i]nterpersonal relationships and day-to-day interactions are central to the project and lie at the heart of the idea of a transformed institution" (HESA, 2010: 46).

Assumptions associated with transformation

In my experience in SAHE, much of what was posed as transformation came through policy channels. The newly 'legislated' and transformation requirements aligned with key performance agreements were dealt with as a matter of instruction without any real debate at an institutional academic level that could have added value. This was done because of assumptions that many of the role players had. Erasmus (2009: 48) captured the essence of these assumptions when he noted the following:

> One side broadly criticises transformation in terms of the fear of falling standards, or the importance of traditions and the undermining of merit and efficiency. The other side bewails the lack of real transformation, alluding to the continuing prevalence of white racism, as well as new forms of racism that feed on old networks and double standards when institutional rules and procedures are being applied.

---

[1] The 2008 report of the Ministerial Committee on Transformation and Social Cohesion and the Elimination of Discrimination in Public Higher Education Institutions became known through popular use as the Soudien report, referring to the chairman of the committee.

To add to the tension created by the above-mentioned assumptions, cognisance should also be taken of the role that culture plays in this process. Erasmus (2009) highlights the need for universities to focus on creating social transformation through recognising cultural differences, although he warns against the assumption that a homogenised 'new' culture must be developed, as it will be artificial. Another issue that would prove to be futile to the transformation process is the assumption that an educator can simply be left to implement transformation policies. The Soudien report highlighted that staff development would have to take place to deal with transformation (Soudien, 2010). Weldon (2010:353) also identified an acute gap in educators' training to openly deal with the "painful legacies of the past".

A vision for transformation

The South African government drafted a vision for transformation in SAHE through the Education White Paper 3 of 1997. The White Paper states the vision for a transformed, democratic, non-racial and non-sexist system of higher education. In summary, it is expected that this transformation process will deal with equity of access, eradicate discrimination, address national development needs, support human rights, advance knowledge and uphold academic quality. The Soudien report found that this vision was implemented on policy level at SAHE institutions, but was rarely evident in everyday campus life (Soudien et al., 2008).

Institutional changes made to the higher education sector since 1994

To realise the transformation vision of government for SAHE, there had to be fundamental institutional changes. The period from 1994 to 1999 was dedicated to setting policy and legislation in place that would lead SAHE into an era of implementation post 1999 (Cloete et al., 2006). The Higher Education Act of 1997 replaced the Universities Act of 1995, the Tertiary Education Act of 1988 and the Technikons Act of 1993, thereby fundamentally reformulating public SAHE into a co-operative governance model with the goal that institutional autonomy should be balanced with public accountability. The aim of this model was to drive the transformation of the higher education system through policies and strategies. This approach was also taken by other countries, but has proven to be unsuccessful (Harpur, 2006). The policy to create a single qualifications framework for all higher education qualifications proved to be one of the most fundamental changes seen in the history of SAHE (Department of Education, 1997).

The institutional mergers that reshaped the SAHE landscape, whereby several universities and technikons merged around 2004, created further fundamental changes. New institutions were created with the anticipation that they would embrace transformation and build a new future for the South African academia; however, this proved to be a myth, as several merged institutions collapsed under the pressures of the process and were placed under administration or unbundled. However, after several years of strive, the current situation can be described as an adolescent, shrugging off growing pains, wanting to focus on future prospects.

Policy, theory and practice – gaps revealed

The process of transformation in SAHE is guided by several policy and legislative documents. It can be argued that the model of co-operative governance with its accountability focus, together with the National Qualifications Framework (NQF) alignment, created major gaps between policy and practice. In theory, although these policies were intended to consolidate higher education, they could, however, cause the opposite.

As an academic, I can attest to the move away from professionalism on which South African academics used to build their reputations to a new dispensation that describes the academic as "the new auditable competitive performer" (Webster & Mosoetsa, 2001: 16). This 'policy-prescribed' accountability has engulfed many academics with a wave of additional administration, leaving them numb with managing expectations from all their constituencies. The HEQSF alignment process has also compromised many experienced industry professionals who are teaching in vocational programmes without formal teacher training. They are now required to deal with issues such as quality assurance, curriculum development and corporate policy, which was previously not expected (Harpur, 2006). This problem was also highlighted by Dineen and Collins (2005: 43), who suggest that "a re-affirmation of experiential evidence is essential to counter the impact of an increasingly audit-driven approach to education which focuses on outcomes rather than process and on systems rather than individuals".

Racism at South African universities

The Education White Paper 3 addressed racism through the following statement: "an enabling environment must be created throughout the system to uproot deep-seated racist and sexist ideologies and practices that inflame relationships, inflict emotional scars and create barriers to successful participation in learning and campus life" (Department of Education, 1997: 22).

The implementation of this statement was never explicit, and it was up to the individual institutions to interpret and put it into action. Within this void of implementation, racism in SAHE took on several 'cloaked' guises. One such an example is 'cultural racism', whereby culture is used as a disguise for exclusive practices (Erasmus, 2009). Pillay (2009) identified the racial character of knowledge production from the still predominantly white academics in research positions in South Africa as another instance of 'cloaked' racism. The paternalistic approach of educators who see themselves as anti-racists can also create an internalised sense of superiority that should not be left unchecked (Santas, 2000).

Transformation within SAHE will only succeed once all the role players have developed a sense of being 'at home'. Thaver (2006) conceptualises the notion of being 'at home' to infer that transformation can be successful when all people involved in the transformation can feel as if they are at home; thereby implying that everyone should have a certain sense of belonging that is created when one feels safe, wanted and cared for and knows that one's opinion matters.

Defining a university of technology

Throughout the process of transformation in higher education, the former technikons had to carve an identity as UoTs. Roy du Pré (2010: 10) notes the definition of 'technology' as described by UNESCO as being useful to define the nature of UoTs: "... the know-how and creative processes that may assist people to utilise tools, resources and systems to solve problems and enhance control over the natural and made environment in an endeavour to improve the human condition."

This description of technology can be closely tied to the nature and function of design, making any design-based programme ideally suited to defining the nature of UoTs. The debate on the nature and role of UoTs in South Africa is mainly driven by the South African Technology Network (SATN). SATN defines UoTs as follows: "A University of Technology offers technological career directed educational programmes, focuses on innovative problem-solving research and engages with government/business/industry with communities as end users" (c2015: n.p.). The discourse on the differentiation between traditional, comprehensive and technological universities in South Africa is still unfolding (Coleman, 2016).

Describing the National Diploma: Graphic Design curriculum

Introduction

The National Diploma: Graphic Design was designed through a 'convenor' system managed by the then Council for Technikon Principals. The then Natal Technikon was the convenor of the National Diploma: Graphic Design. Through this system, a national working committee would constitute the curriculum, and it was then uniformly implemented at all technikons. The convenor system had the advantage that all technikons that employed mostly industry-experienced educators did not have to carry the burden of curriculum development. As vocational training institutions, technikons had a diminished capacity when it came to curriculum development and academic discourse, partly due to the convenor system (Du Pré, 2010). This, together with the challenges related to the "often contested relationship between the professional and disciplinary demands brought together in vocational curricula" (Coleman, 2016: 381), requires that design educators at UoTs interrogate their approach to curriculum development. Design educators at UoTs are faced with the question: "[S]hould a design curriculum focus on developing creativity and ideas, or should it be technically based and prepare the student for professional practice?" (Adams, Hyde & Murray, 2013: 143). With the transformation from technikon to UoT and the implementation of the HEQF, technikon lecturing staff were placed in a precarious position, where lecturing staff with extensive industry experience now had to realign with the world of curriculum development and educational theory.

South African diplomas are pegged at Level 6 of the NQF (Republic of South Africa, 2008), which determines competencies regarding the scope of knowledge; knowledge literacy; methods and procedures; problem solving; ethics and professional practice; accessing, managing and processing information; management of learning; and accountability. These aspects are to a large extent framed into the Graphic Design curriculum by the critical outcomes set for all qualifications in the NQF. The role of the prescribed critical outcomes in the Graphic Design curriculum is central to ensuring that thought is given to the notion of citizenship in said curriculum. The limitation of credits and the implied time allocated by the credits (1 credit = 10 notional hours)[2] impact on the possibilities to address aspects of critical citizenship in the Graphic Design curriculum.

National Diploma: Graphic Design curriculum

The exit-level outcomes and critical outcomes of the National Diploma: Graphic Design are listed on the following page (SAQA, n.d.). This curriculum was carried over from the technikon era to the UoTs and is now in the process of being realigned with the HEQF. In the realignment, project institutions had the choice to make less than 50% changes to the current curriculum and submit as a Category B programme, or they could submit a completely new programme that was classified as Category C. The HEQSF alignment process created the opportunity for institutions to differentiate and claim their niche in the field. Through my involvement with the accreditation process of many of these qualifications, I can state that the opportunities created in this process were not fully explored by all UoTs.

EXIT LEVEL OUTCOMES (Technikon Graphic Design Diploma)

1. Research and develop a creative brief, which meets a client's visual communication needs in the marketing of a formal business.

   1.1 Identify key subjects, problems, targets and objectives in keeping with workable marketing and advertising models. (C) (4 credits) (NQF 6)

   1.2 Set up appointments and conduct interviews and record data. (C) (2 credits) (NQF 6)

   1.3 Conduct research and analyse findings using appropriate research methodology. (C) (3 credits) (NQF 6)

   1.4 Synthesise data and draw up a creative brief, work plan and strategy. (C) (5 credits) (NQF 6)

   1.5 Prepare an estimate of costs. (C) (1 credit) (NQF 6)

2. Visualise original ideas, which meet the requirements of a creative brief.

   2.1 Examine, assess and contextualise relevant historical and theoretical visual models. (C) (30 credits) (NQF 6)

   2.2 Draw a range of suitable visual ideas, which answer the brief, using appropriate historical contexts and theoretical, creative models as a basis. (F) (50 credits) (NQF 6)

   2.3 Group, evaluate and select the most effective visual concept according to the principles of advertising and marketing. (F) (4 credits) (NQF 6)

3. Design the components of a visual communication campaign to give expression to the original concept.

   3.1 Select and arrange the forms of words in accordance with typographic principles to give optimal expression and clarity to the content. (F) (29 credits) (NQF 6)

---

2   A notional hour is equated to the average time required by an average student to complete a task.

    3.2 Draw or otherwise indicate the original pictorial and/or symbolic images required by the concept which will elicit the desired response. (F) (54 credits) (NQF 6)

4. Direct and prepare the production of the design in accordance with professional technical requirements and media specifications.

    4.1 Prepare the final design for production in accordance with the technical requirements of the media. (F) (65 credits) (NQF 6)

    4.2 Specify production components of the visual communication in accordance with the design. (F) (6 credits) (NQF 6)

    4.3 Source and direct specialist suppliers required in the production of the design. (C) (3 credits) (NQF 6)

    4.4 Oversee the production of the final design. (C) (4 credits) (NQF 6)

5. Apply professional ethics and practice in business finance and communication.

    5.1 Make presentations to clients clearly and confidently. (C) (2 credits) (NQF 6)

    5.2 Control income and expenses in accordance with sound business practice. (C) (3 credits) (NQF 6)

    5.3 Manage studio space, equipment and materials effectively. (C) (5 credits) (NQF 6)

    5.4 Maintain accurate records. (C) (3 credits) (NQF 6)

CRITICAL OUTCOMES

- Identifying and solving problems in which responses display that responsible decisions using critical and creative thinking have been made is addressed throughout the course, particularly in 2.1–3.5
- Working effectively with others as a member of a team is addressed in 3.4 and 5.1
- Organising and managing oneself and one's activities responsibly and effectively is addressed throughout the course
- Collecting, analysing, organising and critically evaluating information is addressed in 1.1–2.1
- Communicating effectively using visual, mathematical and/or language skills in the modes of oral and/or written persuasion is addressed throughout the course, particularly in 1.2, 3.4, 5.1, however the primary focus of the course is on visual communication in 2.1–4.1
- Using science and technology effectively and critically, showing responsibility towards the environment and health of others is addressed in 2.1, 4.1–4.4
- Demonstrating an understanding of the world as a set of related systems by recognising that problem-solving contexts do not exist in isolation is addressed in 2.1–2.3
- Contributing to the full personal development of each learner and the social and economic development of the society at large, by making the learner aware of the importance of:
  - i.   Reflecting on and exploring a variety of strategies to learn more effectively is addressed in 1.3, 1.4, 2.1, 2.3;

ii.   Participating as responsible citizens in the life of local, national and global communities is addressed in 1.1, 1.3, 1.4, 2.1, 5.4

iii. Being culturally and aesthetically sensitive across a range of social contexts is addressed throughout the course, particularly in 1.1–1.3, 2.1–3.5, 5.1

iv.   Exploring education and career opportunities is addressed throughout the course and

v.   Developing entrepreneurial opportunities is addressed throughout the course.

Application of the critical citizenship education framework

In this section I will identify outcomes within the National Diploma: Graphic Design curriculum that could facilitate the four major purposes of critical citizenship education, namely to develop the knowledge, skills, values and dispositions of citizens (Johnson & Morris, 2010). This will be discussed under the headings formulated from the different conceptions of critical citizenship, namely:

- Politics/ideology
- Social/collective
- Self/subjectivity
- Praxis/engagement

The political/ideological conception of critical citizenship

Johnson and Morris (2012: 292) describe the political/ideological element of the framework as those elements that could, for example, identify "causes of social problems and the values promoted by the state and its institutions" as well as enable "education to be used for creating cohesion and national identity" if defined clearly, such as in the case of the French educational system.

Development of knowledge

Within the political/ideological conception of critical citizenship education, the National Diploma: Graphic Design curriculum provides design educators with the opportunity to facilitate the development of knowledge and understanding of histories through examining, assessing and contextualising relevant historical and theoretical visual models. Knowledge and understanding of societies could be interrogated when students answer a brief using appropriate historical contexts and theoretical, creative models as a basis. Knowledge and understanding of political systems, oppressions and injustices, power structures and macrostructural relationships could possibly be present in the critical outcome requiring participation as responsible citizens in the life of local, national and global communities. In the curriculum statement it is indicated that the critical outcome addressing 'responsible citizens' could be achieved through the following exit-level outcomes:

1.1   Identify key subjects, problems, targets and objectives in keeping with workable marketing and advertising models.

1.2   Conduct research and analyse findings using appropriate research methodology.

1.3   Synthesise data and draw up a creative brief, work plan and strategy.

1.4   Examine, assess and contextualise relevant historical and theoretical visual models.

I am not convinced that participation as responsible citizens in the life of local, national and global communities could be achieved through these identified outcomes. This could be identified as a lost opportunity to fully engage with the notion of citizenship within the design curriculum. In my experience, design educators are often focused mainly on the requirements of the neo-liberal communication design industry. Especially pre-1994, South African design educators would not have had the freedom to critically engage with political systems, oppressions and injustices, power structures and macrostructural relationships. This observation is supported by Seroto (2012: 63), who states that "former political dispensation as seen through the four dimensions did not create space for critical thinking and dialogue". It must, however, be stated that many pre-1994 South African design educators were involved in a personal capacity as activists, and especially 'green issues' took the forefront (Van Zyl, 2007).

Development of skills

The National Diploma: Graphic Design curriculum design was aimed at achieving the transfer of vocational skills required by the communication design industry. The Diploma is pegged at NQF Level 6, which places constraints on the depth of concepts such as critical and structural social analysis outside the requisites of this diploma. During the technikon era, the apartheid regime created campuses that were officially 'a-political' without any party-political activities allowed, thereby limiting opportunities for dissent and criticism. As a product of technikon design education, my first experience of politicised notions of culture, knowledge and power and the capacity to investigate deeper causalities was when I completed a subsequent Diploma in Public Relations. This knowledge I only fully absorbed at master's level when I enrolled for an MA in Visual Art Education. Through exposure to educational theory, the role of politics, power and the subaltern forever changed the way I approached design education.

Development of values

The development of values within the political/ideological conception of critical citizenship education could be attained through the critical outcome addressing cultural and aesthetic sensitivity across a range of social contexts. In the curriculum, it is stated that this outcome is addressed throughout the course, particularly during the identification of key subjects, problems, targets and objectives. The platform for discussion of political/ideological values is available through the outcome requiring the examinination, assessment and contextualisation of relevant historical and theoretical visual models. As mentioned previously, this platform would not have been used before 1994 when discussions related to politics and ideology were constrained, especially those related to injustice and oppression.

Development of dispositions

Within the political/ideological conception of critical citizenship education, a citizen should develop enduring qualities of mind and character that demonstrate a tendency or inclination towards a critical, questioning interest in society as well as public affairs, while also seeking out and acting against injustice and oppression. In the curriculum being analysed, these qualities could be developed by the critical outcome requiring the demonstration of critical and creative thinking as well as with the exit-level outcome requiring the examination, assessment and contextualisation of relevant historical and theoretical visual models. The exit-level outcome requiring professional ethics and practice in business finance and communication could create a platform for educators to discuss social justice and oppression within the neoliberal design industry.

The social/collective conception of critical citizenship

Johnson and Morris (2012: 292) describe the social/collective element of the framework as having a focus on "dialogue, co-operation and on the ways in which students are encouraged to explore alternative values and identities".

Development of knowledge

Within the social/collective conception of critical citizenship education, the National Diploma: Graphic Design curriculum provides design educators with the opportunity to build student knowledge of interconnections between culture in the process of researching and developing a creative brief. This is supported by Buchanan (2001: 15), who states that "specialized knowledge must be connected and integrated in new ways if the designer is to perform his or her proper function in society and culture". The critical outcome that requires the curriculum to contribute to the full personal development of each student and the social and economic development of society at large is also ideally suited to developing the knowledge required by the social/collective element of critical citizenship education. This can be achieved by making students aware of the importance of participating as responsible citizens in the life of local, national and global communities. As in the political/ideological element, the critical outcomes addressing 'responsible citizens' in the social/collective element could be achieved through exit-level outcomes 1.1, 1.3, 1.4 and 2.1, as it could facilitate dialogue on alternative values and identities. What is, however, problematic is the ability of design educators to engage students with alternative values, identities, non-mainstream writings and ideas in addition to dominant discourses. In a field where the dominant history and theory of graphic design was monopolised by a few authors, graphic design history was not 'democratically' documented as in many other design disciplines (Triggs, 2011).

Critical outcomes aimed at creating cultural and aesthetic sensitivity across a range of social contexts and the demonstration of an understanding of the world as a set of related systems by recognising that problem-solving contexts do not exist in isolation. It is also suited to building knowledge of the social/collective element of critical citizenship education.

Development of skills

The ability to develop skills in dialogue, cooperation, interaction, critical interpretation of others' viewpoints and thinking holistically can be described as central to the armour of a successful designer and is addressed throughout the diploma in almost every outcome. The development of skills through the social/collective element of the critical citizenship education framework is one of the strongest correlations between the purposes of the National Diploma: Graphic Design curriculum and critical citizenship education.

Development of values

The notion of developing an inclusive dialogical relationship with others' identities and values in the social/collective element of the framework could be addressed through the same outcomes identified in the previous section. Dialogical relationships form part of the interactions with clients during the development of a client brief and testing design solutions within a target market. Having a deep understanding of the identities and values of a client and the intended target market is a key success factor in the design process.

Development of dispositions

The concepts of being socially aware, cooperative, responsible towards the self and others and the will to learn with others are key components of the curriculum. These are addressed in almost all critical outcomes. The notion of being responsible towards the self and others could easily be addressed in the outcome requiring the development of professional ethics.

The self/subjectivity conception of critical citizenship

Johnson and Morris (2012: 293) describe the self/subjective element of the framework as "comprising emotions, feelings, introspection, positivity and realism".

Development of knowledge

Within the self/subjective conception of critical citizenship education, it is my experience that especially first-year students struggle to understand themselves and have sparse self-knowledge. Their knowledge of their own position, culture and context and a sense of identity only in rare cases inform their design work. I annually run a project in which South African and American students cooperate in a social awareness campaign. The lack of depth of understanding of their own societal problems (both South African and American) together with their lack of cultural identity annually allows me to highlight the hegemonic quality of the work done by both groups. Students are more likely to adapt a 'student persona' that is aligned with societal expectations than being seen as different or not fitting in. The development of self-knowledge is not explicit in the Graphic Design curriculum. The outcome requiring the development of a creative brief that meets a client's visual communication needs requires from designers to understand people and to be able to identify what 'moves' them. It is stated that the critical outcome requiring being culturally and aesthetically sensitive across a range of social contexts is addressed throughout the course; however, this outcome could include strategies to develop self-knowledge through understanding 'others'.

Development of skills

The development of skills to build capacity to reflect critically on one's 'status' within communities and society could be addressed by the outcome aimed at the full personal development of each student. In South African universities this 'full personal development' is also supported by extracurricular activities. Aspects such as study methods, language proficiency and time and financial management are usually offered. Heller (2006: IX) states that "in many institutions it is no longer adequate to simply have a marketable portfolio – graduates must acquire bona fides through internships, apprenticeships, work studies, and anything else that bulks their résumés". Within the Graphic Design curriculum, the voice of the design student is 'muted' by the requirements of the design brief. Independent critical thinking, speaking with one's own voice, is 'allowed' in so far as it contributes to achieving the goals of the brief that meets a client's communication needs.

Development of values

The development of values within the self/subjective conception of critical citizenship education that would align with concern for social justice and consideration of self-worth could be addressed by design educators through the themes and clients they choose when developing projects for design students. Projects that are done for non-profit institutions and clients such as tobacco companies could create opportunities for such development.

Development of dispositions

The outcome that requires students to draw on a range of suitable visual ideas, which answer the brief using appropriate historical contexts and theoretical, creative models as a basis, could assist in the development of a designer that demonstrates critical perspective; autonomy; responsibility in thought, emotion and action; forward-thinking and being in touch with reality. The historical contexts and theoretical, creative models that are chosen by the design lecturer will be critical in achieving this goal.

The praxis/engagement conception of critical citizenship

The notion of praxis fits squarely into the nature of the UoT and offers the most opportunity for design lecturers to impact how society defines UoTs. Johnson and Morris (2010: 83) describe praxis as "meaning the 'authentic union' of action and reflection which leads to conscientisation".

Development of knowledge

As a communication design educator, I aim to help students to grasp how to collectively effect systematic change through the design campaigns they develop. The idea that knowledge itself is power is supported and perpetuated by the communication design industry. For our students to be successful, they must understand and have the knowledge to influence society. This is done through the outcomes requiring students to research and develop a creative brief that meets a client's visual communication needs in the marketing of a formal business as well as most of the critical outcomes listed.

Development of skills

The development of skills in critical thinking and active participation is facilitated throughout the design process. This is described in the critical outcome that requires the identification and solving of problems in which responses display that responsible decisions using critical and creative thinking have been made. One facet of the participatory nature of the design curriculum is evident in the outcomes requiring setting up interviews and testing the effectiveness of the design in the target group. The notion that designers should be acting collectively to challenge the status quo could be evident in the critical outcomes requiring participation as responsible citizens in the life of local, national and global communities. Decisions on how this is translated into the curriculum are often left to the design lecturer concerned. Designers often by nature of their work have vivid imaginations, hence the ability to imagine a better world will not be a problem. The challenge would, however, be to develop the skills that would transfer imagination into reality. The question that should also be asked is what will be defined as a better world.

Development of values

Within the praxis/engagement conception of critical citizenship education, the development of values that would lead to informed, responsible and ethical action and reflection by design students is supported by almost all the critical outcomes. Again, the translation of these values into the curriculum would be in the hands of the design lecturer involved, and not the curriculum itself.

Development of dispositions

The development of dispositions through praxis that would support commitment and motivation to change society and taking responsibility for decisions and actions is supported by almost all the critical outcomes. The notion of civic courage is not directly reflected anywhere in the curriculum; it could, however, be implied in the outcome requiring participation as responsible citizens in the life of local, national and global communities.

Application of Johnson and Morris's framework

In keeping with the original application of the framework to a curriculum by Johnson and Morris, I will now, through the use of symbols, indicate areas where an element of critical citizenship is present, where there is space for it or where it is missing from the curriculum.

Table 2   The National Diploma: Graphic Design mapped onto the Johnson and Morris framework for critical citizenship education

	POLITICS/ ideology	SOCIAL/ collective	SELF/ subjectivity	PRAXIS/ engagement
KNOWLEDGE	Knowledge and understanding of histories, societies, systems, oppressions and injustices, power structures and macrostructural relationships	Knowledge of interconnections between culture, power and transformation; non-mainstream writings and ideas in addition to dominant discourses	Knowledge of own position, cultures and context; sense of identity	Knowledge of how collectively to effect systematic change; how knowledge itself is power; how behaviour influences society and injustice
SKILLS	Skills of critical and structural social analysis; capacity to politicise notions of culture, knowledge and power; capacity to investigate deeper causalities	Skills in dialogue, cooperation and interaction; skills in critical interpretation of others' viewpoints; capacity to think holistically	Capacity to reflect critically on one's 'status' within communities and society; independent critical thinking; speaking with one's own voice	Skills of critical thinking and active participation; skills in acting collectively to challenge the status quo; ability to imagine a better world
VALUES	Commitment to values against injustice and oppression	Inclusive dialogical relationship with others' identities and values	Concern for social justice and consideration of self-worth	Informed, responsible and ethical action and reflection
DISPOSITIONS	Actively questioning; critical interest in society and public affairs; seeking out and acting against injustice and oppression	Socially aware; cooperative; responsible towards self and others; willing to learn with others	Critical perspective; autonomous; responsible in thought, emotion and action; forward-thinking; in touch with reality	Commitment and motivation to change society; civic courage; responsibility for decisions and actions

Key to symbols

Element present in the curriculum	
Space for element in curriculum, but not explicit	
Null (missing from curriculum)	

From the application of the Graphic Design curriculum to the Johnson and Morris framework in Table 2, the strengths and weaknesses of critical citizenship education can be formulated. The political/ ideological conception of critical citizenship education is the only one of the four conceptions in the model that has a missing aspect in the curriculum. All the other aspects have an element present or have space for it, although not made explicit.

Summary and conclusions

From the investigation, it can be concluded that the critical outcomes of the Graphic Design curriculum facilitate most of the critical citizenship education concepts, while the exit-level outcomes that are discipline-specific need to be unpacked with a critical citizenship lens for them to become relevant. The position of the educator and the impact of the hidden curriculum on the delivery of the curriculum are critical; the presence or absence of aspects of critical citizenship education in the curriculum will in many instances be determined by the educator involved (Apple, 1979). The Johnson and Morris framework guides design educators to ask questions about the curriculum they are designing. The following questions could assist design educators at UoTs in creating curricula that would differentiate from the past practice.

1. In what way will the design curriculum/assignments/projects that I am planning develop
    a. knowledge and understanding of histories, societies, systems, oppressions and injustices?
    b. knowledge and understanding of power structures and macrostructural relationships?
    c. knowledge of interconnections between culture, power and transformation?
    d. an understanding of non-mainstream writings and ideas in addition to dominant discourses?
    e. knowledge by design students of their own position, cultures and context?
    f. a sense of identity by design students?
    g. knowledge of how to collectively effect systematic change?
    h. an understanding that knowledge itself is power?
    i. understanding of how behaviour influences society and injustice?
    j. skills of critical and structural social analysis?
    k. the capacity to politicise notions of culture, knowledge and power?
    l. the capacity to investigate deeper causalities?
    m. skills in dialogue, cooperation and interaction?
    n. skills in critical interpretation of others' viewpoints?
    o. the capacity to think holistically?
    p. the capacity to reflect critically on one's 'status' within communities and society?
    q. independent critical thinking and speaking with one's own voice?
    r. skills of critical thinking and active participation?
    s. skills in acting collectively to challenge the status quo?
    t. the ability to imagine a better world?
    u. commitment to values against injustice and oppression?
    v. inclusive dialogical relationships with others' identities and values?
    w. concern for social justice and consideration of self-worth?
    x. informed, responsible and ethical action and reflection?

2.   In what way will the design curriculum/assignments/projects that I am planning assist in developing design students with the following attributes?

a.   They are actively questioning and have a critical interest in society and public affairs.

b.   They are seeking out and acting against injustice and oppression.

c.   They are socially aware, cooperative, responsible towards the self and others and willing to learn with others.

d.   They have a critical perspective and are autonomous; responsible in thought, emotion and action; forward-thinking and in touch with reality.

e.   They are committed and motivated to change society, possess civic courage and take responsibility for their decisions and actions.

Design educators at UoTs could use the questions above and the findings of this investigation to formulate new design curricula that would assist in the transformation and diversification of design education at UoTs. By focusing on the praxis/engagement conception of critical citizenship education and including skills from the political/ideological conception, there can be a clear differentiation from past practices. The transformation of South African society will be advanced if design educators can capacitate their students with skills of critical and structural social analysis and the ability to investigate deeper causalities within society, and nurture academic freedom that would accommodate the capacity to politicise notions of culture, knowledge and power.

References

Adams, J., Hyde, W. & Murray, B. 2013. Design education: International perspectives and debates. *International Journal of Art & Design Education*, 32(2), 142–145. https://doi.org/10.1111/j.1476-8070.2013.12012.x

Apple, M.W. 1979. *The hidden curriculum and the nature of conflict.* Vol. 2. London: Routledge.

Buchanan, R. 2001. The problem of character in design education: Liberal arts and professional specialization. *International Journal of Technology and Design Education*, 11(1), 13–26. https://doi.org/10.1023/A:1011286205584

CHE (Council on Higher Education). 1996. NCHE report: *A framework for transformation.* Available at http://www.che.ac.za/media_and_publications/other-stakeholder-s-publications/nche-report-framework-transformation-1996 [Accessed 30 April 2014].

Cloete, N., Maasen, P., Fehnel, R., Moja, T., Gibbon, T. & Perold, H. 2006. *Transformation in higher education: Global pressures and local realities.* Vol. 19. Dordrecht: Springer. https://doi.org/10.1007/1-4020-4006-7

Coleman, L. 2016. Asserting academic legitimacy: The influence of the University of Technology sectoral agendas on curriculum decision-making. *Teaching in Higher Education*, 21(4), 381–397. https://doi.org/10.1080/13562517.2016.1155548

Department of Education. 1997. White Paper 3: A Programme for Higher Education Transformation. *Government Gazette*, 58(18207), 324–326.

Dineen, R. & Collins, E. 2005. Killing the goose: Conflicts between pedagogy and politics in the delivery of a creative education. *Journal of Art & Design Education*, 24(1), 43–52. https://doi.org/10.1111/j.1476-8070.2005.00422.x

Du Pré, R. 2010. Universities of technology in the context of the South African higher education landscape: Universities of Technology – deepening the debate. *Kagisano*, 7, 1–44.

Erasmus, P. 2009. The unbearable burden of diversity. *Acta Academica*, 41(4), 40–55. Available at http://reference.sabinet.co.za/sa_epublication_article/academ_v41_n4_a3 [Accessed 30 April 2014].

Harpur, J. 2006. Transformation in higher education: The inevitable union of alchemy and technology. *Higher Education Policy*, 19(2), 135–151. https://doi.org/10.1057/palgrave.hep.8300116

Heller, S. 2006. *The education of a graphic designer*. New York, NY: Allworth.

HESA (Higher Education of South Africa). 2010. *Sector position paper on the report of the Ministerial Committee on Transformation and Social Cohesion and the Elimination of Discrimination in South Africa's Public Higher Education Institutions*. Available at https://www.usaf.ac.za/2010_hesa_position-paper-on-transformation-soudien-report/ [Accessed 30 April 2014].

Johnson, L. & Morris, P. 2010. Towards a framework for critical citizenship education. *Curriculum Journal*, 21(1), 77–96. https://doi.org/10.1080/09585170903560444

Johnson, L. & Morris, P. 2012. Critical citizenship education in England and France: A comparative analysis. *Comparative Education*, 48(3), 283–301. https://doi.org/10.1080/03050068.2011.588885

Lewins, K. 2010. The trauma of transformation: A closer look at the Soudien report. *South African Review of Sociology*, 41(1), 127–136. https://doi.org/10.1080/21528581003676077

Oloyede, O. 2009. Critical reflection on the report of the Ministerial Committee on Transformation, Social Cohesion and the Elimination of Discrimination in Public Higher Education. *Perspectives in Education*. 27 December, 426–434. Available at http://reference.sabinet.co.za/sa_epublication_article/persed_ v27_n4_a10 [Accessed 30 April 2014].

Pillay, S. 2009. Translating "South Africa". In: H. Jacklin & P. Vale (Eds.). *Re-imagining the social in South Africa: Critique, theory and post-apartheid society*. Scottsville: University of KwaZulu-Natal Press, 235–267.

Republic of South Africa. 2008. *National Qualifications Framework Act 67 of 2008*. Available at http://www.che.ac.za/sites/default/files/publications/NQF_act_2008.pdf [Accessed 18 March 2017].

Santas, A. 2000. Teaching anti-racism. *Studies in Philosophy and Education*, 19, 349–361. Available at http://link.springer.com/article/10.1023/A:1005298916161 [Accessed 30 April 2014]. https://doi.org/10.1023/A:1005298916161

SAQA (South African Qualifications Authority). *National Diploma Graphic Design*. Available at http://allqs.saqa.org.za/showQualification.php?id=72594 [Accessed 16 January 2017].

SATN (South African Technology Network). c2015. *Background and role of the SATN*. Available at http://www.satn.co.za/portal/index.php/satn-background [Accessed 10 January 2017].

Seroto, J. 2012. Citizenship education for Africans in South Africa (1948–1994): A critical discourse. *Yesterday and Today*, (7), 63–84. Available at http://www.scielo.org.za/scielo.php?pid=S2223-03862012000100004&script=sci_arttext&tlng=pt [Accessed 4 April 2014].

Soudien, C. 2010. Grasping the nettle? South African higher education and its transformative imperatives. *South African Journal of Higher Education*, 24(5), 881–896. Available at http://reference .sabinet.co.za/sa _epublication_article/high_v24_n6_a2 [Accessed 14 May 2014].

Soudien, C., Michaels, W., Mthembi-Mahanyele, S., Nkomo, M., Nyanda, G., Nyoka, N., Seepe, S., Shisana, O. & Villa-Vicencio, C. 2008. *Report of the Ministerial Committee on Transformation and Social Cohesion and Elimination of Discrimination in Public Higher Education Institutions*. Available at http://www.voced.edu.au/content/ngv:61442 [Accessed 18 May 2014].

Thaver, L. 2006. "At home", institutional culture and higher education: Some methodological considerations. *Perspectives in Education*, 24(1), 15–26.

Triggs, T. 2011. Graphic design history: Past, present, and future. *Design Issues*, 27(1), 3–6. https://doi.org/10.1162/DESI_a_00051

Van Zyl, R. 2007. Design management education: The intersection between design and business. In: *FLUX : Design Education in a Changing World, DEFSA International Design Education Conference 2007*. Available at http://www.defsa.org.za/sites/default/files/downloads/2007conference/van Zyl%2C Ria.pdf [Accessed 14 May 2014].

Webster, E. & Mosoetsa, S. 2001. *At the chalk face: Managerialism and the changing academic workplace 1995–2001*. Available at https://chet.org.za/files/Webster and Mosoetsa 2001 Managerialism.pdf [Accessed 18 March 2017].

Weldon, G. 2010. Post-conflict teacher development: Facing the past in South Africa. *Journal of Moral Education,* 39(3), 353–364. Available at http://www.tandfonline.com [Accessed 30 April 2014]. https://doi.org/10.1080/03057240.2010.497615

Exploring Live and Design-build Projects as Educational Spaces to Foster Critical Citizenship

RUDOLF PEROLD AND HERMIE DELPORT

Introduction

In this chapter we want to share and reflect on our work and experiences in live and design-build projects at the Design Build Research Studio (DBRS). We believe that live and design-build projects are educational spaces in which critical citizenship can be fostered and that it is possible to turn these educational opportunities "into cultures and practices that are weighty enough to challenge the status quo" (Kippen, 2016: 8). To date, the predominant focus in architectural educational and professional practice has been to serve an elite minority who can afford to pay for the services of the architect, thereby neglecting the majority whose quality of life could benefit greatly from architectural design interventions and solutions (Bell & Wakeford, 2008; Perkes, 2009). However, according to Lewis (2014: 2), "even purely private architecture has civic ramifications", and there are signs that the architectural profession is beginning to accept its responsibility towards society. This is echoed by Rosenthal (2013: 1), who states that architectural educators, students and practitioners are becoming increasingly aware of "their ability to promote justice within their social climate".

Internationally, the acceptance of this responsibility is becoming evident through a rise in socially oriented professional practices and live and design-build educational programmes (ACSA, 2014; Anderson, 2012) as well as an increase in research that supports this notion (Design Build Exchange, 2016). Citizenship receives specific attention in many of these practices (Brown, 2012; Christenson & Srivastava, 2005; Crysler, 1995; Jann, 2009). In the South African context, Saidi (2005) devotes an entire chapter of his doctoral thesis, which explores curriculum change in architectural education, to citizenship. It is possible to situate both live and design-build projects within a community, with the aim to make a difference in the lives of others. It is with such projects that our work at the DBRS engages and enables us to draw on this distinct situation in architectural education to negotiate the crossing of several boundaries in the landscape of architectural practices (Delport, 2016).

A live project, as defined by Anderson and Priest (2014: 2), is the "negotiation of a brief, timescale, budget and product between an educational organisation and an external collaborator for their mutual benefit. The project must be structured to ensure that students gain learning that is relevant to their educational development". A design-build project, in turn, is a specific type of live project that has a built structure as outcome. Arguably, the most prominent design-build programme in architectural education is the Rural Studio at Auburn University, founded in 1993 with the aim of contributing to the upliftment of the rural communities of Hale County in Alabama (Rural Studio, 2015). This programme has inspired many schools of architecture to develop their own programmes that are "vernacular, technically sustainable, and community-empowered", with these qualities together forming "the soul of a design-build program, making it a pioneer in sustainable discourse" (Wu, 2007: 9). We find that critical citizenship is, to some extent, embedded in live and design-build projects. At an international symposium on live projects at the Oxford Brookes University School of Architecture in 2012, critical citizenship was one of the symposium themes (Oxford Brookes University, 2012). Brown (2012: 154), in his critique of the live project, writes that the "contribution of critical pedagogy to architectural education is the comprehensive manner in which it associates education with participation and engaged citizenship".

In this chapter our main aim is to introduce the stories of the DBRS and to explore live and design-build projects as spaces to foster critical citizenship. To this end, we will introduce the DBRS and then present two theoretical perspectives that support the notion of critical citizenship. Thereafter we will share our stories and perspectives based on our experiences as participant observers in a number of live and design-build projects undertaken at the DBRS during the past five years. To conclude the chapter, we will highlight aspects of these projects that align with the two theoretical perspectives and the notion of critical citizenship.

The Design Build Research Studio

The DBRS is situated within the Department of Architectural Technology and Interior Design at the Cape Peninsula University of Technology (CPUT) in Cape Town. Since 2011, our work at the DBRS has supported both our doctoral research trajectories and continues to provide us with space for architectural innovation, education and research. The initial doctoral research (Delport, 2016) employed cultural-historical activity theory (CHAT) to explore collaboration as a unique pedagogical construct and educational tool within design-build projects. This research indicated that design-build projects offer inherent instances of and opportunities for collaborative practices, and further explored the possibilities that community-situated design-build projects have for professional architectural practice. The research also explored how students who take part in design-build projects at university gain both the required skills and the necessary inspiration to embark on their own professional design-build practice. The research further drew on the concept of social entrepreneurism – with values underpinning financial, organisational, social and environmental sustainability (Kumar & Gupta, 2013) – to explore design-build as an alternative form of architectural practice.

These explorations of an emergent mode of architectural practice that requires as much soft, social skills as it does hard, technical skills contribute to further doctoral research (Perold, forthcoming). This research conceptualises and explores 'grounded architectural practice', also employing CHAT to study collaborative architectural practice in the context of interventions by non-governmental organisations (NGOs) in informal settlement upgrading projects. The research aims to go beyond individual case narratives – the most prominent mode in which this emergent form of architectural practice is currently reported (Cooke, 2014) – while simultaneously avoiding the abstraction of the modernist tradition in architecture.

Theoretical perspectives

Our experience in live and design-build projects has led us to believe that the projects we do in the DBRS are educational spaces in which critical citizenship can be fostered. We concur with Wenger-Trayner, Fenton-O'Creeve, Hitchinson, Kubiak and Wenger-Trayner (2014: 29) that "as a trajectory through a social landscape, learning is not merely the acquisition of knowledge. It is the becoming of a person who inhabits the landscape with an identity whose dynamic construction reflects our trajectory through that landscape".

Our hope – and indeed one of the intended outcomes of the DBRS projects – is that students who participate in these projects are enabled to inhabit the architectural landscape as critical citizens with a different perspective of their professional potential, status and responsibility. We find two theoretical perspectives, both of which focus on education, especially relevant to our work. The first perspective is a framework of four pedagogical approaches for teaching critical citizenship skills developed by Dejaeghere (2009). For the second we draw on Fullan and Scott (2014) and their framework for new pedagogies for deep learning, which we find to be supportive of the cultivation of critical citizenship. By introducing these two perspectives we aim to provide insight into the pedagogical possibilities of live and design-build projects to foster critical citizenship, and to explore new perspectives to introduce into our own work. We believe that there is evidence of both theoretical perspectives within the projects we have undertaken at the DBRS, and that in future projects we can "actively encourage a critical citizenship disposition, based on the relevant knowledge, skills and values", following Johnson and Morris (2010: 77–78).

A pedagogical framework for critical citizenship education

Dejaeghere (2009: 225) describes critical citizenship education as "teaching and learning strategies to develop young people's engagement in the democratic goals of equality and justice in multicultural societies", and states that educating for critical citizenship is distinct from educating for traditional citizenship. Winton (2007: 6) also draws on Dejaeghere, and describes critical citizenship as an "approach that adopts social reformation as [its] purpose [and] aims to prepare students to critique and change society" as well as a "social reformation model [that] not only encourages active participation, but also examines the relationship between an individual's behaviour and social justice". Dejaeghere proposes a framework of four hands-on strategies with which to approach critical citizenship education (presented in Table 1 below). We believe this framework is a strong conceptual model to use as reference for both exploring completed DBRS projects and designing future DBRS projects.

Table 1   Four strategies for critical citizenship education

Strategy concept	Strategy
Include marginalised knowledge	Including marginalised knowledge and voices in the curriculum to allow for the construction of alternative forms of citizenship, and seeing this knowledge in relation to, and as a critique of, mainstream constructions of citizenship and democracy.
Learn and enact double-consciousness	Learning and enacting double-consciousness, which is examining one's perspectives about and identity related to citizenship through the eyes of another (self-awareness and awareness of others' perspectives) and understanding the complexities of citizen identity affected by discrimination and oppression.
Develop intercultural understanding	Developing intercultural understanding through intercultural learning experiences to engage others in civic relations and spaces.
Utilise collective social action	Utilising strategies for collective social action, such as a collaborative engagement of students, teachers, schools and communities to create social change.

(Source: Dejaeghere, 2009: 228)

Competencies for ethical entrepreneurialism that could support critical citizenship

Coburn (2016) proposes that the critically thinking global citizen requires 21st-century skills. Such 21st-century skills, which, according to McComas (2014), include responsibility, curiosity and adaptability, among many others, are encompassed in the practice of 'ethical entrepreneurialism' conceptualised by Fullan and Scott (2014). They describe ethical entrepreneurialism as …

> … breaking the distinction between being able to work with your hands and your mind and giving a new, deeper meaning to the term 'entrepreneurial'. In our conceptualization entrepreneurialism [it] is not just about making money, but also being able to identify and resolve complex personal and societal challenges locally and globally. For the first time in history the mark of an educated person is that of a doer (a doing-thinker; a thinker-doer) – they learn to do, and do to learn. (Fullan & Scott, 2014: 3)

We find Fullan and Scott relevant, as their perspective ties in with the concept of constructionism (Papert & Harel, 1991) and learning-by-doing (Brillhart, 2014), both of which are an integral part of live and design-build projects. The perspective also resonates with the idea of social entrepreneurialism, which "aims to produce solutions which are sustainable financially, organizationally, socially and environmentally" (Kumar & Gupta, 2013: 10). The principles of social entrepreneurialism and the notion of alternative architectural practice were conceived as a conceptual framework for alternative architectural practice by Delport (2016), consisting of three tiers: sustainable social practice, sustainable environmental practice and sustainable financial practice. Fullan and Scott (2014) identified six competencies – collaboration, creativity, critical thinking, citizenship, character and communication – which one needs to develop in order to practise ethical entrepreneurialism (presented in Table 2 below). We find that these competencies have the potential to support critical citizenship.

Table 2   Competencies for ethical entrepreneurialism, with the potential to support critical citizenship

Competency concept	Competencies
Collaboration	Collaboration refers to the capacity to work interdependently and synergistically in teams with strong interpersonal and team-related skills, including effective management of team dynamics, making substantive decisions together, and learning from and contributing to the learning of others.
Creativity	Having an 'entrepreneurial eye' for economic and social opportunities, asking the right questions to generate novel ideas and demonstrating leadership to pursue those ideas into practice.
Critical thinking	Critically evaluating information and arguments, seeing patterns and connections, construction meaningful knowledge and applying it in the real world.
Citizenship	Thinking like global citizens, considering global issues based on a deep understanding of diverse values with genuine interest in engaging with others to solve complex problems that impact human and environmental sustainability.
Character	Character refers to qualities of the individual essential for being personally effective in a complex world, including grit, tenacity, perseverance, resilience, reliability and honesty.
Communication	Communication entails mastery of three fluencies: digital, writing and speaking tailored for a range of audiences.

(Source: Fullan & Scott, 2014: 6–7)

We agree with Fullan and Scott (2014: 5) that the six competencies described above, when combined into the practice of ethical entrepreneurialism, constitute a framework for new pedagogies of deep learning based on real-world problem solving, with the ability to "build communities, institutions and indeed societies that [are] socially, culturally, economically as well as environmentally sustainable". However, while educating for citizenship is "complex and ambiguous" (Seroto, 2012: 65), educating for critical citizenship is even more so. While the theoretical perspectives we have discussed are two among many that could serve to aid in the conceptualisation of the education of critical citizens, we find them to be clear and supportive of our current educational and pedagogical approach.

DBRS projects

In order to explore the embodiment of pedagogical approaches to critical citizenship education as well as the competencies for practising critical citizenship in our own work, we will present five live and design-build projects that we have undertaken at the DBRS since 2011. The projects are presented in chronological order; the first two projects having informed the doctoral research of Delport (2016), with the latter three informing the doctoral research of Perold (forthcoming).

St Michael's multi-grade school

We constructed three interventions at the St Michael's multi-grade school in Grabouw, the first of which was an outdoor classroom during November 2011. CPUT had already established a relationship with the school through the Centre for Multi-Grade Education, and our aim was to improve the suitability of the building for multi-grade education, where more than one year group is taught in the same classroom. This project represented our first steps into design-build territory and included second-year architectural technology students during the last academic block of their experiential training year. While the rest of their year is spent working in architectural practices, the block format allowed for a two-week construction period on site, with the majority of the design, planning and sourcing of materials having been completed before the block commenced. Working on site would therefore take students to a different site of learning (cf. Garaway & De Villiers Morkel, 2014), beyond that of the studio and the office.

During the initial site visit, some months before the construction period, our students met the principal and teachers, with whom they conversed and discussed ideas, and observed their actual clients – the Grade R to Grade 7 learners – in their classrooms and on the school grounds. After this visit, students studied other conceptual projects involving timber-framed construction in preparation for the design-build project, until the actual design exercise commenced with a collaborative brainstorming session during the academic block in August. Design options were discussed, which ranged from creating platforms for group work within the existing classrooms to the idea of an outdoor classroom and gathering space. Students had to take into account various practicalities, including the fact that they were going to build the intervention themselves while the school was operational, and the availability of transport and materials. These preliminary ideas were consolidated during a reflective discussion session, after which students individually prepared proposals based on the discussion. We then identified the main ideas derived from the individual proposals and discussed these with the school community in order to get their input and determine a collaborative path forward. The process now stepped outside of the available academic blocks, and a core group of ten students volunteered to take part in the final collaborative design process. This process determined materials that could be sourced through recycling and sponsorships as well as those to be purchased through research funding.

The consolidated design centred on an outdoor classroom – essentially three roofs; one solid and two with timber slats – supported by gum pole columns, providing a covered space for formal and informal gatherings and school plays and shelter from the wind and sun. During the two-week on-site construction, we were assisted by a local architect-builder and a natural-building specialist. Students had to travel from CPUT by bus each day, while the core group of students found accommodation in Grabouw, and took it upon themselves to do the site preparation in the morning as well as the final checks and clean-up of the site in the afternoon. Several impromptu opportunities arose on site, including the extension of the stoep in front of the existing classrooms with a timber deck, creating a paved surface at an outdoor drinking tap, building an extra set of stairs to link the outdoor classroom with the playground and food garden as well as making a mural together with the learners (Figure 1). Students worked in small groups that were allocated specific tasks, with some students moving between groups at times and strong alliances forming in some of the groups.

During 2012 we undertook two further interventions at St Michael's. The first involved Extended Curriculum Programme (ECP) students, who did a small project to enlarge and add a screen to the deck built during the first intervention. The design for the screen was completed during the first intervention, and the ECP students therefore learnt about the design process by studying and observing the previous design-build work and then building the deck and screen. Our last intervention involved second-year Architectural Technology and third-year Interior Design students, who converted a shipping container next to the outdoor classroom into a library, complete with custom-designed shelves and furniture as well as a solar protection screen clad with timber from recycled apple crates (figures 2 to 5).

Figure 1   Making a hand-print mural

After the completion of the outdoor classroom intervention, the students involved the learners and made a mural of handprints using environmentally friendly paint sponsored by a local manufacturer. In doing so, students could contribute to the learners' exposure to the concept of sustainability.

Figure 2   Hand-over of outdoor classroom

After completing the mural of handprints, our students and all the learners attended the official hand-over of the outdoor classroom intervention to the school.

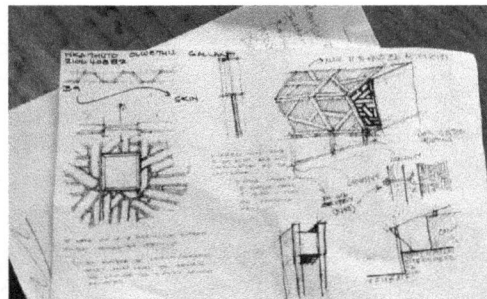

Figure 3   A variety of strategies to enable collaborative work

On-site design development and construction planning involved various media and tools, ranging from cardboard models to three-dimensional computer-aided design software. The variety of strategies used enabled students to work collaboratively and in real time in the construction of the intervention.

Figure 4 Outdoor classroom and shipping
container library

Work underway on our third intervention at the
St Michael's multi-grade school, which involved the
conversion of a shipping container into a library.
The new library faces onto our first intervention,
an outdoor classroom that connects the indoor
classrooms with the playground and a food garden
based on permaculture principles.

Figure 5 Construction of a solar screen for the
shipping container library

A local architect-builder advises students on the
positioning of purlins on the solar protection screen
over the shipping container library. In the background,
the outdoor classroom structure is being re-oiled,
making students aware of their responsibility towards
those who have to maintain the interventions after
their departure.

Sutherland overnight retreat

Three design-build projects were introduced to the third-year studio in 2012, with each project involving around ten students who worked on the conceptual and technological development of their project for a period of eight weeks. Our intent was to build all three of these projects, but unfortunately, due to funding and procurement process constraints, we were not able to do so. Nonetheless, the projects proved to be valuable exercises in intensive collaborative design as a result of the longer time span and smaller groups, which allowed each student to participate fully in the sharing of ideas. For us, experiencing the process of bringing together individual ideas, identifying overlapping intent and then developing the strongest aspects were of great value, and for the first time we fully realised the value of a collaborative design approach.

One of the three projects was the design of an overnight tourist retreat on a farm outside of the town of Sutherland, a remote and climatically extreme part of the Northern Cape. The group of students who participated in this project travelled to the site during the April recess. The owner of the farm provided accommodation for the students as well as funding for the building of the project, which was planned for September that year. On the first day we explored the farm, searching for a suitable site for an overnight retreat (Figure 6). Our students discovered a fountain that provides a constant supply of water at the bottom of a small valley, and then used their bodies as visual height markers for photographs and to establish reference points for views and pedestrian routes. Discussions, which included the farm owner, focused on site selection as well as establishing a range of criteria to guide the development of the project brief.

After the physical immersion on site, our students returned to the studio, where two additional students joined the group. Communicating the physical experience of the site to the new group members was challenging, but it provided an opportunity for group discussion during which the students who had been on the site explained the site verbally and with visual information, which allowed for a mental revisit of the site. Our students then consolidated the site research to ensure that they fully understood the design challenge at hand, and compiled it in a reference document that was used for the duration of the project. The programme allowed for two interactive studio sessions per week, where we acted as facilitators and soundboards to the unfolding process. The key physical outcomes of the project were determined by the group, and these included the shared reference document, a visual pin-up presentation and a series of working models as well as a detailed final model. The collaborative making of physical models as a strengthening of the concept of design-build and learning-by-doing became the central driver of the project.

Students researched appropriate precedents and aspects such as material availability, suitable technology and service options. This exploration uncovered an unexpectedly rich variety of materials available in close proximity to the site, including stone, clay, sand, reeds, wool, straw bales, thicket, steel wire, blue gum and pine, bricks and steel sheeting. They also had to consider the fact that what they proposed was going to be physically built, and this resulted in the bulk of the ideas proposed being practical and executable. Questions were sent back to the owner to establish buildability, available workshop space and artisan skills available on the farm. The students first developed individual design models based on the collective concept statement, reflecting on and individually interpreting this statement by means of sketches, drawings and at least one working model before discussing their findings with the group.

The sharing of design ideas in the group was initially met with apprehension, but the potential for a multitude of creative design solutions soon became clear. Individual idea models were discussed, and strong and overlapping ideas were identified and then formalised into an expanded concept statement to inform subsequent collaborative design work and collaborative idea models. We facilitated the establishment of guiding principles by asking questions and emphasising reflection, allowing all students to voice their opinion about all the aspects of the design. Various iterations of the collaborative design were built on the same working model base and each stage was documented photographically, with each subsequent iteration progressively gaining complexity and detail (Figure 7). As the intention was to eventually build the project, the strong focus on modelling and large-scale technological development was also seen as preparation for the building work on the site.

Figure 6   Exploring the rural landscape

Together with the owner of a farm near the town of Sutherland, students spent the first day of the project exploring the rural landscape. This enabled them to put into practice their academic knowledge relating to building siting and orientation, while compiling a list of natural materials available for use in the structure.

Figure 7   Model-driven design process

Once back in the studio, cardboard models were used to capture the essence of the site and various iterations of the design. This process allowed students to develop a cost-effective structure, respecting both the budget and the natural environment.

Vygieskraal reblocking project

In March 2013 we undertook our first live project in Cape Town, in collaboration with the local NGO Community Organisation Resource Centre (CORC) and residents of Vygieskraal, an informal settlement in Athlone. CORC had been involved in the planning of a reblocking project in the settlement, and we were asked to provide assistance with the visualisation of possible development alternatives based on the strategy of reblocking. The reblocking entailed resident-based mapping (measuring of erven and shacks) and enumeration (a socio-demographic survey of every household) in order to rationalise the layout of their settlements, thereby improving access for emergency vehicles and enabling the installation of municipal services. Prior to their interaction with the community, we sensitised our students to aspects such as different backgrounds, levels of education, languages and cultures as well as the fact that the residents had little or no understanding of design jargon or principles. During the site visit to Vygieskraal for data gathering and on-site analysis, our students witnessed residents' harsh living conditions and the ever-present risk of flooding and fire as well as their everyday challenges to access clean water and sanitation (Figure 8).

CORC expedited the process by providing the information generated by residents during the enumeration and mapping of the settlement. This afforded our students more time to interact with residents on site and to apply critical thinking and creativity in the generation of collaborative options for the improvement of dwellings, infrastructure services and the surrounding environment. The continued engagement with resident volunteers at the design studio in CPUT encouraged the students to employ an approach that demystified the design process and made it accessible enough – both verbally and visually – to allow the direct involvement of the residents in a collaborative design process (Figure 9). At the end of our involvement in the project, the students had developed a slide-show presentation, design proposal posters, a process video and a site layout model, which were presented to CORC in order to support the ongoing upgrading of Vygieskraal.

Figure 8   Informal settlement site visit

Our first site visit at the Vygieskraal informal settlement, during the reblocking project facilitated by the local NGO CORC. This project was introduced to us by a graduate of our department, then employed by CORC, and was fundamental in widening our perspective of the potential of live and design-build projects as educational spaces to foster critical citizenship.

Figure 9   Collaborative design workshop

Students and residents discuss a site layout model based on decisions made during the collaborative design workshop held in our design studio. This process enabled residents to provide students with insight into their living conditions and aspirations for the reblocking of their settlement, which our students then interpreted into spatial design proposals for further discussion.

Lwazi Park post-reblocking upgrading

While the live project at Vygieskraal developed our confidence in engaging with residents and their living environment in a more direct manner, we felt that the focus on reblocking (based on the reinstatement of informal dwellings) did not offer a substantive technological challenge to our students. As such, we were excited to engage with CORC and the residents of Lwazi Park, an informal settlement that had already been reblocked. For CORC this was one of the first projects exploring incremental housing typologies for a reblocked settlement and as such it reflected the potential cumulative nature of informal settlement upgrading. Lwazi Park is located next to the Lotus River canal, in Gugulethu, and the reblocking had occurred during 2011 as part of a canal-widening project to reduce the risk of flooding. The project had been contentious, as an external consultant employed by the City of Cape Town (CoCT) prepared a conventional, uniform settlement layout that could accommodate only 26 households, meaning that some households would have to be relocated elsewhere.

When the residents rejected the proposed layout, CORC was called on to assist. The residents saw the intervention as an opportunity to upgrade their settlement and indicated that they wanted CORC to assist them with planning and negotiations. The CoCT agreed to this and allowed time for a participatory design process, during which residents expressed their real concerns on the proposed layout: wide streets posing a thoroughfare to Barcelona informal settlement, insufficient perimeter security and a lack of space for communal services such as washing and laundry areas (CORC, Lwazi Park Community & South African SDI Alliance, 2011). CORC and the CoCT mediated between the residents and the external consultant, and they agreed on the co-designed layout, minimally revised in order to satisfy fire safety regulations. Within a week of this agreement, residents moved their informal dwellings in accordance with the layout.

This initiated a process where residents began to imagine the next phase of settlement upgrading. In April 2015, we undertook a live project with CORC and the Lwazi Park residents to contribute towards this process. Our intention was to develop alternative settlement layouts and housing typologies suited to incremental upgrading. The project commenced with a site visit to Lwazi Park, where students met with residents and discussed their needs and priorities. The collaborative design process started with a site analysis based on information provided by CORC and the CoCT as well as interviews conducted on site, which facilitated an understanding of the physical context and spatial planning issues, most of which pertained to the relationship with neighbouring settlements, the challenges of everyday life and community needs. As before, our students became aware that many things they took for granted were absent: heating, piped water, toilets and showers. They then started negotiating the difficulties of planning, urban design and landscape architecture in an unfamiliar context, and developed settlement layouts in an interactive and fluid collaborative design process punctuated by real-time input from residents and CORC (Figure 10). Having to adjust their design based on the input received challenged their critical thinking skills and creativity, making clear the complexity of balancing residents' needs with one's own design intent.

Individually developed conceptual settlement layout diagrams were discussed in groups, and the best ideas were combined into a new iteration. This was a rich process due to the variety of voices present, and different settlement layout options were tested as overlays over existing maps and aerial photography. Different strategies that allow for passive surveillance and sufficient access to shared facilities were tested, while ensuring that residential areas are private and secure. Residents required each housing unit to have a direct relationship with the ground, preferably with a small front yard, and that units should allow for incremental expansion so that each household can adapt their unit to their own evolving needs over time. In order to facilitate this, our students designed a core structure, to be funded from the housing subsidy for which residents were planning to apply. Appropriate materials and construction methods were explored in terms of cost, performance and availability. While this was within the realm of expert knowledge, which the students are accustomed to applying in their design projects, residents provided crucial information about the relation of spaces and functions as well as the internal layout of housing units (Figure 11). As with the Vygieskraal project, the alternative settlement layouts and housing typologies were presented to CORC and the residents as a contribution to their ongoing negotiations with the CoCT.

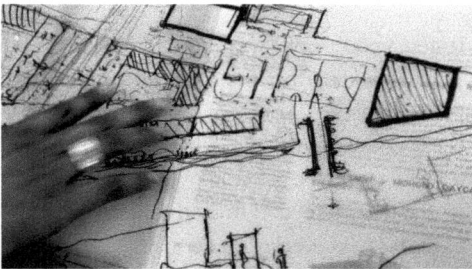

Figure 10   Site layout proposals

A student explains their initial site layout proposal for the post-reblocking upgrading of Lwazi Park. The proposals were directly informed by residents' concerns, many of which related to security, which were voiced during both the site visit facilitated by CORC and the collaborative design workshop at CPUT. These provided students with clear and tangible informants to steer the development of spatial layout options for the settlement.

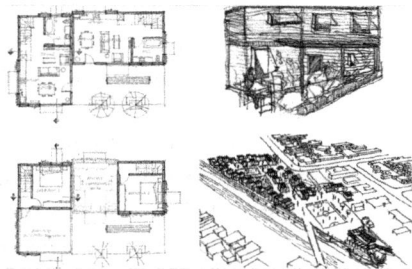

Figure 11   Exploring various aspects of the project together with residents

The strategic move to a post-reblocking project provided the architectural and technical complexity that we found lacking in our first informal settlement project. At Lwazi Park, our students had the opportunity to explore urban design, dwelling layout and structural technology in the work they co-produced with the residents.

Lotus Park public space intervention

After the two live projects in collaboration with CORC, we felt confident enough to tackle a design-build project in an informal settlement. To this end, we collaborated with Violence Prevention through Urban Upgrading (VPUU), which was in the process of consolidating a public space intervention in Lotus Park, an informal settlement adjacent to the Nyanga Junction train station in Gugulethu. In response to service-delivery protests, the CoCT asked VPUU to adapt its violence-prevention methodology to an informal settlement context, using an in-situ developmental approach. The public space is centred on a neighbourhood centre (NHC), completed in 2014, which functions as a safety catalyst and provides community facilities. These include offices for local organisations, meeting rooms, a hall, early childhood development facilities and an *emthonjeni* – a multifunctional space with a selection of utilities (e.g. water points), places for gathering, playing, washing and conducting business (Ewing, 2015).

The live project took place during April and May 2016, involving the design and building of a public space intervention at the NHC. It commenced with a site visit and guided walkabout, during which an architect from VPUU described the history of its involvement in Lotus Park to the students, followed by a site analysis in the NHC. Based on the site analysis and discussions with residents who volunteered to take part in the live project, possible interventions were proposed. These were then designed collaboratively in groups consisting of students and residents, working in the studio as well as at the NHC. Concept designs were presented to residents at the NHC during the last week of April (Figure 12), after which a group of 12 students were identified to proceed with the technological design and construction of the proposed intervention. Residents from Lotus Park reviewed the proposed interventions and selected a design for implementation by means of a vote. The selected design was then developed further by our students, in liaison with their Construction Technology lecturer and a structural engineer. The design of the steel brackets and reinforcement bars had to be finalised urgently to allow sufficient time for manufacturing.

The character of our students (as well as ours) was tested a couple of days before construction was to commence, when we received an e-mail from VPUU reporting that the proposed intervention was discussed at its weekly meeting with resident representatives, some of whom felt that they had not been sufficiently consulted in the design process, and were concerned about the form and function of the intervention. This was in part due to a misinterpretation of computer renderings that were displayed at the NHC, and with the use of a cardboard model and revised renderings one of our Xhosa-speaking students addressed the concerns at the next weekly meeting.

This delay had postponed the construction by one week, meaning that we would only have half the time we allowed for this part of the project. Nonetheless, as the construction work was to take place in two groups – six students working on site under supervision of a local contractor, doing excavations and preparing for the concrete to be cast, and six students working in an off-site workshop to prepare and test-assemble the timber structure – we decided to attempt to complete the entire project in one week. Progress was slower than expected due to the risk of theft on site and cumbersome procurement processes, which resulted in a delay in the delivery of material. However, the delays allowed more time for planning, which resulted in our students being able to work more efficiently once the material had been delivered. At the end of the week, the concrete work had been completed and the timber structure had been test-assembled (Figure 13), but there was not sufficient time to erect the timber structure on site. As a result, the assistance of a local construction company was obtained to complete the intervention (figures 14 and 15).

Figure 12   Design presentation to residents

A design presentation to the residents of Lotus Park, held at the NHC that was recently completed by VPUU. For this project we wanted to build our first intervention in an informal settlement, which proved to be a very challenging learning trajectory for all concerned.

Figure 13   Test assembly of timber frames

The building work at Lotus Park took place with one group of students assisting a local contractor with the on-site concrete and masonry work, while another group of students cut and test-assembled the timber frames at a workshop. These were then transported to the site, where they were to be bolted onto the masonry platform and receive their roof purlins and sheeting in order to complete the intervention.

Figure 14   The completed structure

The intervention was completed with the assistance of a local contractor, and the timber structure completes the one edge of the sports court by extending the façade of the NHC.

Figure 15   Detail of the completed structure

A close-up view of the completed timber structure, with roof sheeting over the seating area and a pergola towards the rear.

Discussion

The four strategies of Dejaeghere (2009) and the six competencies of Fullan and Scott (2014) resonate with the principles underpinning the work we undertake at the DBRS. We see both existing evidence and future opportunities for these approaches in our projects. In tables 3 and 4 we have responded to the two frameworks with a brief reflection from our own experience.

Table 3   DBRS reflection on evidence of the four strategies for critical citizenship education in our work

Strategy concept	DBRS reflection on evidence of strategy
1. Include marginalised knowledge	Our work is a critique against both conventional studio education and professional practice (Delport, 2016) and as such is often characterised by what Carter (2013) refers to as an explicit anti-professional ideology. Students are provided with the opportunity to engage with marginalised knowledge and voices through engagement with real clients in the real world and the lessons derived from these experiences are incorporated into the curriculum to inform future projects. Furthermore, students are exposed to an emerging mode of professional architectural practice, which stands well outside of the mainstream of architectural professional possibilities predominantly on offer for young graduates.
2. Learn and enact double-consciousness	Through collaborative group-based design projects, drawing on our partnerships with local NGOs, our students are provided with opportunities to learn and enact double-consciousness. This refers to both exposure to the relative strengths, skills and knowledge of other students within the group projects and the situated knowledge of the community as client, such as the informal settlement residents who volunteered to take part in the design projects as co-designers.
3. Develop intercultural understanding	By drawing on the expertise of our local NGO partners, these projects provide facilitated intercultural encounters in contexts that are often foreign to our students and immersion in these contexts provides the opportunity to explore the world from a different perspective. Students have to examine the context and realities of each community in which they work, and we believe that this provides an opportunity for more explicit examination of different identities, histories and contexts.
4. Utilise collective social action	Strategies for collective social action are inherent in live and design-build projects. In the doctoral research of Delport (2016), collaboration among students emerged as the unintended consequence of such projects. When students work together on a common goal – usually related to social justice – they become interdependent, developing group working skills and relying on self-management in order to achieve their goal. Collective action in design-build projects can be conceptualised as three types of collaboration: collaborative learning, collaborative design and collaborative construction (Delport, 2016). Of these three, we find collaborative construction to be the most effective space for practising collaboration.

(Source: Dejaeghere, 2009)

Table 4   DBRS reflection on evidence of the six competencies for ethical entrepreneurialism in our work

Competencies for ethical entrepreneurialism	DBRS reflection on evidence of competencies
1. Collaboration	Students themselves acknowledged the value of group work and collaboration. The following are verbatim quotes from students who participated in our projects: This project could never have been completed without the teamwork and willingness to work by everyone. We did a good job and I am proud of my team. Feels good solving problems on site instead of doing it on the computer. … the best learning experience was working well in a group. I am gaining more and more knowledge with regard to teamwork; this is a tough issue, as everyone has their own ideas and thoughts, yet is very much a part of life and the working profession. It was great learning about the coordination, commitment and effort needed from all members of the team to allow a flow of construction.
2. Creativity	When confronted with the need to obtain recycled material for use in our projects, students responded with both innovative materials and sources of material. Observations made en route to the project sites also led to opportunities that were not evident beforehand, such as sourcing timber mulch for a floor surface at the St Michael's outdoor classroom. Drawing on the resources available in the rural landscape of the Sutherland project also informed novel technological choices with regard to the concept design and detailing of the overnight retreat. In the projects that engaged informal settlement residents, students drew on the tacit knowledge and everyday practices of the residents and incorporated aspects thereof into their designs.
3. Critical thinking	Students had to bring together a varied range of information – both familiar and unfamiliar to them – in order to design real solutions to real problems. In the design-build projects, the requirement that they had to execute their designs themselves led to them becoming more critical in their decision making. The same occurred when students were confronted with the scarcity of means that characterised the live projects in informal settlement contexts.
4. Citizenship	Working in financially and socially deprived areas made students aware of diverse values. Referring again to Wu (2007), the spirit of design-build projects encompasses human and environmental sustainability. We found that students' participation is intrinsically motivated by the difference that they can make in the lives of others. The following verbatim quotes from students who participated in our projects support this observation: This experience will unify us … towards achieving a common goal, which is to make a success of the St Michael's design-build project. … one thing stands out for me: the little girl who thanked us, and painting everyone's hand to handprint the wall we painted. Now the hard sweating on that ladder wasn't just for nothing. That was the proudest moment of my two weeks, in fact the whole year. We were there and we made that change.

Table 4   DBRS reflection on evidence of the six competencies for ethical entrepreneurialism in our work (…continued)

Competencies for ethical entrepreneurialism	DBRS reflection on evidence of competencies
5. Character	The characteristics of grit, tenacity, perseverance, resilience, reliability and honesty are called for by Fullan and Scott. The physical aspect and on-site location of the DBRS projects ask of students to work in hot, windy and rainy conditions, which are foreign in an academic environment. One has to be resilient and have grit to persevere under such circumstances. The principle of collaboration or teamwork requires reliability and interdependence; the team cannot move forward without relying on one another. Honesty as a characteristic is not outright measurable or visible in our experiences and warrants investigation into how one would integrate learning about honesty into a live and Design-build project.
6. Communication	Communication in the completed DBRS projects involved both verbal and visual skills. Students had tos communicate with a range of different stakeholders, all with differing levels of prior knowledge and understanding of architectural and design processes. Students had to engage with one another, with other professionals as well as with their client, the community, and explain their ideas by means of verbal, written and graphic communication.

(Source: Fullan & Scott, 2014)

Conclusion

In this chapter we have shared and reflected on our experiences in live and design-build projects at the DBRS, and argued that these projects are educational spaces that enable the development of critical citizenship. The theoretical perspectives provided by Dejaeghere (2009) and Fullan and Scott (2014) enabled us to elaborate on our experience of learning as the "becoming of a person who inhabits the landscape with an identity whose dynamic construction reflects our trajectory through that landscape" (Wenger-Trayner et al., 2014: 29). Our investigation into the pedagogical possibilities of live and design-build projects to foster critical citizenship was undertaken by reflecting on our own work, and identifying evidence of strategies towards critical citizenship education as well as competencies for ethical entrepreneurialism. It is our hope that in drawing on these strategies and competencies, we can continue to cross boundaries in the landscape of architectural practices (Delport, 2016) and support the emergence of a more grounded architectural practice that supports the principles of critical citizenship.

*   *All photographs by the authors, including those of students' work.*

References

ACSA. 2014. *ACSA Fall Conference Paper Proceedings*. Washington, DC: ACSA Press. Available at http://www.acsa-arch.org/programs-events/conferences/fall-conference/2014-fall-conference [Accessed 18 August 2015].

Anderson, J. & Priest, C. 2014. Developing an inclusive definition, typological analysis and online resource for live projects. In: H. Harris & L. Widder (Eds.). *Architecture live projects: Pedagogy into practice*. Abingdon: Routledge, 9–17.

Anderson, N.M. 2012. Public interest design: A vehicle for change in architectural education and practice public interest design. In: *ACSA International Conference proceedings*, 20–22 June, Barcelona. Washington, DC: ACSA Press, 268–274. Available at http://lib.dr.iastate.edu/arch_conf/38 [Accessed 23 January 2017].

Bell, B. & Wakeford, K. (Eds.). 2008. *Expanding architecture: Design as activism*. New York, NY: Metropolis Books.

Brillhart, J.L. 2014. A machine to reflect on the infinite city. In: *ACSA Fall Conference Proceedings*, 16–18 October, Halifax. Washington, DC: ACSA Press, 8–9. Available at http://www.acsa-arch.org/programs-events/conferences/fall-conference/2014-fall-conference [Accessed 18 August 2015].

Brown, J.B. 2012. A critique of the live project. PhD thesis. Belfast: Queen's University Belfast.

Carter, F. 2013. Structures of knowledge and pedagogy. *Architecture South Africa*, 61, 36–45.

Christenson, M. & Srivastava, M. 2005. A proposal for a cross-disciplinary design pedagogy: Generative full-scale investigations. In: *International Conference on Design Education Proceedings*, 2–4 March, Brussels. Ahmedabad: National Institute of Design, 231–238. Available at http://www.ndsu.edu/fileadmin/mchriste/2005_DETM.pdf [Accessed 23 September 2014].

Coburn, J. 2016. *Why the world needs critically thinking global citizens? Innovative strategies to prepare your students for a future of uncertainty*. Available at http://blog.worldvuze.com/blog/2016/06/02/why-the-world-needs-critically-thinking-global-citizens-innovative-strategies-to-prepare-your-students-for-a-future-of-uncertainty/ [Accessed 2 August 2016].

Cooke, J. 2014. Two worlds – to narrow the gap. *Architecture South Africa*, 66, 1.

CORC (Community Organisation Resource Centre), Lwazi Park Community & South African SDI Alliance. 2011. *Moving towards land tenure: Relocation of Lwazi Park* [Printed report provided by CORC].

Crysler, C. 1995. Critical pedagogy and architectural education. *Journal of Architectural Education*, 48(4), 208–217. https://doi.org/10.1080/10464883.1995.10734644

Dejaeghere, J.G. 2009. Critical citizenship education for multicultural societies. *Revista Interamericana de Eduacion para la Democracia*, 2(2), 223–246.

Delport, H.E. 2016. Towards design-build architectural education and practice. DTech thesis. Cape Town: Cape Peninsual University of Technology.

Design Build Exchange. 2016. *Projects*. Available at http://db-x.org/projects/ [Accessed 18 August 2016].

Ewing, K. 2015. Violence prevention through urban upgrading: Approach to reclaiming the public realm. *Architecture South Africa*, 71, 28–30.

Fullan, M. & Scott, G. 2014. *New pedagogies for deep learning*. Available at http://michaelfullan.ca/wp-content/uploads/2014/09/Education-Plus-A-Whitepaper-July-2014-1.pdf [Accessed 4 September 2016].

Garraway, J. & De Villiers Morkel, J. 2014. Learning at sites of practice. *Progressio*, 36(2), 22–37.

Jann, M. 2009. Revamping architectural education: Ethics, social service, and innovation. *International Journal of Arts and Sciences,* 3(8), 45–89.

Johnson, L. & Morris, P. 2010. Towards a framework for critical citizenship education. *The Curriculum Journal,* 21(1), 77–96. https://doi.org/10.1080/09585170903560444

Kippen, H. 2016. *Place is the space*. Available at http://collaboratecic.com/place-is-the-space-ca8d51fb16fd#.he6dtts9t [Accessed 1 December 2016].

Kumar, S.S. & Gupta, K. 2013. Social entrepreneurship: A conceptual framework. *International Journal of Management and Social Sciences Research*, 2(8), 9–14.

Lewis, M.J. 2014. *Architects and citizenship*. Available at http://www.citizenship-aei.org/2014/02/architects-and-citizenship/#.wmfjrnkgouk [Accessed 25 January 2017].

McComas, W.F. 2014. 21st-century skills. In: W.F. McComas (Ed.). *The language of science education: An expanded glossary of key terms and concepts in science teaching and learning*. Rotterdam: Sense, 1.

Oxford Brookes University. 2012. *Architecture Live Projects Pedagogy International Symposium*. Edited exhibition. Available at http://architecture.brookes.ac.uk/research/symposia/liveprojects2012/documents/ArchitectureLiveProjectsCatalogue2012.pdf [Accessed 2 February 2016].

Papert, S. & Harel, I. 1991. *Constructionism*. Norwoord: Ablex.

Perkes, D. 2009. A useful practice. *Journal of Architectural Education*, 62(4), 64–71. https://doi.org/10.1080/03057240.2010.49761510.1111/j.1531-314X.2009.1005.x

Perold, R. (Forthcoming). Informal capacities: Exploring grounded architectural practice in transitions to sustainable urbanism. PhD thesis. Hasselt: Hasselt University and Stellenbosch: Stellenbosch University.

Rosenthal, H. 2013. *Expanding architectural practice to advance social justice: Social architecture creates equitable shelter*. MSc thesis. Ames: Iowa State University. Available at http://lib.dr.iastate.edu/etd/13337/ [Accessed 21 June 2016].

Rural Studio. 2015. Available at http://www.ruralstudio.org/ [Accessed 26 April 2016].

Saidi, F.E. 2005. Developing a curriculum model for architectural education in a culturally changing South Africa. PhD thesis. Pretoria: University of Pretoria.

Seroto, J. 2012. Citizenship education for Africans in South Africa (1948–1994): A critical discourse. *Yesterday & Today,* 7, 63–84.

Wenger-Trayner, E., Fenton-O'Creeve, M., Hutchinson, S., Kubiak, C. & Wenger-Trayner, B. (Eds.). 2014. *Learning in landscapes of practice.* New York, NY: Routledge Taylor & Francis.

Winton, S. 2007. Does character really support citizenship education? Examining the claims of an Ontario policy. *Canadian Journal of Educational Administration and Policy,* 66, n.p. Available at http://www.umanitoba.ca/publications/cjeap/articles/winton.html [Accessed 18 August 2016].

Wu, S. 2007. *A new trend of architectural practice and education community-based design / build programs.* Available at http://www.mcgill.ca/mchg/files/mchg/wu_isd_essay.pdf [Accessed 15 September 2013].

Community Engagement, Catalysts in the Built Environment and Reflections on Teaching Architecture with a Focus on Housing Design

AMIRA OSMAN

Introduction

I am an architect and professor at the Tshwane University of Technology (TUT), previously lecturing in housing and urban policy. This chapter was written in the context of South African university turmoil around the #FeesMustFall campaign and the demands for free decolonised education. My teaching revolves around the themes of housing and urban environments (HUE). I established HUE as a research field at the University of Pretoria (1998–2009) and at the University of Johannesburg (2016) and am currently developing a similar programme at TUT.

My design teaching practice has focused on instilling the values of citizenship and design activism by emphasising the belief that design can make a difference and serve a higher purpose. I have done this by tapping into the unique skills of architects in addition to borrowing from other disciplines, as innovation is not necessarily embedded in the narrow confines of a single discipline, and mostly exists at the interface between disciplines. In my courses, architecture is presented as a social act, based on social agreements, serving the needs of the individual as well as the collective, and helping to manage the relationship between them.

By premising my pedagogical approach on these concepts, I aim to enable my students and our partner communities to achieve more awareness of their agency, influence and decision-making capacity in the built environment. In projects that I led (I predominantly use my University of Pretoria experience in this chapter), activism has mostly been in the form of service learning and in providing documentation, design and/or building services with the intention of achieving education, empowerment and improved negotiating power for all participants.

In the contexts I used for student projects, mostly inner city and township settings, I have aimed to combine learning goals and community service in a manner that aims towards knowledge exchange as opposed to knowledge transfer. It is also to encourage a search for design and technical solutions through deeper understanding of people, place and context, rather than deriving solutions in isolation, using abstract theories that may not have relevance to partner communities. It is important to understand the inherited realities of post-apartheid South African cities in order to appreciate the unique characteristics of inner city and township settings. South Africa is a divided nation with divided cities as a result of its political history. The idea of complete, integrated, sustainable, human(e) settlements and multi-layered environments, realised through alternative design, finance and delivery mechanisms, which acknowledge built environment levels and diverse agents of decision making, is still a far-away ideal.

This teaching approach is presented here, underpinned by a theoretical framework based on ecosystemic thinking and open building. Case studies / studio projects are preceded by definitions of architecture, housing and participation. Finally, the concept of 'catalysts' is explained as an approach to community engagement.

Pedagogical premise

African educational institutions have a tendency to isolate people from their communities, as elaborated by bwa Mwesigire, citing Mazrui: "The high priests of Western civilization in the continent are virtually all products of those cultural seminaries called 'universities'" (bwa Mwesigire, 2014: n.p.). I have aimed at dismantling these barriers between campus and context in my teaching approach. My housing studio briefs have aimed at documentation, analysis and developing practical design solutions at various built environment levels (residential units; mixed-use, multi-family urban blocks; urban design / neighbourhood / precinct levels).

Dewey's educational theories, summarised in a concise book in 1938, question the relationship between the learner and the teacher and bring to focus the experience of the learner as well as commentary on the methods, format and space of teaching/learning (Dewey, 1938). In *Democracy and education: An introduction to the philosophy of education* (Dewey, 1916) the ground was set for progressive, relatively unstructured education, which focuses on both content and process. These concepts have influenced my approach to a great extent. These theories have been described by Saltmarsh (1996) as decentring of the teacher, connected knowing through extension of teaching spaces beyond the campus and recognition of multiple ways of teaching and learning towards the achievement of connected institutions through contact with proximate communities. Saltmarsh (1996: 15) further explains: "[C]onnected knowing treats education not as something separate from 'life', but as life itself, and education becomes a lifelong process carried forward by an individual provided with the proficiencies of a self-directed learner." Education is perceived as 'a way of life' that does not divorce people from context, and is a process of living as opposed to being prepared for life (Saltmarsh, 1996).

I have taken Dewey's concepts of education and applied them to the architectural studio. This led to a re-think of the format and methods of delivery, the drafting of studio briefs, places of learning being extended beyond the studio and a focus on the experience of the student. This practically translated into the city becoming the training ground – the laboratory where partnerships and networks are built. This process has contributed towards the development of a more enlightened approach to professionalism, challenging elitist, expert-driven approaches, acknowledging and respecting local ways of doing as well as improving practice through the application of the wealth of knowledge available at universities (*cf.* Osman, 2007).

I have had to deal with the complexities that arise when working with real communities in real time. To address this complexity, I have adopted what I refer to as 'adaptive' teaching strategies. In other words, I have followed leads in the form of time, people and place, and constantly changed direction when I needed to, as I strongly believe Jones's (1976) proclamation that an adaptive strategy is the most intelligent strategy. While it is understood that academic programmes are restricting, I learnt to develop strategies that allow for a level of flexibility in terms of the set brief and the expected outcomes of the projects. The outputs of the studios that I managed over the years were not predetermined and were usually quite unexpected. I have constantly had to adapt to changing circumstances, perspectives and new information. This is especially important in the context of transforming communities and dynamic conditions. This positioned the way of thinking in the university setting and within set university systems it has been a complex process. Community-engagement projects had to be reconciled with university administrations and academic calendars and negotiated with the various funders.

My design and teaching approach is rooted in concepts of ecosystemic thinking as well as open building. A brief description of both is important. The links with concepts of citizenship, agency and participation will become evident.

Ecosystemic thinking

Ecosystemic thinking pertains to eco-philosophy as a way of thinking. It acknowledges the interconnectedness of things and ideas. No 'thing' stands alone; things are what they are by virtue of their relationship to one another.[1] Ecosystemic thinking applies to the built environment, looked at in its totality rather than as individual buildings, in opposition to the approach taken by institutional architecture. Yet, an ecosystemic understanding of the built environment allows for definitions of architecture to be broadened. It is also key to understanding how to harness alternative and innovative concepts as tools towards transforming space and built environment production systems in South Africa (Osman, 2004, 2015). Open building is one such tool.

Open building

Open building has different interpretations across the different levels of the built environment. It can imply the way a building is 'put together', how it is assembled in terms of long- and short-life components and how the interface between building components allows for disassembly, replacement and upgrading with no disruptions to other building systems or components. However, open building also implies the interface between building level and urban design level and between spaces within

---

[1]   This way of thinking was due to the influence of Professors Roger Fisher and Karel Bakker at the University of Pretoria. It was also the philosophy underpinning my PhD thesis presented at the same university under Professor Bakker's supervision.

and outside of buildings and how people manage their relationships within the built environment through negotiation, transaction and deal making.

Habraken (cited in CIB 104, 2004) declares that modernism was a regressive movement, as it failed to acknowledge the complexity evident in older contexts in terms of multiple decision makers and articulation of the different levels of the built environment. Habraken and Teicher (2000) further illustrate this concept through the study of historical cities in their book *The structure of the ordinary: Form and control in the built environment*, demonstrating how ancient cities have developed as a 'fine-grained living fabric' with no single party controlling the whole and where control is hierarchically structured.

The principles of open building were first articulated in the book *Supports: An alternative to mass housing* (published in Dutch in 1961 and in English in 1972) (Habraken, 1999). Habraken's argument regarding housing is that it …

> … must always recognise two domains of action – the action of the community and that of the individual inhabitant. When the inhabitant is excluded, the result is uniformity and rigidity. When only the individual takes action, the result may be chaos and conflict. This formulation of a necessary balance of control had implications for all parties in the housing process, including architects. (Wikipedia, 2017, n.p.)

The term 'open building' was coined by Age van Randen; the 'movement' aimed to reinvigorate housing industrialisation through a research agenda focused on the relationships between the profession of architecture and the housing industries, emphasising the varied roles users could take in the process (ETH Zürich, 2015).

'Open' can mean 'receptive': Open buildings have 'capacity' and are described as being 'lovable', as coined by Frank Bijdendijk, a Dutch developer, to explain how buildings have resonance with many users over time – time being an important aspect of the concept of open building. Open building is used both as a noun and a verb, expressing both thinking/practice and the architectural products thereof. Open building has socio-political, technical, financial and management implications at many levels of the built environment.

The concept of open building implies a very particular approach to the concepts of 'agency' and 'community engagement', where the spatial/physical is seen to have a profound impact on socio-cultural and economic conditions and allows for ongoing participation rather than ineffective once-off participation at the start of a project. The products of open building thinking usually have great built-in capacity to adapt and change in terms of spatial and functional variation. This adds value and quality to the day-to-day experience of users, and is a deeper understanding of change beyond cosmetic, surface and facade variation.

This also allows for the possibility of cost variation and rental/ownership diversity within the same development, thereby avoiding solutions that perpetuate difference between people with diverse income levels. Open building also dissolves the distinctions between the urban level and the architectural level, making decisions across the two levels simultaneously in some cases, but also acknowledging the dominance of the higher-level decisions in other cases (UJ_UNIT2, n.d.). One way of defining 'agency' that supports this approach is "the relationship between the motivation of the participant and the solidarity of the group" (Segalowitz, 2012: ii).

I believe that this 'open way' of building is very relevant to addressing accessibility and affordability issues in South Africa as well as ensuring more participation and acceptance from the various role players in the process of developing sustainable human settlements. The educational programmes I have developed have all been based on open building thinking. This includes the housing programmes I taught at the University of Khartoum (1992–1996), the HUE research field at the University of Pretoria (2003–2009) (see HUE, n.d.) and the University of Johannesburg's UJ_UNIT2 (Architecture and Agency: DESIGN | MAKE | TRANSFORM) (2015) (see UJ_UNIT2, n.d.).

Architecture definitions within the context of citizenship debates

Architecture is people's spatial response, patterns of space appropriation and use. Architecture creates places that support society, social practices and social interactions. In studying architecture, the boundaries between the disciplines dissolve, because to understand the built environment, one needs to build up an understanding of the culture, religion and social setup of a community as well as the geography and history of the region in question. The intangible aspects of the culture, such as values, ideas, emotions, rituals, social practices and linguistics, influence the practice of architecture.

For the purpose of this chapter, it is important to explain that the decision not to build is also an architectural decision (Crysler, 2015; Osman, 2004). Crysler (2015: 94–95) explains how Rittel's rethinking of design problems as "wicked problems means not only that there is no definitive solution or endpoint to the design process, but also that in some cases what is initially posed as an 'architectural problem' might be best addressed in an entirely non-architectural way".

The history of architecture has generally been a history of 'important' buildings and of patrons who could afford the services of an architect. The limitations of traditional approaches to architecture, its history and theory exclude not only vernacular architecture from architectural debates, but also vital aspects of so-called developing societies:

> ... in our own culture, both in domestic and nondomestic situations, semifixed-feature elements tend to be used much – and are much more under the control of users; hence they tend to be used to communicate meanings. Yet, they have been ignored by both designers and analysts who have stressed fixed-feature elements. (Rapoport, 1990: 92)

Open building thinking in terms of built environment levels and agents of control in the various levels acknowledges these 'lower-level' elements and the users interacting directly with them.

Despite its social intentions, modernism aimed to create new, healthier environments for the masses, environments with light and air and urban parks (Glazer, 2009; Gold, 1997); modernist design generated highly controlled environments, which were sometimes perceived as de-humanising. This failure "expressed the dwindling belief in the capacities of human beings to shape socio-spatial reality" (Lindblom, 1959, cited in Oosterlynck & Albrechts, 2011: 2).

Today, architects are still engaging in intense debates on relevance, social justice and professional values; they have to invent new roles for themselves and develop new methods of practice. This has led to questions regarding professionalism, practice and the political function of architecture, and most importantly regarding how design and technical solutions are generated, and by whom. Present-day practice entails thinking beyond the confines of the site and acknowledging the role that a building has to play within its broader urban context and the fact that space must be co-produced. We have moved away from the architect as maverick artist, a "solitary genius" (Buchanan, 2012: 92), a so-called grand tradition of design, where architects operate in isolation and produce masterpieces serving the elites. We are under pressure to explain the importance of what we can offer to the 98% of people who do not use our services (Bell, 2004).

Housing design in architectural education

Housing is not just about the individual living unit, but encompasses all aspects in the macro and micro environment in which it is located. Understanding housing as a process rather than a product demands an understanding of informal economies, settlements and structures and our role as professionals in interacting with diverse systems and 'ways of doing/living'. There is a level of informality in every context; an expression of the will of people to shape their personal space. Informal systems could become catalysts for future interventions in a process of "negotiated reactions" (Dewar & Uytenbogaardt, 1991: 42).

Despite a successful programme of government-subsidised housing in South Africa, the housing backlog/waiting list is not being reduced (Cooke, 2014). It seems that the more government delivers in terms of house numbers, the more the demand increases. The current trend towards peripheral growth and social exclusion is constantly being contested. There are more voices calling for spatial justice. Exploring alternative housing-delivery mechanisms is fundamental to the success of cities and the support of people's lives and livelihoods. Housing needs a major re-think; a shift in the way we think about the morphology of human settlements and the processes by which they are created. Practice in the housing field that recognises this complexity is as important as current approaches are simplistic.

In 2010, in a partnership of various agencies, we developed a vision for sustainable human(e) settlements in South Africa. The vision aimed for vibrant, attractive, integrated, mixed (in terms of tenure, typology, income groups, functions) environments in which the pedestrian is the priority, with densities that support small and medium enterprises. The vision addressed the whole built environment ecosystem, reinforcing the idea that there can be no solution to low-cost housing if it is not recognised as an integral part of the city – and therefore the debate on low-cost housing should be integral to any debate about the city as a whole, including the wealthy suburbs (Tsela Tshweu Design Team, n.d.).

Norberg-Schulz (1979) believes that to dwell means to belong, and that a house repeats the basic structure of the environment – it becomes a microcosmos. He compares the role of the house in the cold north ('my home is my castle') to other contexts where daily life takes place outdoors and the house serves a semi-public purpose. In medieval city typologies and vernacular contexts, individual houses are also not easily identified within the urban fabric. This means that the single building is characterised by anonymity and dependence, as compared to a building being an autonomous object of identification. Most architectural theory focuses on the latter and therefore it is unsuited to the study of vernacular contexts. Architecture as a discipline is unable to effectively deal with the complexity of collective decision making, dynamic social processes, informal systems or multiplicity of voices in design processes.

Unpacking concepts of participation

Arnstein (1969: 216) equates 'citizen participation' to 'citizen power':

> It is the redistribution of power that enables the have-not citizens, presently excluded from the political and economic processes, to be deliberately included ... It is the strategy by which the have-nots join in determining how information is shared, goals and policies are set, tax resources are allocated, programs are operated, and benefits ... are parceled out ... the means by which they can induce significant social reform which enables them to share in the benefits of the affluent society.

While I agree with these principles, I find current approaches to 'design participation' simplistic and problematic. Yet they are being presented to students in educational institutions as the way to practise and teach. As an example, the use of the term 'community architect' in South Africa seems to be at odds with globally accepted convention, according to which qualified architects are further trained in working directly with communities in complex situations (Community Architects Network, n.d.) and rather seems to focus on providing community members with a minimum of training to be able to make design decisions (Fieuw, 2012). The change from using a community 'planner' rather than an 'architect' is still problematic (Goethe Institut et al., 2012). It is an approach that fails to acknowledge that the community architect is a fully trained architect (Hackney & Sweet, 1990). This attitude withholds vital professional services from the communities that most need them. In some cases, it appears to be an approach promoted by government agencies in a defeatist mechanism, as it fails to deliver on basic services they are mandated to deliver. This seems to be evident in strong support for 'reblocking' as an approach to informal settlement upgrading (26'10 South Architects, n.d., Hennings, Mollard, Moreschi, Sawatzki & Young, n.d.). It is also a process supported by the so-called experts who have no idea about how to intervene in complex residential situations. We have simply not been trained to do so – nor have our professional institutes set out guidelines for this form of practice.

The National Upgrading Support Programme states that the "planning and designing of the upgrade is done by the partnership, with the help of the technical experts and professionals. This means that the experts must first listen to the partnership members as they explain their needs and priorities" (NUSP, n.d.: n.p.). However, the decision about who is included in this consultative process is not as easy. As stated by Crysler (2015: 25):

> In Participatory Design the conventional way of thinking is that users have a right to partake in the design process because they are the ones who will be affected by the outcome of the project ... non-users are also considered to be affected by the outcome of the project, and therefore must be considered.

It is also not clear whether 'user inclusion' always leads to project success (Segalowitz, 2012).

This process of consultation assumes that 'needs' are stagnant and that stakeholders are unchanging. It over-simplifies the dynamic context of informal settlements – indeed, it simplifies the dynamics present in any settlement, planned or unplanned, and leads to further isolation of an informal settlement by emphasising difference rather than attempting to integrate the settlement within it context: "Among the arguments against community control are: it supports separatism; it creates balkanization of public services; it is more costly and less efficient; it enables minority group 'hustlers' to be just as opportunistic …" (Arnstein, 1969: 15).

Despite the problems mentioned, Arnstein (1969) says that other ways to end the victimisation of vulnerable groups have failed. But how can 'victimisation' be addressed in processes that neglect power imbalances and covert forms of dominance? He proceeds: "In the name of citizen participation, people are placed on rubberstamp advisory committees or advisory boards for the express purpose of 'educating' them or engineering their support" (Arnstein, 1969: 5). Arnstein (1969) found terminology such as 'self-help', 'citizen involvement' and 'absolute control' to be misleading.

My approach to these complexities is to emphasise that the capacity for participation can be 'built into' a design, spatial and technical solution. This leads to a debate on the relationship between activism and expertise. In Arnstein's ladder of participation, the topmost rung excludes experts, something with which I strongly disagree. Crysler (2015: 99) explains how this is problematic and is a position that Rittel would oppose, as …

> … [h]e argued for a 'symmetry of ignorance' in which there was no a priori hierarchy or value judgment imposed on those taking part in decision-making processes. His position was not 'anti-professional'. He regarded professional epistemologies as one distinctive way of knowing amongst many others. In his view, architects and ordinary citizens could, under the right circumstances, recognise that each had knowledge to share of different but equal value.

Questions on expertise and design activism have exposed a paradox articulated by Crysler (2015: 108), in that sometimes design activism is transformed into what it sought to challenge:

> The goals of social transformation through collective participation were initially developed to challenge expertise. The same techniques of participation and community outreach now operate as forms of expertise in themselves, with their own well-defined and formulaic problem-solving techniques … technical rationality, previously used to instrumentalize state power and manage the economy through Keynesian strategies, now emerging as means to do the same thing, but this time through the mechanisms of the free market. The target of both operations is the poor, and from the standpoint of today's economy, a potentially dangerous precariat. These techniques attempt to achieve an alignment between 'economic potential' and 'social need' through practices that conflate the free market with freedom.

George Elvin (2004, cited in Bell, 2004:35–26) considers the 'reconfiguring' of architecture, using tools such as remodelling, custom systems, off-the-shelf collage and mass-produced customisation: "Construction systems should encourage participation in design and redesign by end users. They should do so with an eye not only for up-front costs, but also life-cycle costs, including repair and maintenance." This strongly relates to Habraken's approach. Milgrom (2008, cited in Goonewardena,

Kipfer, Milgram & Schmid, 2008: 264–281) also explains a similar process in describing the well-known, though somewhat controversial, Kroll student housing, where …

> … a system of key structures could be placed permanently in the urban environment, to support the infill elements provided by future residents. The idea was to provide accommodation that would meet the needs of future generations, as well as those who first occupied the sites, since infill could be changed with no negative effects on the structural integrity of the whole

This is a way to manage co-production, as it implies a focus on spatial transformation (Attoe, 1989). Social innovation here implies the empowerment of socially disadvantaged groups and non-conventional actors in strategic planning processes (Attoe, 1989).

In addressing the issues of community engagement in the teaching of architecture, and in my focus on housing design within the context of these complexities, the idea of catalysts in the built environment has come out strongly as something to consider in building partnerships and service learning.

Catalysts in community projects

The idea of catalysts is key in terms of achieving an intimate understanding of the settings within which students and staff operate and where project sites are located; that is, identifying where interventions could take place and what kind of interventions it would be and anticipating the kind of influence it would have. Some individuals/groups are perceived as institutions and champions within their communities in the sense that they are known, respected and accepted and many activities are initiated by them, supported by them or revolve around them. Identifying these individuals/groups is paramount to the success of a project. These individuals/groups become agents of change. Planning and design interventions may either enhance or undermine this agency capacity and the potential to institutionalise it (Oosterlynck & Albrechts, 2011).

Eng (2016: n.p.) shares her experience with Shyam in Dharavi, saying "Find the person who knows everyone", and describes how, when walking through the streets of his neighbourhood, "you'd think he was a Bollywood star or a well-known politician, because he shakes hands with everybody! He knows everyone. He helped us find makers to work with and got them to trust us". Hamdi (2004) explains the complexities of working with communities. He questions whether we are ever certain that we are interacting with the real community representatives and portrays the problems of communicating through 'gatekeepers'. Some agencies may not necessarily have enough community backing to make them truly representative. This risk remains and demands sensitivity and experience in managing it. It is also important to use this approach to balance between 'visioning' and 'action', where the short-term interventions are conceived within a long-term vision (Van den Broeck, 2010, cited in Oosterlynck & Albrechts, 2011: 7).

Attoe (1989: xi) describes 'catalytic architecture' as …

> … the positive impact an individual urban building or project can have on subsequent projects and, ultimately, the form of a city. It encourages designers, planners, and policy makers to consider the chain-reaction potential of individual developments on civic growth and urban regeneration. It advocates design control as part of a catalytic strategy for urban design.

The author continues: "Catalysis … is both an appealing metaphor and an appropriate process for rebuilding, one that is sensitive to its context and also powerful enough to restructure it" (Attoe, 1989: xii). It is interesting to note that it is recognised that the 'catalyst' may be transformed, merged or disappeared, or may remain identifiable in the context (Attoe, 1989).

The catalyst may be an individual or group:

> A discussion of the chemistry of urban architecture would be incomplete without reference to the people who make it happen. The urban chemist does not stand outside the process but is integral to it and influenced by it … effective people are as important to the catalytic process as a well-conceived appropriately staged development. People get the process going. In one city a corporation executive might be instrumental, in other cities a development corporation, a highly respected individual, a popular mayor, or an alliance of citizens. (Attoe, 1989: 73)

Attoe continues with the chemistry analogy by explaining that the urban context is less predictable than the laboratory, needing 'nudging at the right time' and 'appropriate finesse' to keep the process going. The researcher is also a change agent, as indicated in participatory action research literature, independent of macro-social organisations, and research is transformed into an interactive communal enterprise (Babbie & Mouton, 1998; Osman, 2007).

Guidelines for the use of catalysts as an approach to community engagement

As presented, it is important to identify potential catalysts in any given context before embarking on any interventions, similar to a process of 'reading context' explained by Hamdi (2004), where pickle jars and bicycle shops and bus stops were identified as the potential catalysts that could be used to generate change in community and context. Also, referring to the concepts presented by Hamdi (2004), these initial interventions need not be costly or large. While identifying 'community' might be difficult to achieve in some situations (Hamdi & Majale, 2005), using key individuals as potential catalysts might be an approach that facilitates the harnessing of the energies of a diverse group of people who may not necessarily be in complete agreement, but who are able to join together in a common vision for their community.

Another aspect to be used in guiding the use of catalysts in the form of individuals and small projects for the teaching of community architecture is the fact that any immediate intervention needs to be understood in the context of a long-term vision for the area where the projects and research investigations are being carried out. Several aspects should be considered towards the achievement of these intentions:

- While rapid assessment is needed and indeed rapid interventions in some cases, this should always be combined with long-term thinking. As preliminary appraisals are being carried out, students should be trained in searching for design clues for the development of the long-term vision.
- Every project/intervention, however small, should consider decision making regarding the key structuring elements for the settlement/context (these may not necessarily be confined to spatial elements), as planning needs to be understood in terms of social and economic development.

- Managing the relationship between community and educational institutes as well as managing expectations is crucial. Ethical considerations and accountability systems need to be considered upfront. Agreements between the university and partner community need to be in place. This has not been the norm. Consider 'parachute architects' coming into African contexts, building and leaving as quickly as they came – or even our own practice of community engagement over the years where real impact and/or benefits and risks have not been measured, and where no one has been held accountable for failures. This continues today, as an example, in informal settlement upgrade projects, where the name of the 'invisible' architect is rarely mentioned under the pretence that it is a community-generated design. This means that no one is held accountable for failures and no clear practice guidelines are enforced to ensure that communities achieve a high-quality service.
- Students must be encouraged to explore the achievement of more diversity in settlements through studying the 'not-so-obvious' solutions. This may mean, as an example, consideration of alternative tenure/ownership options and/or using interventions, construction methods, material selection or process decisions as an income-generation opportunity for a community. To achieve this, they may investigate design from its various angles. One way is to investigate finance options – questioning where government funding stops or extends – and linking that to thinking about where the "city ends and the building begins" (Kendall, n.d.: n.p.), and equally where planning ends and architecture begins. This means being able to offer insight into community and individual resources and the innovative use of funds. In a similar manner, it means constantly addressing issues of integration and social cohesion through spatial and design interventions.
- Consideration should be given to how technological know-how may be shared through participatory workshops and an approach to technological and cultural exchange should be adopted, which takes into account locally available skills as a starting point for a design process. For students and communities equally, this translates into 'knowing by doing'.

A multi-year research and educational experiment across countries and institutions

In projects carried out over a number of years at the University of Pretoria, the students, in consultation with lecturers and identified community collaborators, identified where interventions could take place and what kind of intervention it would be and anticipated the kind of influence it would have on the surroundings. This was initiated by a mapping exercise, where existing energies and forces provided indicators as to where input may have the most potential for triggering a variety of responses. The ultimate aim was to intervene where it will generate a response, thereby allowing more agents to become involved in the formulation of the built environment. It is important also to note that "a strategic approach to spatial planning entails choosing certain goals and places above others" (Attoe, 1998: 3).

Participatory approaches can best be explored through real-life design projects, so design-build processes became an integral part of the courses I presented. Currently, more reflection is needed on these past experiences – especially with regard to the question of the ethics of practice in contexts of poverty and informality. One challenge with the approach to teaching presented in this chapter is the distinction between the projects as an 'educational process' versus the intention to deliver a 'community service'. This is further complicated by the fact that the projects undertaken have a strong research component. Ideally, the university would have a long-term partnership agreement with the community, as this both guarantees a level of continuity for the receptive community and creates a teaching environment where there is a strong sense of partnership and a high level of understanding between the parties involved and their expectations.

What became evident was that coordination of community-engagement projects and design-build studios need to be aligned with academic programmes and university schedules in order to ease administration tasks. The collaboration needs to be conceptualised as a multi-year collaboration for it to add value to both the students and the community. In our South African setting, and if studios are run as electives, students would typically change every quarter (seven weeks). It is therefore important that the project is ongoing while students come and go. To achieve this, we must distinguish between the *project* and the *studio*, because the project must not be disrupted by the changing studios and vice versa. There needs to be continuity built into the project and an efficient system of handover built into the studio. This allows for many students to participate and ensures minimum disruptions to the project(s). Students may be involved in conceptualising projects, establishing partnerships, identifying service providers and raising funding. These contributions may of course continue on a voluntary basis during holidays, summer/winter schools, etc. That is, the participation of students may continue outside of the academic schedules and studios. If projects are reasonably well funded, research assistants may be appointed to continue data gathering, maintain connections with partner communities, identify project sites and opportunities, etc. This allows for the project to continue even during the holidays or during semesters when no studio is running. Some of the projects carried out based on these principles and processes are described below.

In a project titled "Exploring participation and flexibility in partnership with small-scale, local industries in Mamelodi and Nellmapius, Pretoria", locally based, small-scale construction enterprises in the case study areas were researched in terms of operation methods, material suppliers, techniques, economic viability, legislative restrictions, target groups, clients and legality. A workshop approach was followed: 'knowing by doing', through using existing builders' yards and building sites as locations for technological and cultural exchange. These localities are interesting in terms of being positioned in an area removed from the city – being not easily visible or accessible in the manner of typical apartheid planning – yet they are in close physical proximity to the city and mostly comprised of mono-functional residential areas, isolated from the central business district and job opportunities, with poor-quality housing and a large component of informal settlements. The most visible industry as one drives through the area is no doubt that of the 'zozos' or shacks, usually made from corrugated metal sheeting on a timber frame and which can be considered as a rudimentary form of modularisation. Modular coordination generally facilitates quicker construction and saves costs and is easy to assemble and dismantle, therefore the project solutions focused on retaining these positive qualities of informal structure.

The student projects during the course of this project addressed various issues, including design, finance and technical experimentation. One project proposed a new zozo system mostly focused on improving the quality of shelters using the same materials and the juxtaposition of smaller elements; maintaining the benefits of existing systems, modularisation and entrepreneurship opportunities (Peeters, 2005) (see Figure 1). A project titled "Out of context" aimed to target a wider client base by constructing furniture and partitioning systems at the construction yards out of materials already available at those yards. This was important acknowledgement of an open building approach of separating built environment levels. One student developed a system to produce papercrete insulation for zozo panels. Another group of students developed a concept for a multi-purpose wall, extending the definition of 'wall' to include seating, storage, play equipment and planting. This project won the Des Baker Award in 2007 (Figure 2).

Figure 1   The "Out of Context" project   Figure 2   The multi-purpose wall project

We also implemented a structure to host an arts centre at The Mamelodi Heritage Forum. The arts centre was constructed within an existing shed structure in 2007 (Figure 3). The project collaborators were mostly local artists. The project brief specified that materials and workmanship be sourced from as close to the site as possible. A classroom was built in 2009 (Figure 4). During that year, we ran a highly successful vertical studio where groups of first-year students were partnered with honours students. The teams undertook various building, gardening, maintenance and cleaning tasks on the site of the school in the informal area (Figure 5). We were also able to raise funding for Felicia's House in Nelmapius, Pretoria. Felicia's House is located within a medium-density, low-cost neighbourhood and is known as an 'RDP' house, referring to the Reconstruction and Development Programme, and implies a 'give-away house' under the Housing Subsidy Scheme. Felicia looks after orphaned children and the small RDP at times accommodated up to 20 children. University of Pretoria and Technical University of Eindhoven (TU/e) students collaborated (remotely) on designing extensions to the house and funding was provided via TU/e. The project research component explored how a typical housing development may be densified using readily available material and local labour (Osman & Davey, 2011).

Felicia proceeded to expand the house with a linear addition on one side of the plot, not linked to the RDP unit. This highlighted how our proposal failed to acknowledge the limited skills of her builder, who avoided a solution that was directly connected to the existing building. It may also have been a lack of understanding of the spatial/functional benefits of the alternative design solution, which could have been better presented/communicated to her by the research team (Figure 8). This being said, the collaboration certainly led to improvements in the conditions of the house and a better living environment was achieved for the children.

Figure 3

The HUE UP studio implemented a structure, within an existing shed, and in collaboration with local artists, to host an arts centre at The Mamelodi Heritage Forum in 2007

Figure 4

In 2009, the HUE UP students built a classroom, the only building structure, at the time, in an informal school yard where classes were housed in old army tents and shacks.

Figure 5   The vertical studio run in 2009

More recently, UJ UNIT 2 students have been exposed to 'neighbourhood immersion' exercises, where they aimed to better understand a city context by being on site full-time for a number of days and nights, thereby experiencing the context at a deeper level through documentation, observation and direct interaction rather than hurried site visits and interviews (Figure 6). We took our activities off campus on several occasions (Figure 7). The same students were tasked to graphically communicate the intangible processes in the built environment through interpretations of project sites visited in Nairobi in August 2015 (Figure 8). These intangible processes are seen to manifest as space and product (territory and ownership, negotiation and deal making and socio-cultural structure generating space). This was presented for review to a panel from Shack Dwellers International and UN Habitat representatives (Figure 9).

Figure 6

The UJ_UNIT 2 students have been exposed to 'neighbourhood immersion' exercises, mostly at the premises of Bjala Square in Jeppestown, Johannesburg and the surrounding city context. Some of the crit sessions and exhibitions were also done on site.

Figure 7

We took the activities of the UJ_UNIT 2 off campus on several occasions; in this image the students are shown in Fietas, Johannesburg, a project done in a collaboration with departments across FADA/UJ and with community members.

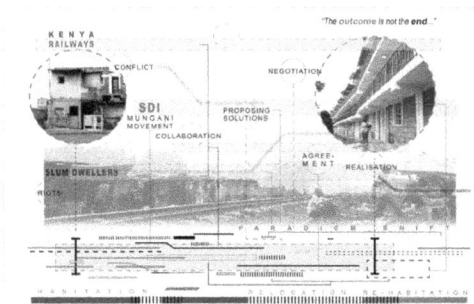

Figure 8   Interpretations of project sites visited in Nairobi in August 2015

Figure 9   Panel from Shack Dwellers International and UN Habitat

Conclusion

This chapter has presented a particular pedagogical approach based on ecosystemic thinking and open building. Architecture has been defined within the context of citizenship debates and the teaching of housing design was linked to these concepts with a focus on the balance between individual and collective aspirations and needs. The chapter presented a critique on current thinking about participation and suggested that there is a role for design, spatial and technical decision making to enhance ongoing participation in decision making and engagement in the built environment. The idea of catalysts in the form of people and project interventions was presented as a method to teach where simplistic interpretations of participation are avoided and the larger visions are reconciled with small design interventions. A set of guidelines was presented to facilitate this process and some project examples were shared from various studios managed by the author. This is a two-way process and implies the creation of a mutual learning ground: from students/researchers/lecturers to local workers (skilled and unskilled), local entrepreneurs and the general community, and vice versa.

In training future professionals, universities need to instil understanding of informal economies, settlements and structures and the role of the professional. While it is important to train future architects in the methods that acknowledge the co-production of space and permit participation, it is also equally important to understand that this multiplicity has technical and spatial implications when making design decisions. A distinction between the permanent and fixed components of the environment is crucial in achieving legibility, robustness and identity. The adaptable, changeable and transitory is just as crucial towards facilitating for complex and democratic decision-making processes and broader representation. There also needs to be a balance between the planned and unplanned through disentanglement of physical and administrative systems at various levels of the environment, so change in one system does not disrupt the others.

Our work with communities in the past has been a process of mutual learning. Community members have contributed in project criticisms and our students have made presentations to subsidy beneficiaries, local councillors and various government officials, where we have managed to portray alternative approaches to housing design. Our partners in the townships have assisted us in identifying projects; they have been our guides and have helped us gain more insight into various city contexts. Extending learning sites beyond the campus has led to more complexity in terms of liability and ethical responsibility and questions on managing relationships with partner communities, the fairness of representation, the quality of service and the dynamics of power relations.

Catalysts, in the form of individuals and small projects, have been identified as important vehicles for collaboration, development and learning. However, catalysts and short-term and acupunctural interventions are promoted in light of the larger, longer-term visions that should drive them. Training of the future architect will have to achieve a balance between the individual and the community, between the small intervention and the larger vision, between a building and its neighbourhood, between respect for what is already there and a new envisioned future, between the benefits of a specific community and the links with the wider city context, between what is permanent and what is transient.

Acknowledgements and funders

University of Johannesburg; UJ_UNIT2 students 2015; Housing and Urban Environments (HUE_UP) students, University of Pretoria 2005–2007; University of Pretoria; National Research Foundation

References

26'10 South Architects. N.d. Available at http://www.2610south.co.za/gallery24.php [Accessed 15 March 2017].

Arnstein, S. 1969. A ladder of citizen participation. *Journal of the American Planning Association,* 35(4), 216–224. https://doi.org/10.1080/01944366908977225

Attoe, W. 1989. *American urban architecture: Catalysts in the design of cities.* Berkeley, CA: University of California Press.

Babbie, E. & Mouton, J. 1998. *The practice of social research.* Oxford: Oxford University Press.

Bell, B. 2004. *Good deeds, good design: Community service through architecture.* New York, NY: Princeton Architectural Press.

Buchanan, P. 2012. *The big re-think Part 9: Rethinking architectural education.* The Architectural Review. Available at https://www.architectural-review.com/rethink/campaigns/the-big-rethink/the-big-rethink-part-9-rethinking-architectural-education/8636035.article [Accessed 17 March 2017].

bwa Mwesigire, B. 2014. 5 Strategies for de-Westernising globalisation by Ali Mazrui. *This is Africa,* 21 November. Available at https://thisisafrica.me/5-strategies-de-westernising-globalisation-ali-mazrui/ [Accessed 15 March 2015].

CIB 104. 2004. *Proceedings of the 10th International Conference: Open Building and Sustainable Environment.* Paris.

Community Architects Network. N.d. Available at http://communityarchitectsnetwork.info/about.php [Accessed 17 March 2017].

Cooke, J. 2014. Upgrading, not eradicating, informal settlements: Listening to Steve Topham. *Architecture SA,* (66), 2–27. Available at http://saia.org.za/wp-content/uploads/2014/06/66.pdf [Accessed 17 March 2017].

Crysler, G. 2015. The paradoxes of design activism: Expertise, scale and exchange. *Field,* 2, 77–124.

Dewar, D. & Uytenbogaardt, R. 1991. *South African cities: A manifesto for change.* Cape Town: Urban Problems Research Unit, University of Cape Town.

Dewey, J. 1916. *Democracy and education: An introduction to the philosophy of education.* New York, NY: The Free Press.

Dewey, J. 1938. *Experience and education.* New York, NY: Kappa Delta Pi.

Eng, K. 2016. *How to create a museum – wherever you are.* Available at http://ideas.ted.com/how-to-create-a-museum-wherever-you-are/ [Accessed 15 March 2017].

ETH Zürich. 2015. *Open building.* Available at http://www.openbuilding2015.arch.ethz.ch/background.html [Accessed 15 March 2017].

Fieuw, W. 2012. *No more white elephants: Mshini Wam community architects assisted by University of Botswana planning students.* Available at http://sasdialliance.org.za/no-more-white-elephants-mshini-wam-community-architects-assisted-by-university-of-botswana-planning-students/ [Accessed 17 March 2017].

Glazer, N. 2009. *From a cause to a style: Modernist architecture's encounter with the American city.* Princeton, NJ: Princeton University Press. https://doi.org/10.1515/9781400827589

Goethe Institut, University of Johannesburg, 26'10 South Architects, Informal Settlement Network, CORC, FEDUP & Ikhayalami. 2012. *Informal Studio: Marlboro South – between and within processes of engagement.* Available at http://blog.goethe.de/weltstadt/uploads/wsg140414_JOHANNESBURG_RZ.pdf [Accessed 15 March 2017].

Gold, J.R. 1997. *The experience of modernism: Modern architects and the future city, 1928–53.* London: Taylor & Francis.

Goonewardena, K., Kipfer, S., Milgram, R. & Schmid, C. (Eds.). 2008. *Space, difference, everyday life: Reading Henri Lefebvre.* New York, NY: Routledge Taylor & Francis.

Habraken, N.J. 1999. *Supports: An alternative to mass housing.* Second edition. Exeter: Urban Press.

Habraken, N.J. & Teicher, J. 2000. *The structure of the ordinary: Form and control in the built environment.* Cambridge, MA: The MIT Press.

Hackney, R. & Sweet, F. 1990. *The good, the bad, and the ugly: Cities in crisis.* London: F. Muller.

Hamdi, N. 2004. *Small change: About the art of practice and the limits of planning in cities.* London: Earthscan/James & James.

Hamdi, N. & Majale, M. 2005. *Partnerships in urban planning: A guide for municipalities.* London: Intermediate Technology.

Hennings, Z., Mollard, R., Moreschi, A., Sawatzki, S. & Young, S. N.d. *Supporting reblocking and community development in Mtshini Wam.* Available at http://wp.wpi.edu/capetown/files/2012/11/Final-Project-Executive-Summary-for-Mtshini-Wam.pdf [Accessed 15 March 2017].

HUE. N.d. Available at http://h-ue.co.za [Accessed 17 March 2017].

Jones, J.C. 1976. *Design methods: Seeds of human futures.* London: Wiley.

Kendall, S. N.d. *Open building.* Available at http://skendall.iweb.bsu.edu/Research.html [Accessed 10 July 2013].

Norberg-Schulz, C. 1979. *Genius loci: Towards a phenomenology of architecture.* New York, NY: Rizzoli.

NUSP (National Upgrading Support Programme). N.d. Available at http://www.upgradingsupport.org/index.php/content/page/part-5-the-planning-process [Accessed 15 March 2017].

Oosterlynck, S. & Albrechts, L. 2011. *Strategic spatial projects: Catalysts for change.* New York, NY: Routledge Chapman & Hall.

Osman, A. 2004. Space, place and meaning in northern riverain Sudan. PhD thesis. Pretoria: University of Pretoria.

Osman, A. 2007. Building a bridge from the studio to the townships. *Innovate,* (2), 26–30.

Osman, A. 2015. *Open building versus architecture or open building as architecture?* Available at http://uj-unit2.co.za/open-building-versus-architecture-or-open-building-as-architecture/. UJ_UNIT2 2015 [Accessed 15 March 2017].

Osman, A. & Davey, C. 2011. *Sustainable building transformation in the South African housing sector: CSIR case studies.* Available at http://openarc.co.za/sites/default/files/Attachments/CSIR%20housing_case_studies_report_June2011.pdf [Accessed 15 March 2017].

Peeters, N. 2005. Generating an improved quality of informal housing: A case study in South Africa. MA thesis. Pretoria: University of Pretoria.

Rapoport, A. 1990. *The meaning of the built environment: A nonverbal communication approach.* Tucson, AZ: University of Arizona Press.

Saltmarsh, J. 1996. Education for critical citizenship: John Dewey's contribution to the pedagogy of community service learning. *Michigan Journal of Community Service Learning,* 3, 13–21.

Segalowitz, M. 2012. "Participation" in participatory design research. Master's thesis. Queensland: Queensland University of Technology.

Tsela Tshweu Design Team, N.d. Available at http://uj-unit2.co.za/architecture-and-agency/tsela-tshweu-design-team-ttdt/ [Accessed 15 March 2017].

UJ_UNIT 2. N.d. *UJ_UNIT2, Architecture and Agency: DESIGN | MAKE | TRANSFORM.* Available at http://uj-unit2.co.za [Accessed 15 March 2017].

Wikipedia. 2017. *Open building.* Available at https://en.wikipedia.org/wiki/Open_building [Accessed 15 March 2017].

WPI (Worchester Polytechnic Institute) & CORC (Community Organization Resource Centre). N.d. *Reblocking: A partnership guide – a handbook to support the reblocking of informal settlements though a multiple stakeholder effort.* Cape Town: WPI, Cape Town Project Centre.

A Potential Difference Model for Educating Critical Citizen Designers: The Case Study of the Beegin Appropriate Technology Beekeeping System

5

ANGUS DONALD CAMPBELL AND IVAN LEROY BROWN

Introduction

Renowned design thinker and educator Ezio Manzini (2010: 8) claims that "[t]he only sustainable way to get out of the current worldwide financial and ecological crisis is to promote new economic models, new production systems, and new ideas of well-being". Many definitions of design describe a goal-orientated process of "solving problems, meeting needs, improving situations, or creating something new or useful" (Friedman, 2003: 507–508). Design is therefore well placed to deal with the systemic crises Manzini describes; however, the practice of design is extensively shaped by the way it is taught, which does not necessarily generate designers capable of dealing with such systemic complexities. There is therefore a need for design education that provides graduates with a critical mindset, methodologies, tools and skills for appropriate change making embedded in complex contexts. Borrowing from Johnson and Morris's (2010) framework for critical citizenship education, we describe such graduates as critical citizen designers.

The context of South Africa provides a multitude of opportunities for student designers to use their expertise to bring about appropriate change. However, in order to encourage positive outcomes, an appropriate pedagogy, strengthened through praxis and grounded in economic, social and environmental realities, is required to prepare students for critical and sustainable change making. This chapter explores the education of industrial designers in South Africa utilising a 'potential difference' model for critical citizen design. The model attempts to consider stakeholder relationships through a lens of power and love (Kahane, 2010) in order to increase people's capabilities (Nussbaum, 2011; Sen, 1999) through appropriate technology (Schumacher, 1975). This is contextualised through a case study of the design and implementation of an appropriate technology beekeeping system for urban farmers in Johannesburg. We begin the chapter with an exploration of critical citizen design pedagogy.

Critical citizen design pedagogy

The concept of citizenship tends to align with "the promotion of a common set of shared values (e.g. tolerance, human rights and democracy), which prepare young people to live together in diverse societies and which reject the divisive nature of national identities" (Johnson & Morris, 2010: 77–78). The addition of the descriptor 'critical' to citizenship education points to the expectation of graduates with a certain level of social understanding and obedience, but also a level of critical reflection and creativity (Johnson & Morris, 2010). Both of these aspects are beneficial in enabling stable societies, but also dynamic and innovative economies.

Such a duality is also evident in design education. The Eurocentric origin of design can be divided between two ideologies: one more consumer-focused and the other more socially orientated. Consumer-focused design has concerned itself with rapidly satisfying needs and wants, creating jobs and opportunities for people to become wealthy while developing innovative technologies that generally improve people's quality of life. Social design has long been concerned with freeing society from the ills that capitalism has brought to bear, which include rampant consumerism, selfish and exclusionary practices, growing inequality and cultural deterioration. After over a century of consumer-focused design and a few decades of socially responsible design, we need to reflect on the ability of both these approaches to address the challenges of social, environmental and economic unsustainability (Steen, 2011; UN, 1987; UNDP, 2014). In the global South, this reflection can be expanded to also include the recognition of other forms of knowledge, as highlighted in the recent call by South African 'fallists' to decolonise South African academic institutions.

Postcolonial theorist Achille Mbembe (2015: n.p.) explains as follows:

> In order to set our institutions firmly on the path of future knowledges, we need to reinvent a classroom without walls in which we are all co-learners; a university that is capable of convening various publics in new forms of assemblies that become points of convergence of and platforms for the redistribution of different kinds of knowledges.

Critical pedagogue Paulo Freire (2004) was clear in highlighting how uncritical education tends to reproduce scholars who conform to a system of thinking as opposed to those who are free in their ability to critique, engage with and transform their world. More recently, agriculturalist-turned-economist Anil Gupta from the Indian Institute of Management and founder of the Honey Bee Network questioned: "Why is it … that the designers of pedagogies and curricula, policies and programmes the world over neglect the need for learning from knowledge rich-economically poor people?" (2012: 29).

Social impact design has positively taken design education out of the classroom into the field; however, although it is a burgeoning field in design education, it has too often favoured the designer's expertise over those being designed for (Campbell, 2017). This can result in a problematic development model focused on handouts to divested beneficiaries (Bunch, 1991). Both consumer-focused and social design tend to be based on the idea that needs and wants are universally similar, with design taking place in a traditional producer–consumer relationship. Such top-down approaches have produced design solutions for the needs and wants of both the mainstream and the marginalised, but have failed to significantly impact on social, environmental and economic issues (Lissenden, Maley & Mehta, 2015).

The design discipline has therefore mostly been concerned with design *for* the other 90%,[1] but after criticism of such power differentials (Baelden & Van Audenhove, 2015) it has more recently been reorientated, breaking ties with the traditional producer–consumer approach, opting for a more democratic design *with* the other 90%. Design pedagogy and praxis have therefore shifted from more quantitative studies of ergonomics and technology-centric design (Krippendorff, 2006) towards more qualitative human-centred or co-design (Steen, 2011). In this more inclusive approach, design researchers recognise the knowledge that people have accumulated through their own lived experiences and integrate this into the design process through empathic and participatory research (Maguire, 2001). People are therefore partners in the development of solutions for their own contexts, which develops an important aspect of ownership of the process and outcome, and hence investment in the project (Campbell & Harrison, 2015). Contemporary social designers have realised that impactful design cannot rely on far-removed or de-contextualised perspectives of what people need, but requires the knowledge, input and investment of local experts.

It is widely accepted that designers have a role to play in developing interventions for marginalised people, yet the ability to effect measurable impact through their philanthropic endeavours or to make a career in responsible design is seldom achieved (Margolin, 2007). In developing countries such as South Africa, emphasis is placed on designing for the needs of the marginalised majority (Campbell, 2008), but at the same time emphasis is placed on design as a means of development. In most cases this equates to the capitalisation of local or international consumer demands in order to increase economic growth (Design Council, 2015). All projects, whether they are undertaken in academia or in industry, have time and resource constraints. Great effort may be taken in developing participatory design interventions, but this does not amount to positive benefit for intended users if the solutions cannot be correctly implemented. In industry an ideological focus on commercialisation results in the need for a product to be successfully rolled out in order to support the livelihood of the designer or client, but often sacrifices social and environmental concerns. Academic design research has the luxury of being able to spend extensive resources on social and environmental design so long as research publication and/or qualification outputs are met. However, the focus on academic outputs tends to result in limited and ineffectual outcomes and hence severely limits the tangible benefit for those for whom the intervention was designed. When those participating in the research do not receive equitable benefit, design research tends to take a problematic colonial turn (Gupta, 2016; Smith, 1999).

Thus far we have described the concept of critical design pedagogy in terms of the ideologies, methodologies and various knowledge(s) represented in design education. Johnson and Morris (2010) describe critical citizens at the intersection of critical pedagogy and the more abstract concept of critical thinking. Within this framework, Johnson and Morris present the concepts of "politics; society and interaction; the self; and reflection, action, engagement and possibility" (2010: 92) as themes that need to interact with the knowledge, skills, values and disposition of people to encourage critical citizenship. Such a framework provides a way to approach curriculum design in order to provide students with the critical faculties to navigate the complex realities when they enter the 'real' world,

---

[1] Where the 90% are the majority who cannot afford or benefit from 'designer' products intended for the wealthiest 10% of the population.

or when they straddle the world of academia and the world of the people with whom they are designing. In our experience of educating critical citizen designers in South Africa we have found two additional concepts that have proven useful for design students to navigate their positionality and the impact of their work. The first is Adam Kahane's lens of 'power and love' as a means to navigate the complex relational dynamics in social design, and the second is Amartya Sen (1999) and Martha Nussbaum's (2011) 'capability approach' as a means to consider the effective impact of, in the case of industrial designers, 'appropriate technology' (Schumacher, 1975). In combination we describe this as the *potential difference* model for critical citizen design; we begin by exploring the concepts of power and love.

Power and love

The famous line of the second president of IBM, Thomas Watson Jr, "Good design is good business", contrasts with the renowned graphic designer Milton Glaser's equally famous line "Good design is good citizenship" (Heller & Vienne, 2003: 1). They represent the dilemma of design classified under the two binary headings of consumerism and humanitarianism, or competition versus cooperation. Educators similarly face a dichotomy between didactic and dialogic education (Freire, 1970). These binaries can generally be aligned to represent either of the concepts of 'power' or 'love'. In 1967 Martin Luther King Jr (2002: 186) highlighted the interdependence of these two concepts in one of his landmark speeches:

> Power properly understood is nothing but the ability to achieve purpose. It is the strength required to bring about social, political, and economic change. .... And one of the great problems of history is that the concepts of love and power have usually been contrasted as opposites – polar opposites – so that love is identified with the resignation of power, and power with the denial of love. Now we've got to get this thing right. What [we need to realise is] that power without love is reckless and abusive, and love without power is sentimental and anaemic ... It is precisely this collision of immoral power with powerless morality which constitutes the major crisis of our time.

Inspired by King Jr's speech, change maker Adam Kahane (2010) explores power and love as a theory and practice of social change. Kahane describes the two most common methods to solve social problems as either violent aggression or endless negotiation and compromise; these two methods are underpinned by the drive for power or love. Kahane (2010) describes power as resolute, orientated towards business and productive activities and mostly aligned with self-serving agendas, and love as empathic, orientated towards socially responsible activities and mostly aligned with collective benefit. Kahane echoes King Jr in that both these approaches have to be combined in order to solve complex problems. For example, in academic design research, much time and effort are taken to collaborate towards outcomes; this is much more aligned towards love. Although the outcome may be theoretically successful, the impact of the design may be limited due to constraints of implementation. Timothy Prestero, chief executive officer of Design that Matters, explains that "compared to the whole process that leads to implementation – which includes financing, manufacture and distribution, training, and adoption – design is the least hard part" (Cooper-Hewitt, 2013: 24). The opposite is also possible. For example, a designer in industry may find him-/herself under the powerful watchful eye of corporate clients who, due to time and financial constraints, find collaborative design methods arduous and therefore forgo processes of defining appropriate purpose, participatory development, testing and refinement in order to meet implementation deadlines. This results in a high probability that the outcome does not fully meet the needs of those for whom the product was intended.

Power is particularly difficult to manage in participatory projects (Nelson & Wright, 1995) and even more so when working in contexts where poorly considered community projects and complex historical racial power hierarchies have perpetuated notions of "white as knowledgeable and black as needy"(Biko, 2004: 23) (see also Costandius & Rosochaki, 2012). Projects that attempt to 'do good' can unconsciously be focused more on making the initiators feel good about themselves (helping behaviour), but do they truly empower participants to feel good about themselves so that in the future they have the confidence to continue their own emancipation? In order for critical citizen designers to bring about systemic and sustainable change, they need to become aware of the complexities of maintaining equilibrium between the drives of power and love in their education. Such critical minds will help uncover and mitigate the various requirements of self and society, humanitarianism and consumerism. This can result in good design that does good (love/social/ citizenship) and makes good (power/self/business). However, in a context of strong power disparities, an additional rudder is needed to help designers navigate the difference they have from those with whom they are designing.

Capabilities and appropriate technology

Keeping the approach of power and love in the fore requires a level of intimacy between the various participants in design research projects. Relationships are formed due to shared concerns, views and interests, and through these relationships the worldview of all participants is changed (Kasulis, 2002). Ultimately, such embedded design projects aim to improve the well-being of all those involved in the project. However, well-being is a particularly difficult concept to define: Is it defined in terms of happiness, or in terms of wealth? Neither of these is particularly appropriate, as our individual concepts of happiness and wealth shift as our circumstances change. Hence we have found in our design research projects that the capabilities approach developed by Amartya Sen (1999) and Martha Nussbaum (2011) is a more appropriate means to help steer design projects towards valued outcomes. Robeyns (2011: n.p.) describes the capability approach as follows:

> The capability approach is a theoretical framework that entails two core normative claims: first, the claim that the freedom to achieve well-being is of primary moral importance, and second, that freedom to achieve well-being is to be understood in terms of people's capabilities, that is, their real opportunities to do and be what they have reason to value.

The freedom that people have to do and be, or not to do and be, is intrinsic to well-being (Nussbaum, 2011). Sen is particularly interested in how people are able to participate in economic, social and political action, both in terms of "functionings" ("what a person values doing and being") and "capabilities" ("the alternative combinations of functionings that are feasible for her to achieve") (1999: 75). Functionings are either realised or effectively possible based on the person's opportunities and freedoms (Oosterlaken, 2009, 2015). Nussbaum (2011) defines people's functionings as created by their own abilities (internal) or the social, political and economic context (external). Nussbaum (2011: 33–34) defines ten "central human capabilities" for human flourishing, namely life; bodily health; bodily integrity; senses, imagination and thought; emotions; practical reason; affiliation;

other species; play; and control over one's political and material environment. The capabilities approach is a means to assess quality of life and the effect things have on it (Robeyns, 2011). It is therefore well positioned to act as a rudder in guiding design research projects, particularly in terms of how design interventions can improve or hinder people's capabilities.

In a paper exploring human dignity and the principles of human-centred design, Richard Buchanan (2001) explains that designers should be sufficiently responsible and socially productive to provide people with the capability to support themselves. One of the means that industrial designers have to enhance people's capabilities is through the development of appropriate technology (Oosterlaken, 2009). The concept of appropriate technology was developed by Fritz Schumacher (1975) in order to offer an indirect method for easing poverty by developing products for/with marginalised communities that support skills development and economic growth. Schumacher (1975) understood that products should be developed in their context of use to provide a medium for local social entrepreneurship, as opposed to typical development-based 'all-round solutions' or 'aid'. In his paper on the socio-economic development for Third World countries, Anthony Akubue (2000) indicates that appropriate technologies are the most suitable tools to provide opportunities for development and although these technologies are often simplified, they must be progressive, allow for future advancement or create progress through innovation. Ian Smillie (2008: 91) defines appropriate technology as meeting the following criteria:

- It meets the needs of the majority, not a small minority, of a community.
- It employs natural resources, capital and labour in proportion to their long-term sustainable availability.
- It is ownable, controllable, operable and maintainable within the community it serves.
- It enhances the skills and dignity of those employed by it.
- It is non-violent both to the environment and to the people.
- It is socially, economically and environmentally sustainable.

Appropriate technology can therefore provide people with the means to extricate themselves from poverty and satisfy their needs and wants simultaneously. The key lies in undertaking participatory design research to determine the entrepreneurial desires of a community, assessing possibilities and working together to realise a system that allows them to achieve what they value. We describe this process as a potential difference model of critical citizen design (Figure 1), which balances power and love to increase people's capabilities through appropriate technology.

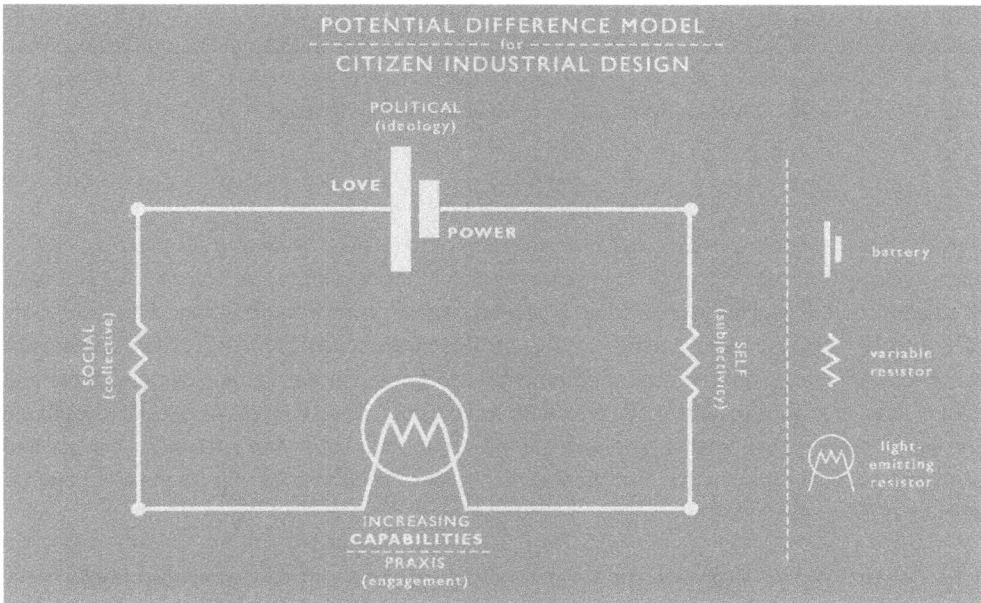

Figure 1 The potential difference model for citizen industrial design

The model in Figure 1 is a diagrammatic representation of critical citizen design that utilises the potential difference created by balancing the two ideological approaches to change, of love, which drives to unite with others, and power, which aims at achieving individual purpose. This balance enables the circuit to meet through engaged design praxis and results in an appropriate technological outcome that has the potential to increase people's capabilities. In the reduction of a complex process, the model becomes a circuit diagram with an illuminated light bulb that represents a system of appropriate technology, but what is not evident are the people involved in the process or the complexities of facilitating participation to identify the value and need for light. In order to make this model and process more tangible, we will now present a case study that explores the design of an appropriate beekeeping system for urban farmers in Johannesburg. This project began as a BTech (honours) project in 2015 and continued as an MTech (master's) project into 2016–2017 in the Department of Industrial Design at the University of Johannesburg.

Case study: The Beegin Appropriate Technology Beekeeping System

Pedagogy

The University of Johannesburg (2016: n.p.) is "alive down to its African roots, and well-prepared for its role in actualising the potential that higher education holds for the continent's development". Within the university, the Department of Industrial Design (2016) has four central principles that drive the education on offer. These include social responsibility, sustainability, human-centeredness and contextual relevance. Staff and students of the department engage in a number of community-centred design projects and social development initiatives, including the Design Society Development

DESIS Lab (2016a), various postgraduate design research projects and the service-learning urban agriculture[2] initiative "iZindaba Zokudla" (Conversations about Food) (Design Society Development DESIS Lab, 2016b), which is a collaborative interdisciplinary project based at the University of Johannesburg focused on systemic change in Johannesburg's food system.

Social initiative background: Political ideology

According to the Food and Agriculture Organization of the United Nations (FAO) (2015), in 2015 approximately 780 million people in low-income communities worldwide did not have access to adequate food. Although food security has improved in recent years, issues regarding the sustainability of modern agriculture are threatening food supplies worldwide (Allen, 2010; FAO, 2015). Commercial agriculture is widely criticised for its detrimental effects on biodiversity, ecological systems and natural resources (Thrupp, 2015). For people to achieve the central capabilities of bodily health, life and bodily integrity, they need to have access to healthy food. In South Africa, the social, political and economic contexts are such that many people do not have access to healthy food and are therefore defined as 'food insecure'.

In Africa, rapid population growth and urban migration, coupled with slow economic development, have resulted in widespread urban poverty (Crush, Hovorka & Tevera, 2011). The growing demand for food in cities has placed strain on agricultural production (Allen, 2010). The food imported into the cities comes at high costs financially and environmentally. In reaction to the structural and systemic problem of food insecurity, some cities have begun to move towards localised food production through small-scale urban farming (Carpenter & Rosenthal, 2011). In the FAO publication exploring the state of food insecurity, they clearly indicate that "[e]conomic growth is a key success factor for reducing undernourishment, but it has to be inclusive and provide opportunities for improving the livelihoods of the poor. Enhancing the productivity and incomes of smallholder family farmers is key to progress" (2015: ii).

As part of the City of Johannesburg's flagship programme, "A city where none go hungry" (2012) and the Integrated Development Plan (2013), urban agriculture has been implemented as a local food security strategy. iZindaba Zokudla aims to promote urban agriculture in low-income communities to increase access to food and income generation (Malan & Campbell, 2014). iZindaba Zokudla focuses on the creation of farmers' markets, participatory technology development, skills enhancement, school gardens, security of tenure and a farmer's school in Johannesburg's southwestern township (Soweto) (Malan & Campbell, 2014). In addition, iZindaba Zokudla develops research opportunities and interdisciplinary projects that emanate from the University of Johannesburg and intend to form sustainable food systems for the community stakeholders (farmers, retailers and customers/ recipients) (Malan & Campbell, 2014). The Department of Industrial Design, working in conjunction with iZindaba Zokudla, has produced a variety of products with the aim to increase urban farmer productivity in order to improve their livelihoods (Campbell, 2013: 12). Some of the products have

---

[2]   "[Urban agriculture] is an industry located within (intraurban) or on the fringe (peri-urban) of a town, a city or a metropolis, which grows and raises, processes and distributes a diversity of food and non-food products, (re-)using largely human and material resources, products and services found in and around that urban area, and in turn supplying human and material resources, products and services largely to that urban area" (Mougeot, 2001: 10).

been more successful than others (Malan, Campbell, Sibeko, Van Zyl & Benecke, 2015), but the greatest hurdle has been to feasibly implement technology developed as part of a design curriculum back into the communities that co-designed it, to their benefit. This is where the Beegin[3] Appropriate Technology Beekeeping System for emergent farmers has made significant strides.

Beegin: Industrial design project

Beegin (Figure 2) is an ongoing participatory design research project that aims to use a long-term, human-centred design process to develop and implement an appropriate technology system for emergent beekeepers. The research goals are to assist urban farmers, promote apiculture and help ensure the ongoing survival of the honeybee. The project engages with food insecurity in two ways: indirectly, by bringing additional income to marginalised, small-scale farming communities; and directly, by protecting the pollination source of 70% of food crops (*cf.* UNEP, 2010).

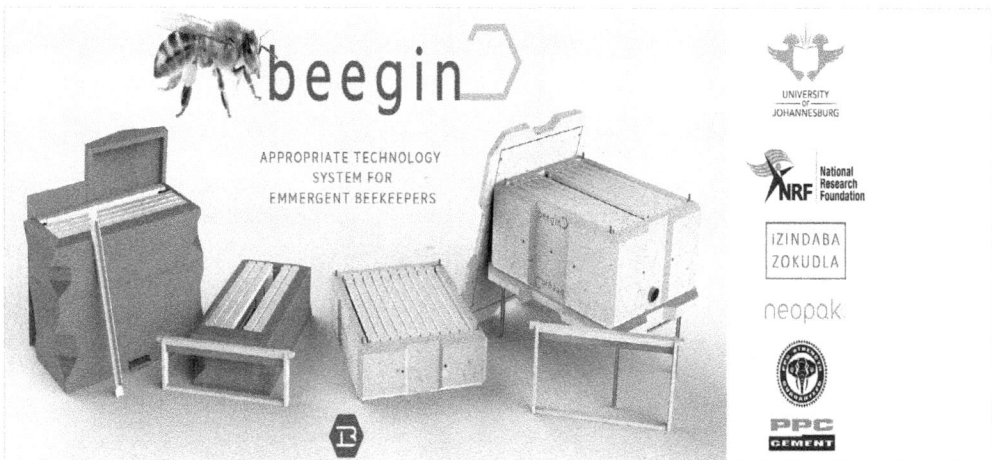

Figure 2   Entry-level cardboard and permanent concrete beehives developed and used in the Beegin project; project supporters to the right

Although the success of urban agriculture has been called into question with concerns regarding income generation, food production and social interest (Crush *et al.*, 2011; Frayne, McCordie & Shilomboleni, 2014), the Beegin project began with a search for opportunities to increase the income capabilities of urban farmers through either bettering existing crop yields or the benefit of an additional high-value crop to sell (honey). To mitigate some of the concerns about the efficacy of urban agriculture, we found examples of the implementation of apiculture (agricultural beekeeping) projects in rural Ethiopian, South African, Tanzanian, Nigerian and Kenyan communities that had successfully created socio-economic growth by increasing crop yields and providing additional sources of income (Girma, Ballo, Tegegne, Alemayehu & Belayhun, 2008; Illgner, Nel & Robertson, 1998; UNEP, 2010). The additional income generated from beekeeping can be significant, with South African beekeepers earning between R2 000 and R40 000 per hive annually (Johannsmeier, 2001; TTA, 2008).

---

[3]   Beegin is the name of the project, derived from 'beginning' 'beekeeping'.

In interviews with local urban farmers (Figure 3), their studious and entrepreneurial spirit was noted, along with their concern for environmental sustainability. As a key foundation to the intervention, urban farmers were identified to participate in the project based on a desire to keep bees due to their pre-existing knowledge of the value of having bees on a farm (Figure 4). However, it became apparent that they had not yet been able to easily take up beekeeping, mostly due to a lack of access to skills and equipment. The farmers therefore indicated an understanding of the benefit of beekeeping to their farming system, but lacked the 'power' to sustainably initiate beekeeping endeavours. We then interviewed expert beekeepers to determine the power factors (skills, knowledge and capital) involved in making a successful beekeeping business. It was clear from the expert beekeepers that they also possessed an underlying 'love' in their beekeeping practice (innovation, bee appreciation and environmental sustainability). An additional unexpected finding was the serious problem that the South African beekeeping industry faces from theft, vandalism (Figure 5), fires, diseases and pests, resulting in 30% asset (equipment, hives and colonies) losses annually. This was a power factor out of their control.

Leading South African bee expert Martin Johannsmeier (2001:5) indicates that "with available natural resources, the industry could expand twice or three times its present size"; however, the beekeeping industry has been declining annually for the past two decades. In addition, the world is facing a "pollinator crisis", or a global decline in insect pollinator species, particularly the honeybee (UNEP, 2010:1). A recent Harvard study indicated that up to 56% of the population in developing nations is at risk of becoming food insecure as a result of this pollinator crisis (Ellis, Myers & Ricketts, 2015). It is also clear that modern apiculture and mass agriculture practices are contributing directly to the demise of the honeybee (Ellis et al., 2015; UNEP, 2010).

Figure 3
Urban farm on the grounds of a primary school in Soweto.

Figure 4
Urban farmer harvesting honey from a wild swarm living under a rock near his farm in Orange Farm, Johannesburg.

Figure 5
Vandalised beehives collected from a commercial beekeeper's apiaries in South Africa.

The culmination of centuries of apiculture has led to a general universal system of beekeeping that relies on beehives (to house a swarm of bees), gear (to protect the beekeeper while working with the hive), know-how (skills, knowledge, practices and techniques for beekeeping) and extraction equipment (to process and package the bee products). The beehive tends to define the other three, as different beehive designs require different gear, knowledge and extraction processes. Two contemporary systems dominate the practice: the top-bar beehive (R600) and the Hoffman frame beehive (R900). The former is more suited to marginalised communities through its lower cost, simplicity and emphasis on harvesting the entire honeycomb. The latter is more suited to commercial apiculture through its efficiency, standardisation and emphasis on high-production output. Although effective in bringing beekeeping to two different markets, the distinction has also widened the gap between the two groups and both have proved ineffective at mitigating the losses currently experienced as a result of theft, vandalism, fire, pests and disease.

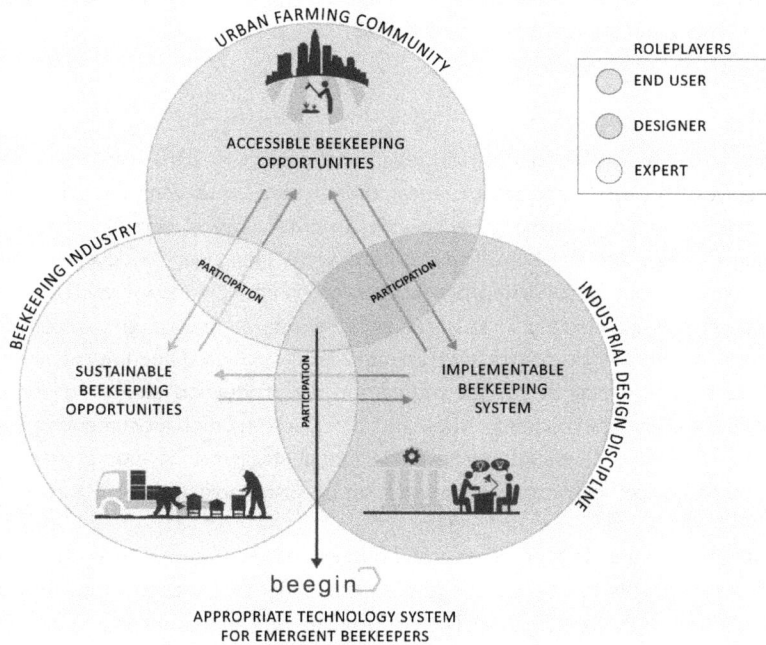

Figure 6   Diagram of participatory research towards increasing capabilities

Theoretical framework: Capabilities

Three distinct groups of stakeholders were identified as participants in the Beegin project, namely industry (expert beekeepers), society (emerging urban farmers) and academia (the design researcher). This triangle of relationships was initially defined in terms of their position in the spectrum of power and love. A sustainable, appropriate beekeeping system has the potential to greatly benefit the beekeeping and small-scale farming industries (love). Existing beekeepers are well versed in the commercial aspects of profiting from long-term beekeeping (power). Small-scale farmers are motivated to become beekeepers to escape poverty and become food secure (power). The design researcher understands the requirements for successful appropriate technology interventions as an academic endeavour (love), but is also motivated to complete a degree (power) and implement the system as a potential career opportunity to the benefit of all stakeholders (power and love). These relationships are captured in Figure 6 below.

It was recognised that it was the desire of the design researcher to affect meaningful change. The expert beekeepers and the farmers had the desire to easily and sustainably keep bees and everyone had a basic need for food security. The Beegin project therefore aimed to enhance the various stakeholders' capabilities towards these ends. The current lack of an appropriate technology system for local beekeeping contributes to an unsustainable industry and limits economic opportunities for emergent farmers. By way of a collaborative research effort between the three groups, the intention was to create an accessible and sustainable system. The envisioned system would need to be adoptable by expert beekeepers for its appropriateness to industry, accessible and operable by urban farmers, and implementable by the design researcher.

Practical application: Balancing power and love

Beegin started as a BTech Industrial Design final project in 2015 with the development a series of beehives. Through participatory research (interviews, site visits and discussions) with expert beekeepers and urban farmers, beehive design criteria were identified that would benefit both the human users and the bees. These criteria were then used to develop new beehive designs and low-tech,[4] community-driven production mechanisms for new hives. The iterative design and production process resulted in low-cost, durable, easy-to-make, highly insulated and easy-to-use beehives. The product outcomes were an entry-level cardboard beehive (retail R275), a permanent concrete beehive (retail R800), the mould and die production equipment for each of the hives (retail R3 400 for the concrete hive) and a mini-dissertation documenting the design process (Brown, 2015). All of these catered to a conceptual, staggered initiation process, conceived to help low-income novices learn to keep bees and set up sustainable apiaries (Figure 7).

The narrative on the initiation process and business model (Figure 7) was developed, in conjunction with the participants, to balance love (the societal benefits) and power (the ability to administer the system) in the most viable manner. The concept centred on the designer producing the production tools and distributing them to beekeepers or farmers interested in manufacturing their own hives without electricity or expensive machinery. The farmers needed to be sufficiently established (capital and resources) to undertake training and purchase ancillary equipment and tools. They would become a point of access for other farmers to acquire hives, training and equipment within the community. Low-income farmers could easily incorporate the entry-level cardboard beehive due to its low cost. Using the entry-level hive to house a swarm of bees for up to two years, the farmers would become acquainted with the practice and begin harvesting honey, which could be sold in order to raise money to invest in permanent beehives, gear and equipment.

---

[4]   'Low-tech', short for 'low technology', is a term used to describe technologies that can be produced and delivered with minimal capital investment, specialisation or compartmentalisation (Wikipedia, 2017).

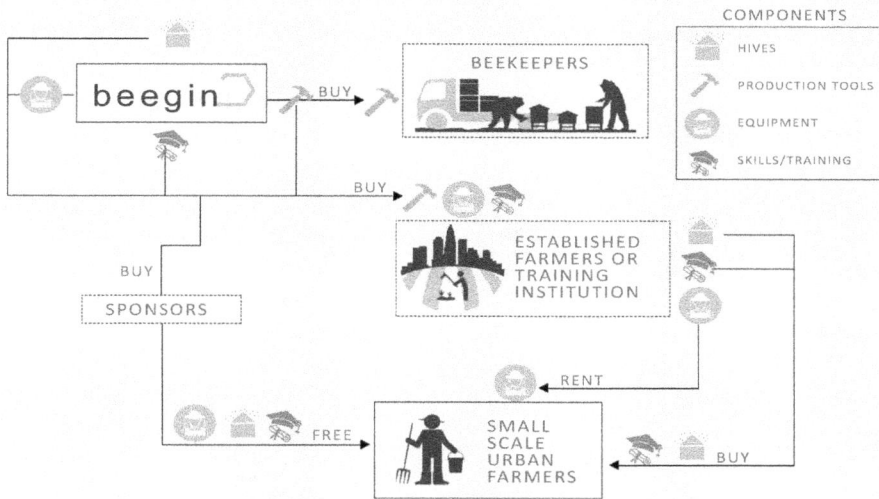

Figure 7   Business model for the Beegin Appropriate Technology Beekeeping System

Central to the accessibility and implementability of the Beegin system was the localised, community-based production of the beehives, and potentially other ancillary products. Instead of the design researcher setting up a business to retail the products directly to the community, the low-tech production tools could be sponsored or subsidised through sales to existing beekeepers. It can also be sold to individuals who could become an access point for others in their community and this can create additional community-driven businesses. This would allow the design researcher the flexibility to move on and scale the system rapidly in other places. If further design research was necessary, at least the tools and skills would be owned by the urban farmers, immediately benefiting their participation in the project.

Praxis: Test, refine, scale and repeat

The concept hives were initially tested by the design researcher, who became certified as a licensed beekeeper during the course of the project, to verify their basic functioning (their ability to keep bees and yield honey). The majority of academic design research projects end at this point, with an initial, potentially viable, solution. In industry, the solution would generally be rolled out immediately without batch testing in different contexts to ensure the validity of the solution. However, initial implementation usually presents complications that require further iterations of the solution (IDEO, 2011). In line with the human-centred design process, further user testing, development and refinement needed to be undertaken to determine the actual appropriateness (function, usability, commercial viability and accessibility) of the Beegin system.

The next phase of the Beegin project was undertaken as the main focus of a two-year MTech Industrial Design degree and the phase was midway at the time of writing this chapter. This phase of

Beegin was particularly focused on refining implementation[5] through the small-scale field testing[6] of the products and trial running the initiation process. This is often referred to as 'second-tier research and development' through the production of a batch of the products to be intensively field-tested over an appropriate period to gather data for further refinement. The cyclical human-centred design process, as per IDEO's model, ends with implementation; however, if further cycles are undertaken, each preceding cycle begins with implementation (IDEO, 2011). Figure 8 illustrates the cyclical human-centred design process that was adopted in the Beegin project and indicates continual refinement and scaling built into the design process. At each stage we referred back to the capabilities of the urban farmers to determine whether the project direction was still true to their values. In addition, we worked towards balancing the drives of power (the delivery of the solution) and love (the societal benefit) in order to arrive at a sustainable system.

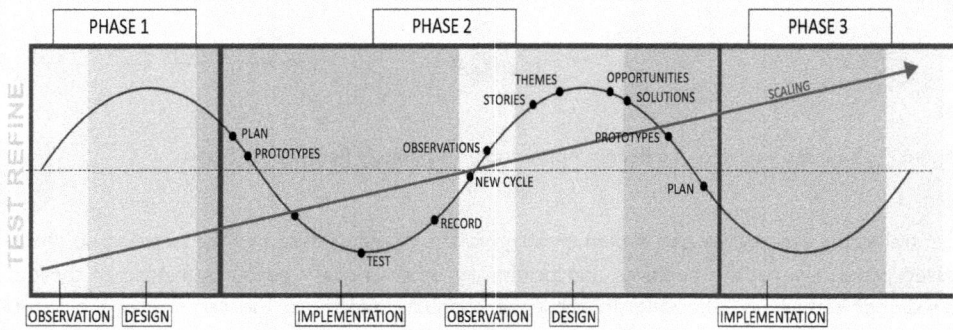

Figure 8   Cyclical testing, refinement and scaling process for citizen design projects
(based on IDEO, 2011)

In keeping with the qualitative nature of the project, an appropriately sized, and varied, group of participants were identified. This group consisted of five expert beekeepers and five urban farmers who all indicated a distinct understanding of the value of beekeeping. In the spring of 2016 the expert beekeepers were tasked with integrating the Beegin beehives into their existing operations and comparatively measuring their function against their existing hives (wooden, Hoffman-frame beehives). The urban farmers were provided with an entry-level cardboard beehive, complete with a swarm of bees, to test the initiation process (see figures 10 and 11). The expert beekeepers operated autonomously, while the urban farmers were assisted by the design researcher to inspect, document and keep their hives through monthly site visits. Ongoing self-testing took place with the design researcher's own concrete and cardboard hives to further inform opportunities for refinement. The initial batch production of the beehives used in the testing provided useful insights into more efficient community production out of the control of the design researcher (Figure 9). During the roll-out of the hives, one of the urban farmers additionally volunteered to test the concrete hive production

---

[5]   Implementation refers to the commercial roll-out, or commercialisation, of the solution, requiring a system that can be scaled to provide different markets with access to the technology through a sustainable business or businesses.

[6]   Field testing refers to the production of a small batch of products to be tested in the environment or context in which they are to be used.

tools, and will become an important access point for skills and knowledge for the other urban farmer participants and any future beekeepers in the area.

Within three months of testing the hives, the beekeepers have already begun harvesting honey, leading to requests for additional hives as well as enquiries about the purchase of the hive production tools. One of the expert beekeepers simultaneously placed new swarms in a pre-existing empty wooden hive as well as the Beegin concrete hive. He was very surprised to witness a 40% increase in productivity in the concrete hive. This equates to almost half the time needed to fill the hive to capacity with honey. We consider this increase in bee productivity as due to the insulating properties of the concrete hive, which means the bees spend less time regulating hive temperatures, particularly in the very hot weather Johannesburg experiences in summer. It is presumed that this will also extend hive productivity in winter.

Although the testing is still underway, not everything went to plan. Three of the farmers voiced their concerns about the cardboard entry-level beehive at the start of the testing. They did not see the benefit of buying a low-cost temporary cardboard in the long run, indicating they would prefer to purchase permanent concrete hives outright. The expert beekeepers were also vocal about their issues with the longevity of the cardboard hive, highlighting that unless it is kept under cover and dry, it would become damaged too quickly, as they found with existing cardboard catch boxes. As testing progresses, concerns for longevity of the cardboard may be exacerbated even further, with evidence of some of the bees 'eating' the cardboard hives in places. It is clear from this that good design intentions do not supersede the realities of those being designed with, whether human or animal.

Figure 9	**Figure 10**	**Figure 11**
Producing concrete beehives.	Testing cardboard beehive with urban farmer.	Testing concrete beehive with urban farmer.

The business model for the Beegin system has been reliant on limited funding for materials, equipment and other expenses necessary to undertake the field testing. The social development orientation of the project enabled support to be leveraged through the University of Johannesburg Research Committee and the National Research Foundation (NRF) of South Africa. It is clear through the initial field testing of the Beegin hives that the expert beekeepers see value in the concrete hive. Further testing and buying from the urban farmers and expert beekeepers will be required to form a sustainable decentralised business for the Beegin project, but the progress thus far has already provided significant benefit to those who participated in its conceptualisation.

With regard to the other ancillary items on which the Beegin system relies (gear, know-how and equipment) (cf. Brown, 2015), the development of a low-cost honey-extraction system, a booklet on beekeeping information and different frame-production methods have already been undertaken. Other systemic considerations of training, protective clothing, harvesting equipment, apiary construction, colonies of bees, networking media, record keeping, sponsorships and expanding community-based production will still need to be explored in the coming year in order to complete a sustainable and resilient system that can be refined and scaled to different communities of urban farmers.

Conclusion

Critical citizen designers need to be provided with the opportunity to discover that good design does good and makes good. This can be encouraged through the exploration of relational tools such as the potential difference model as a means to achieve a sustainable equilibrium between power and love, while developing appropriate technologies that enhance all stakeholder capabilities. Although the model is a simplification of the complexity of participatory design interventions, it is a useful educational tool for the design researcher to keep in mind and manage power and love, both of which are required for sustainable change. The education of critical citizen designers therefore requires appropriate pedagogies that balance the didactic (teaching skills and theories) and dialogic (providing a platform to question and reform those theories). Critical citizen design pedagogy also needs to balance the theoretical and practical experience of students. Such praxis needs to move from the studio into the field. The complex task for design educators is to ensure that all those involved in social design projects, including the students, the university, community stakeholders and experts, benefit equally from such design research. It is this complexity that encouraged the potential difference model and a focus on people's capabilities as a means to evaluate both the improvement and the impact in participatory projects.

The success, thus far, of the Beegin project has been the fact that it has extended from a final fourth-year project into a master's research project, enabling the continuation of the iterative human-centred design cycle while constantly refining the technological system. The time span of the project has also allowed for meaningful relationships to be built between the triangle of stakeholders, which brings with it more authentic trust and honesty in feedback, which is particularly important in iterative projects. No promises have been made that could not be met and even if the project does not roll out into a fully-fledged business, all stakeholders have benefited to some extent from being involved. The student benefitted through the real-world design experience, potential enterprise and qualification he will ultimately be awarded. The urban farmers benefitted through the co-creation, use and ownership of new technologies that potentially allowed them the opportunity to improve their livelihoods. Lastly, the expert beekeepers benefitted from a new technology that enabled them to increase their productivity and expand their existing businesses. Along the way, the student has learnt to navigate the dynamics of power and love by utilising the potential difference model to reflect on his position in the design research process. This is the core of social design and yet it cannot be taught – it can only be learnt through getting one's design hands dirty through projects such as Beegin.

Acknowledgements

This work is based on the research supported in part by NRF for Thuthuka grant no. 88030 held by Angus D. Campbell, titled *Designing development: An exploration of technology innovation by small-scale urban farmers in Johannesburg.* Any opinion, finding and conclusion or recommendation expressed in this material are those of the authors and the NRF does not accept any liability in this regard.

References

Akubue, A. 2000. Appropriate technology for socioeconomic development in Third World countries. *The Journal of Technology Studies*, 26(1), 33–43. https://doi.org/10.21061/jots.v26i1.a.6

Allen, P. 2010. Realising justice in local food systems. *Cambridge Journal of Regions, Economy and Society*, 3, 295–308. https://doi.org/10.1093/cjres/rsq015

Baelden, D. & Van Audenhove, L. 2015. Participative ICT4D and living lab research: The case study of a mobile social media application in a rural Tanzanian university setting. *Telematics and Informatics*, 32, 842–852. https://doi.org/10.1016/j.tele.2015.04.012

Biko, S. 2004. *I write what I like.* Johannesburg: Picador Africa.

Brown, I. 2015. An improved beehive design to support local urban agriculture. BTech mini-dissertation. Johannesburg: University of Johannesburg.

Buchanan, R. 2001. Human dignity and human rights: Thoughts on the principles of human-centered design. *Design Issues*, 17(3), 35–39. https://doi.org/10.1162/074793601750357178

Bunch, R. 1991. People-centred agricultural improvement. In: B. Haverkort, J. van de Kamp & A. Waters-Bayer (Eds.). *Joining farmers' experiments: Experiences in participatory technology development.* London: Intermediate Technology Publications, 23–48.

Campbell, A.D. 2008. Industrial design education and South African imperatives. *Image & Text: A Journal for Design*, 14, 89–99.

Campbell, A.D. 2013. Participatory technology design for urban agriculture in South Africa. In: P. Lyle, J.H.-J. Choi, S. Lawson, C. Lueg, A. Chamberlain, M. Foth, A. Meroni & M. Brereton (Eds.). *Proceedings of the Urban Agriculture: A Growing Field of Research Workshop at INTERACT 2013–14th IFIP TC13 Conference on Human-Computer Interaction.* Cape Town: INTERACT, 8–16.

Campbell, A.D. 2017. Lay designers: Grassroots innovation for appropriate change. *Design Issues*, 33(1), 30–47. https://doi.org/10.1162/DESI_a_00424

Campbell, A.D. & Harrison, P.H. 2015. A framework for socio-technical innovation: The case of a human-powered shredder. In: L. Collina, L. Galluzzo & A. Meroni (Eds.). *Proceedings of the Cumulus Conference, Milano 2015: The Virtuous Circle: Design Culture and Experimentation.* Milan: McGraw-Hill, 211–230.

Carpenter, N. & Rosenthal, W. 2011. *The essential urban farmer.* London: Penguin Books.

City of Johannesburg. 2012. *A city where none go hungry: Operational strategy document.* Johannesburg: Johannesburg Metropolitan Council.

City of Johannesburg. 2013. *2013–2016 Integrated Development Plan (IDP): Implementing the Joburg 2040 strategy.* Available at http://www.joburg.org.za/images/stories/2013/March/March2/2013-16%20IDP.pdf [Accessed 10 June 2016].

Cooper-Hewitt. 2013. *Design and social impact: A cross-sectoral agenda for design education, research and practice.* New York, NY: Cooper-Hewitt, National Design Museum, Smithsonian Institution.

Costandius, E. & Rosochacki, S. 2012. Educating for a plural democracy and citizenship: A report on practice. *Perspectives in Education,* 30(3), 13–20.

Crush, J., Hovorka, A. & Tevera, D. 2011. Food security in southern African cities: The place of urban agriculture. *Progress in Development Studies.* 2(4), 285–305. https://doi.org/10.1177/1464993410011100402

Department of Industrial Design. 2016. *About.* Available at http://www.uj.ac.za/industrial [Accessed 3 October 2016].

Design Council. 2015. *The design economy: The value of design to the UK: Executive summary.* Available at http://www.designcouncil.org.uk/sites/default/files/asset/document/The%20Design%20Economy%20executive%20summary_0.pdf [Accessed 10 November 2016].

Design Society Development DESIS Lab. 2016a. *About.* Available at http://www.designsocietydevelopment.org [Accessed 5 August 2016].

Design Society Development DESIS Lab. 2016b. *iZindaba Zokudla (Conversations about Food).* Available at http://www.designsocietydevelopment.org/project/izindaba-zokudla [Accessed 20 November 2016].

Ellis, A., Myers, S. & Ricketts, T. 2015. Do pollinators contribute to nutritional health? *PLOS ONE,* 10(1), 1–17. https://doi.org/10.1371/journal.pone.0114805

FAO (Food and Agriculture Organization). 2015. *The state of food insecurity in the world: Meeting the 2015 international hunger targets – taking stock of uneven progress.* Rome.

Frayne, B., McCordie, C. & Shilomboleni, H. 2014. Growing out of poverty: Does urban agriculture contribute to household food security in SA cities? *Urban Forum,* 25(2), 177–189. https://doi.org/10.1007/s12132-014-9219-3

Freire, P. 1970. *Pedagogy of the oppressed.* Los Angeles, CA: Penguin.

Freire, P. 2004. *Pedagogy of indignation.* Boulder, CO: Paradigm.

Friedman, K. 2003. Theory construction in design research: Criteria, approaches, and methods. *Design Studies,* 24(6), 507–522. https://doi.org/10.1016/S0142-694X(03)00039-5

Girma, M., Ballo, S., Tegegne, A., Alemayehu, N. & Belayhun, L. 2008. *Approaches, methods and processes for innovative apiculture development: Experiences from Ada'a-Liben Woreda Oromia Regional State, Ethiopia.* IPMS Working Paper 8. Kenia: ILRI.

Gupta, A.K. 2012. Innovations by the poor for the poor. *International Journal of Technological Learning, Innovation and Development,* 5(1/2), 28–39.

Gupta, A.K. 2016. *Grassroots innovation: Minds on the margin are not marginal minds.* Haryana: Penguin Books India.

Heller, S. & Vienne, V. 2003. *Citizen designer: Perspectives on design responsibility*. New York, NY: Skyhorse.

IDEO. 2011. *Human-Centered Design Toolkit.* Second edition. San Francisco, CA.

Illgner, P.M., Nel, E.L. & Robertson, M.P. 1998. Beekeeping and local self-reliance in rural southern Africa. *The Geographical Review*, 88(3), 349–362. https://doi.org/10.2307/216014

Johannsmeier, M.F. (Ed.). 2001. *Beekeeping in South Africa: Plant Protection Research Institute handbook no 14.* Pretoria: Agricultural Research Council.

Johnson, L. & Morris, P. 2010. Towards a framework for critical citizenship education. *The Curriculum Journal*, 21(1), 77–96. https://doi.org/10.1080/09585170903560444

Kahane, A. 2010. *Power and love: A theory and practice of social change*. San Francisco, CA: Berrett-Koehler.

Kasulis, T. 2002. *Intimacy or integrity: Philosophy and cultural difference*. Honolulu: University of Hawaii Press.

King, M.L. Jr. 2002. Where do we go from here? In: C. Carson & K. Shepherd (Eds.). *A call to conscience: The landmark speeches of Dr Martin Luther King, Jr.* New York, NY: Grand Central Publishing, 165–200.

Krippendorf, K. 2006. *The semantic turn: A new foundation for design*. Boca Raton, FL: Taylor & Francis. https://doi.org/10.4324/9780203299951

Lissenden, J., Maley, S. & Mehta, K. 2015. An era of appropriate technology: Evolutions, oversights and opportunities. *Journal of Humanitarian Engineering*, 3(1), 24–35.

Maguire, M. 2001. Methods to support human-centered design. *International Journal of Human-Computer Studies*, 55, 587–634. https://doi.org/10.1006/ijhc.2001.0503

Malan, N. & Campbell, A.D. 2014. Design, social change and development: A social methodology. In: *Design with the Other 90%: Cumulus Johannesburg Conference Proceedings*. Johannesburg: Cumulus Johannesburg, 94–101.

Malan, N., Campbell, A.D., Sibeko, J., Van Zyl, C. & Benecke, R. 2015. Service learning for food security: The iZindaba Zokudla experience. Paper presented at The Fourth Conference of the South African Development Studies Association (2015): Development in Troubled Times, Nelson Mandela Metropolitan University, Port Elizabeth.

Manzini, E. 2010. Small, local, open, and connected: Design for social innovation and sustainability. *Journal of Design Strategies*, 4(1), Spring, 8–11.

Margolin, V. 2007. Design, the future and the human spirit. *Design Issues*, 23(3), 4–14. https://doi.org/10.1162/desi.2007.23.3.4

Mbembe, A. 2015. *Decolonizing knowledge and the question of the archive*. Available at https://africaisacountry.atavist.com/decolonizing-knowledge-and-the-question-of-thearchive [Accessed 25 May 2016].

Mougeot, L.J.A. 2001. Urban agriculture: Definitions, presence, potentials and risks. In: N. Bakker, M. Dubbeling, S. Gündel, U. Sabel-Koschella & H. de Zeeuw (Eds.). *Growing cities, growing food: Urban agriculture on the policy agenda: A reader on urban agriculture*. Feldafing: German Foundation for International Development, 1–43.

Nelson, N. & Wright, S. 1995. *Power and participatory development: Theory and practice.* Rugby: Practical Action. https://doi.org/10.3362/9781780445649

Nussbaum, M. 2011. *Creating capabilities: The human development approach.* London: Harvard University Press. https://doi.org/10.4159/harvard.9780674061200

Oosterlaken, I. 2009. Design for development: A capability approach. *Design Issues*, 29(4), 91–102. https://doi.org/10.1162/desi.2009.25.4.91

Oosterlaken, I. 2015. *Technology and human development.* London: Earthscan.

Robeyns, I. 2011. The capability approach. *The Stanford Encyclopedia of Philosophy.* Available at http://plato.stanford.edu/archives/sum2011/entries/capability-approach/ [Accessed 17 April 2016].

Schumacher, E.F. 1975. *Small is beautiful: Economics as if people mattered.* New York, NY: Harper Perennial.

Sen, A.K. 1999. *Development as freedom.* Oxford: Oxford University Press.

Smillie, I. 2008. *Mastering the machine revisited: Poverty, aid and technology.* Rugby: Practical Action.

Smith, L.T. 1999. *Decolonizing methodologies: Research and indigenous peoples.* London: Zed Books.

Steen, M. 2011. Tensions in human-centred design. *CoDesign: International Journal of CoCreation in Design and the Arts*, 7(1), 45–60.

Thrupp, L.A. 2015. Linking agricultural biodiversity and food security: The valuable role of agrobiodiversity for sustainable agriculture. *International Affairs*, 76(2), 265–281. https://doi.org/10.1111/1468-2346.00133

TTA (Total Transformation Agribusiness). 2008. *Situation analysis of beekeeping industry: Situation analysis of the beekeeping industry in Botswana, Lesotho, Malawi, Mozambique, South Africa, Swaziland, Zambia and Zimbabwe.* Available at http://www.apiservices.biz/documents/articles-en/beekeeping_regional_situational-analysis.pdf [Accessed 17 April 2016].

UN (United Nations). 1987. Towards sustainable development. In: *Our common future: Report of the World Commission on Environment and Development*. Geneva, 41–58.

UNDP (United Nations Development Programme). 2014. Human Development Report 2014. *Sustaining Human Progress: Reducing Vulnerabilities and Building Resilience.* New York, NY.

UNEP (United Nations Environment Programme). 2010. *Annual report 2010.* Nairobi.

University of Johannesburg. 2016. *About.* Available at https://www.uj.ac.za/about [Accessed 30 November 2016].

Wikipedia. 2017. *Low technology.* Available at https://en.wikipedia.org/wiki/Low_technology [Accessed 9 March 2017].

'Socially Responsibilised' Designers: The Evils of Entrepreneurship Ideology in Citizenship Education

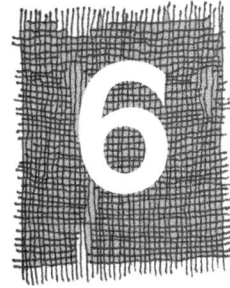

6

Introduction

The idea of agency in citizenship, certainly as it is presently understood, may be ideologically inflected with what are at times opposing understandings of human agency. Neoliberal workfare notions and social democratic notions of citizenship based on welfarism (Wacquant, 2009), economistic-instrumental and political-cultural orientations (Muller, 2000) contend with each other in defining what citizenship means or ought to mean in education in the 21st century. These tensions are certainly evident in discourses of local public higher education expressed in disjunctures between economic and social justice imperatives (Leibowitz, 2012). Tensions are present in global citizenship education (Haste, 2010) as well as in the lack of a clear policy direction in community engagement in South African higher education (O'Connell, Favish & Simpson, 2016) and are certainly also present in the design disciplines, whose instrumental orientations raise difficult questions about the purpose of education. Emerging design discourses such as 'human-centred design' (Steen, 2011) register similar tensions. This contestation about what citizenship and agency means is not of small concern. It is central because it raises key questions about education itself, design education in society and "graduatedness" in the 21st century (Barnett, 2006: 55).

In this chapter, I explore the ideological implications of conceptualising agency within citizenship in terms of neoliberal ideas of 'active' enterprise and entrepreneurship subjectivities (*cf.* Ball, 2013). This is in contrast to notions of social democratic citizenship centred on human welfare and democracy. Specifically, in terms of design education, I critique the curricular activation of design students as 'creatives' as one that produces an 'active' entrepreneurial habitus that I feel is resistant to and largely in tension with critical citizenship. Finally, I take issue with the imposition of entrepreneurship within community-engagement settings. I show that an over-determination of the 'preneurial' habitus averts attention away from the causes of community problems that necessarily stem directly and indirectly from capitalist domination. My position presents entrepreneurship as an *ideology*, one that propagates a neoliberal understanding of social reality. The aim is to deflect and undermine public notions of critical citizenship and one that must be exposed in order for designers to do good work.

I reflect on the implications of this ideology in education and argue that design educators who advocate critical citizenship must directly challenge the assumptions upon which neoliberalism is based and reject entrepreneurial approaches in teaching critical citizenship. I signpost approaches to teaching citizenship in design education that are perhaps more genuinely emancipatory.

The new worker of neoliberal capitalism

In and of itself entrepreneurship is not a bad thing. The problem is that at the same time as it is evangelised in popular culture as a commonsensical standard of individual excellence, it is also posited, in quite a serious sense, at the level of policy and education, as a viable approach to solve a range of serious social problems such as unemployment, inequality, poverty and related problems such as xenophobia, crime, corruption and racism. It is difficult not to find academic articles that do not appeal to these problems in their arguments for entrepreneurial education (Chimucheka, 2014; Jesselyn & Mitchell, 2006; North, 2002) as a vital component.

The narrative of economic growth and growth acceleration (National Planning Commission, 2011) is central to claims that entrepreneurship is a solution. National economic growth is everywhere posited as leading to greater prosperity for the citizenry. In order to achieve it, every effort must be made to encourage enterprising behaviour (Chang, 2012). By dismantling inflexible labour laws, trade protections and human, labour and environmental rights frameworks and imposing corporate governance on state management, as neoliberal orthodoxy proposes (Harvey, 2007), government can remove the barriers that prevent the market from thriving and expanding. In the narrative of economic growth, government unleashes entrepreneurial energy through liberalisation, de/re-regulation and processes that encourage innovation and capital investment and by spreading enterprising values throughout society.

Importantly, this new view involves perceiving and educating humanity differently. The economy, rather than society, becomes the sovereign category in defining what it means to be collectively human. Citizens are free and rational economic actors ('homo economicus' rather than political agents or 'citizens') acting in their own interests to maximise their returns. In this narrative, rather than seeing society as expressing an essentially exploitative relationship between a dominating capital and vulnerable labour – in which a democratically formed state critically intervenes to manage the conflict growing out of this antagonistic relationship – capital itself and the market are idealised as beneficent actors; if not actors, then impersonal and deified forces acting in the name of the greater good with labour as the beneficiary. In this narrative, capitalists are cast as 'entrepreneurs'. Capitalist development is reframed as 'development' and nations are characterised as brands competing for market share. National growth leads to all-important 'job creation' and social stability and the market comprises the primary mechanisms and avenues through which prosperity is shared. This arrangement overrides democratic, public and welfare concerns and makes them secondary to economic growth. Everything must be done, including disciplining the political sphere, state (for example through ratings agencies and via the media) and broader population to ensure that growth occurs.

Within such a scheme, work is conceived of as a privilege. In order for growth to occur and for labour to profit from the opportunities presented by economic growth in the form of jobs, it must cooperate with capital under the terms of a new social compact (Standing, 2011). Part of this deal requires that labour compromises. It must surrender its power and become more 'flexible'. This is because with high labour inflexibility, national economies cannot grow. In the terms of the new compact, the working class must be fragmented, and the working population targeted for subjectivation and activation by a range of agencies, including civil society, the market and various state apparati, so that it is amenable to re-organisation under global capitalism. Labour must be shifted, reconfigured and directed by dictates of capital manifest in terms of increased precarity, casualisation, income insecurity, temping, migrancy and so on. Labour must at the same time be adaptable to imperatives of market competition, accept the conditionalities of new forms of work demanded by innovation, commodified and finally willing to surrender some of it rights in exchange for other rights, particularly those associated with free choice, insurance and the market (Standing, 2011). This radical reconfiguration of the nature of work in the 21st century, commonly advocated by neoliberals, means educating the worker differently and with this new educative regime – 'skills development' – comes a moral imperative pointing to what it means to be a 'good citizen'. This largely supplants a transformative pedagogy (Baatjes, Baduza & Sibiya, 2014).

Entrepreneurship is presented as an imperative and it is this that I take issue with in this chapter. It usefully subjectivises labour in the terms required by global capital. As an unemployed worker, you are taught through the ideology that the reason why you don't have a job is a personal affair. It might be your personality, your hair, your skills, the colour of your skin, your family, your accent, your connections, your age, your attitude. There is something about you that needs to be fixed and then your unemployment problem will be solved. By becoming entrepreneurial, that is, by reforming yourself in the image of the market and by becoming negatively predatory, selfish, future-fit, hyper-individualistic, opportunistic and positively creative, innovative, passionate and 'go-getting' you will not only save yourself from oblivion and survive, but also contribute to national prosperity through economic growth. Paradoxically, it is by behaving exploitatively – harnessing the labour of others for a profit – that you will become a 'job creator' and will be in a better position to 'give back' to your community. Here exploitation is re-semanticised as a positive value.

In the narrative of entrepreneurship, the worker is re-educated to believe that resolving individual deficiencies through self-reform rather than collective and political action is the key to control over one's destiny and economic salvation. A dispositionally oriented education (Bowles & Gintis, 1976, 2001), focuses on reforming attitudes towards work and on filling the mythical 'skills gap' (Treat, 2014) that will address the all-important question of economic growth. This holds promise to secure work in a chaotic and unstable world in which jobs are scarce and the dream of stable employment is a distant fantasy.

A vocational, entrepreneurially geared education will address the fact that the masses do not have the wherewithal to create jobs because they are not sufficiently invested in themselves or have the confidence to imagine themselves differently. The configuration of 'human capitals' that workers have accrued over the course of their lives, freely on the market as it were or through older forms of work, is no longer relevant. Experience and education are no longer guarantees of employment, as they might not be sufficiently aligned with the needs of the market. In the neoliberal trope of 'the 21st century', it is the lack of creativity, inappropriate skill sets, outdated knowledge and, importantly, *inflexibility* that holds back the individual from employment and survival. By adapting to the needs of the market characterised in terms of information, knowledge and flows of goods and services and by reshaping their identity as vulnerable, responsibilised, insecure and adaptable, labouring subjects, attuned to the needs of new capital are offered the promise of what could be construed materially and symbolically as economic salvation.

Debunking the myths of entrepreneurship

Understanding why driving down labour costs and the exploitation and degradation of labour are beneficial is key to explaining why the narrative I have outlined above is so disingenuous. Exploiting and degrading labour remains, despite the rhetoric of newness, the main driver in the process of capitalist accumulation and innovation even in the 21st century. This is essentially a process of appropriating the social surplus (profit) through various forms of social domination (Laclau & Mouffe, 2001). Capitalism can neither survive nor flourish without this arrangement being in place. In every respect, driving down labour costs sits at the heart of any capitalist enterprise, regardless of context. According to Marx (1961, cited in Singer, 1980: 73), capitalism as a development of modernity provokes …

> … a coercive relation, which compels the working class to do more work than the narrow round of its own life-wants prescribes. As a producer of the activity of others, as a pumper-out of surplus-labour and exploiter of labour-power, it surpasses in energy, disregard of bounds, recklessness and efficiency, all earlier systems of production based on directly compulsory labour.

Owners all over the world will do whatever they can, and draw on a range of strategies, from the manipulative (government lobbying, control of the media), to the outright coercive (capturing the state to repress), to achieve the goal of exploiting labour for a profit. Deriving from this fact, from what is a set of legally sanctioned social arrangements centred on the protection of private property rights, is a variety of contradictory social outcomes. These outcomes threaten the system of capitalism itself by creating crises of all kinds (see Harvey, 2010, 2014) and political instability, but also these outcomes contribute to its continuance as a system. In this process, the outcomes of poverty, inequality and unemployment feature prominently, and according to Marxist theory (Marx, 1887), actually maintain the reproduction of capitalist domination:

- Unemployment is an outcome of capitalism and is one that is encouraged by capitalists. The existence of what Marx termed a 'reserve labour army' compromises the bargaining power of labour so as to drive down labour costs, which increases profits.
- Technical innovation (such as automation, shop floor optimisation) is an outcome of the competitive nature of capitalist development. Technical innovations are encouraged by owners in a bid to lower production costs and replace costly labour, contributing again to unemployment.
- Given the vulnerable position of labour – as the class that owns nothing but its labour – accumulation and dispossession quickly grow out of control, resulting in widening class inequality.
- In a system where this inequality is not managed (a weak, corrupt state), owners quickly assert their control over the institutions that challenge their advantages and redirect them to reproduce their power, adding political inequality to social inequality.
- The inability of certain sections of the population to participate economically in their society results in deepening poverty and marginalisation.

The common sense of entrepreneurship turns this logic on its head. Paradoxically, it promotes capitalist domination as a good thing. It achieves this magical turn by painting social relations in personalist and culturalist rather than structural terms. In doing so, it shifts the blame for unemployment, inequality and poverty away from where the blame should lie – with the system of capitalism – and places it at the feet of the individual worker. In the neoliberal imaginary the social outcomes of capitalism are framed in innatist-evolutionary terms (Schumpeter, 1934, 2012) of 'social ills' or caricatured as cultural or personal deficiencies:

- Unemployment grows out of an individual lack of industriousness and of commitment to capitalist growth and personal empowerment.
- Poverty is the result of irresponsible and irrational behaviour and is cultural in origin. Poverty can be traced to overspending, lack of a culture of saving, crime, a sense of entitlement and so forth.
- Poverty and unemployment are a social pathology. Poor communities have only themselves to blame for their lack of enterprise and must be reformed to change their conditions. A lack of family values and respect for the rule of law results in social deprivation.
- Inequality is a natural outcome of struggle for the survival of the fittest on the open market. Inequality should be encouraged to foster competition and personal betterment, which are drivers of progress.

Aside from the obvious hermeneutic problems with the personalist and subjectivist approach to understanding human motivation (Bourdieu, 1990), the main basis for this point of view is the idea that human selfishness is the engine for human growth, social development and prosperity. This is reflected in the unexamined promotion of entrepreneurship as educational innovation (Papagiannis, Klees & Bicketl, 1982). What remains to be understood is how the reform of education on an entrepreneurial basis leads to growth and what distributive mechanisms will make the benefits of this growth shared by the citizenry. Growth, irrespective of whether it flows from human selfishness or not, does not necessarily mean that wealth will 'trickle down' to the working masses. Growth does not magically translate into greater equality and distributive justice via the invisible and mysterious workings of the market, and without an equality of a substantial kind and a significant investment in cooperation between human beings, meritocracy has no meaning.

Without correct social regulation, control and the correct democratic institutions and mechanisms being in place (Piketty, 2014), growth will not necessarily lead to greater prosperity and lesser inequality. Institutions must be created to protect equal opportunity, give access to and moderate the distribution of resources and curb destructive growth that, for example, threatens the environment. Some have argued that what has not changed is the fact of capitalist accumulation and domination. What has changed and grown exponentially is the power of capital to exploit human labour and influence political decisions through the globalisation and the language of globalism (Fairclough, 2008; Harvey, 2014).

The key point to be made here is that the growth narrative is exactly that, a narrative, that may have little basis in reality. In a world of global brands, corporate monopolies, multinational capital and rentier capitalism, do many entrepreneurs survive long on the open market? When limits are not placed on capital, when it is not regulated and controlled, monopolies quickly develop, driving out innovation and entrepreneurial spirit. The successful entrepreneur may be the exception rather than the rule in capitalist societies. Entrepreneurs who succeed do so not because they have both exploited market opportunities and found the means to exploit the labour of vulnerable others successfully. Those dependent on capitalists for their survival constitute the vast majority of the population. Under the conditions of globalised capitalism they are doomed to a life of few opportunities, insecure wage labour, underemployment and, increasingly, a lifetime of unemployment.

In a great irony, given that neoliberalism advocates the privatisation of essential services such as education, the vulnerable subject of new capitalism has even a slimmer chance of succeeding as an entrepreneur in a highly competitive environment. That is because he or she ironically becomes excluded from precisely those educative processes that will increase his or her chances of success and susceptibility to the ideology of responsibilisation. In the new regime of global accumulation, the truth is that it will be labour's vulnerability to market discipline, debt enslavement and the punishing apparatus of the state, rather than through the encouragement of entrepreneurial fervour, that will ultimately drive it on to be more willing to work and more enterprising, responsible and flexible in a situation that ultimately benefits existing capitalists.

This contradiction is well expressed in the intensity of the rhetoric of personal enterprise versus the reality of soaring inequality (Oxfam, 2016) and exponential growth of the precariat. False claims are designed so that they must seem true and self-evident to the oppressed and be useful to protect the interests of the powerful in the form of hegemony. Arguments, myths and rhetorics must be invented by the dominant classes to ensure that the oppressed – labour – does not gain consciousness of its exploitation by the dominant class and rise against it. Over time, ideologies are not only newly invented, but old ideologies are also updated to accommodate the evolving productive arrangements of societies. Entrepreneurship seems to me to be such an ideology. It is ingenuous in the sense that it successfully convinces workers to accept ever-increasing levels of vulnerability and insecurity, which increases their productivity and neutralises their political radicalism. This increases the chances for exploitation *while hiding from the workers the very fact of their exploitation.* It effectively takes attention away from what are structural problems arising from capitalist development and locates most of the problems it generates, imaginatively, at the level of the private. It is ingenuous because the problem (capitalism) is here advocated as the solution (entrepreneurship).

Responsibilisation and the labouring society

If the welfare state failed to alleviate the worst features of capitalist development (some of which I have outlined above) by addressing the symptoms rather than the causes, the workfare regime of neoliberalism (Wacquant, 2012), by contrast, ignores causes and symptoms of capitalism altogether. Neoliberalism reinvents the cause of social ills as located in the deficiencies of the working individual and attempts, through the universalisation of entrepreneurial values, to change what capitalism itself means, normalising and naturalising its operations. Welfarism is characterised by neoliberal orthodoxy as misdirected charity, one that encourages idleness and entitlement through handouts to welfare recipients. The neoliberal state replaces the passivity associated with the dispensation of universal and human rights under welfarism with the activity of receiving limited market rights in exchange for work. In the framework of workfare, human and labour rights are re-conceptualised as a privilege, *earned* through personal enterprise, competitiveness and risk taking and in the failure of this, subjects are reformed through the pedagogy of prisonfare.

In the logic of neoliberalism, welfarism is delinked from the systemic outcomes of capitalism and seen as an ineffective institutional means of managing social deviancy. In neoliberal thinking, the state must reject the welfarism of social democracy without entirely dispensing of the discourse of rights, essential to the functioning of liberal democracy. Rights are reconceptualised in relation to the bearing of risk. The role of the state is to offer equal opportunities to responsibilised citizens by ensuring that goods and services (such as transport, electricity, water, health and education) are not universally free, but available, accessible and 'affordable'. If they are not to be found on the market, they must be dispensed to subjects that are found to be deserving, for example through means testing. The state ends its social role at arbitrating who is deserving and in doing so passes all sorts of risks onto citizens, creating a society of risk, where individuals, without the benefit of state support, must take personal responsibility for their failures without the benefit of a safety net. Under neoliberal capitalism, the social, maternal bosom of the state has shrunk, its ability to regulate has been shrunk or directed to enhancing the functioning of the market and significantly, its disciplining, punishing arm and "penal fist" has grown (Wacquant, 2009: 4) to create what Standing (2011) largely describes in his book as a growing and anxious precariat.

The changing nature of work under globalisation, a crisis of work and work identities and the increase of risk in the late 20th and early 21st centuries have been well documented (Crompton, 2008; Du Gay, 2006). More than 30 years of neoliberal policy has been stunningly successful. It has meant that globally, in very real terms, the formal labour market has shrunk, workers' wages have stagnated and the labour force has become globally migrant and the working population insecure. The middle classes, the flabby stabiliser of developed nations around the world, have shrunk, leading to ever-greater levels of social instability, anomie, alienation, anxiety and anger (especially for the youth), while an elite class of billionaires has become visibly ascendant (Kotkin, 2014).

Some have argued that labour, after 30 years of what is in fact onslaught by the Right and capital, is being punished. Labour is increasingly casualised, workers are being denied the ability to save, the power of working people to own property and gain stability is shrinking dramatically and debt is rampant, ultimately making for a class that is exploitable precisely because it is vulnerable. Without a government to protect its wages, moderate its working conditions and ensure its job security to maintain labour laws, ensure that social and public spending meets social needs and corporate taxes are paid to finance this, labour is being punished for the political gains made prior to the 1960s.

We now see states and governments that are, to all intents and purposes, indifferent to labour. Some are being seduced by multinational capital and some have been captured. States are increasingly mandated by a disciplining and punishing capital (through rating agencies, the International Monetary Fund, the World Bank and other agencies) to not only manage, but also contain the dangers associated with the rise of unemployment, underemployment and general insecurity of the working population. Controlling labour insecurity under deindustrialised and desocialised citizenship stands as central to the task of neoliberal government and its various governmental modalities. Key to this is targeting sections of the population to cooperate with the needs of global capital through education, securitisation, surveillance and ultimately repression and violence.

At the high point of capitalist development, where poverty and unemployment reach dangerous levels, new ideological devices (war rhetoric, anti-immigration rhetoric, religious fundamentalism, patriotism) are always conveniently summoned to alleviate and mediate social crisis. The ideology of entrepreneurship seems to be such a device, aimed to persuade an alienated and desocialised working class, immigrant labour and a disenchanted precariat class that the crisis of capital does not in fact exist. Entrepreneurship ideology attempts to convince us that what we face is a cultural crisis that can be overcome through education. This requires a suitable educational ideology to responsibilise the citizenry.

Educating the designer for hustling in the gig economy: The case of the 'creative'

I have outlined in a somewhat over-elaborate way how citizenship is conceived in neoliberal terms as the education of the active, responsibilised, flexible and vulnerable worker. This stands in stark contrast with the social democratic notion of educating the critical citizen worker, who under Fordism and socialism was the privileged subject of the state. The contrast between these two approaches (Table 1) could be reduced to a simple binary or class antagonism expressed in the difference between a world dominated by capital and another by labour:

Table 1 Comparing the educational orientations of politically dominant groups

Politically dominant group	Educational orientation	Political system
Labour (1950–1970)	Educating workers to resist and protect themselves from exploitation by capital	Social democratic – socialist
Capital (1970–present)	Educating workers to be willing to be exploited by capital	Neoliberalism, liberal democracy

I have done this to contextualise why these tensions are represented at the level of education policy throughout the world. These tensions have found definite expression in the adoption of outcomes-based education in South Africa, a national 'competence' approach in which learners are taught in somewhat behaviourist terms to reach specified well-defined and observable outcomes in the learning process. As Tikly (2003: 164–165) remarks, the tension between the outcomes where preferable to capital and workers was acutely expressed in the shape and form that outcomes-based education was supposed to take in South Africa in the early 2000s:

> [B]oth the construction of the 'entrepreneurial individual' and of the 'critical citizen' implied by the two sides of this debate are reflected in national policy documents … It is the former, however, that is increasingly likely to predominate as it is more overtly linked to the development of an enterprise culture in keeping with the new market discipline. Indeed, the trajectory of the new curriculum does appear to be moving more towards a neo-liberal view of citizenship. What is also emerging in the new curriculum is a reformulated version of critical citizenship that emphasises national unity based on 'core values'. In place of a radicalised notion of workers' rights, the new construction of citizenship is more in keeping both with classical liberalism and with recent shifts in neo-liberal thought globally.

The tension between these conceptions of worker versus entrepreneur is reflected in the national critical cross-field outcomes statement in its understanding of development (SAQA, 2016: 19):

> In order to contribute to the full personal development of each learner and the social and economic development of the society at large, it must be the intention underlying any programme of learning to make an individual aware of the importance of ... participating as responsible citizens in the life of local, national and global communities, being culturally and aesthetically sensitive across a range of social contexts; exploring education and career opportunities, and *developing entrepreneurial opportunities* [my emphasis].

How does this relate specifically to the *education of designers* in the contemporary South African situation?

In this regard, I find it interesting that many design students are increasingly referred to and refer to themselves in class terms as 'creatives' – members of what is a creative class (popularised by theorists such as Richard Florida [2014]) – and much of their education prepares them for this role. 'Creatives' refers to a class of workers who are largely defined not in terms of their discipline, subject, profession or expertise, but by their ability to independently apply their creative skills and their passion to a given problem or task. The 'creative' is generally associated with those aspects of architecture, design and the arts that are informal, short-term and contractually based. Creatives may be trained as artists, digital artists, multimedia designers and graphic designers and as scientists, technologists and anthropologists, but in order to qualify with this designation they must show a capacity to be productively flexible. They are able to depart from convention, discipline and traditional socialisations in order to find new areas of intersection and applicability in the market, applying 'mode 2' competences (Muller, 2000) to benefit industry.

The 'creatives' are largely valorised within entrepreneurial mythologies as being figures to be aspired to: cutting-edge, innovative, free. However, at the same time as the creatives stand out as a symbol of new class distinction, they strike me as tragic figures. Creatives are becoming, I believe, an archetype of what it means to be a flexible and vulnerable cognitive worker, experiencing themselves simultaneously as members of the creative class, service class and the multitudinous precariat. The designers-as-creatives are neither the alienated workers of the factories described by Engels or the call centre workers of a multinational outfit, but nor do they occupy the privileged position in the professional salariat, being largely roaming characters. The creatives are the distinctive animals of the cultural intermediary class and lumpen members of the urban precariat.

They are not necessarily temporary or part-time workers. In broad terms they are the immaterial, interstitial labourers of the post-Fordist regime cut loose from formal employment and the iron cage of the class structure. The creative stands out as being quintessentially "an entrepreneur of the self" (Dilts, 2011: 130), self-made, self-determining, but always within the bounds of the market.

Given this positioning, creatives are neither sucked into the anxiety, anomie, alienation and anger of the precariat, nor enjoy "joyful ideas of communality" (McRobbie, 2010: 65) associated with workerism. They do not entirely fall prey to the "powerful regime which inculcates cynicism and opportunism, manifest in the context of the party and the events culture of network sociality where self-promotional public relations holds sway" (McRobbie, 2010: 65). The creative is a place of some power, but also intense vulnerability "where work and leisure are dissolved" (McRobbie, 2010: 65) and human feeling and sentiment have gone beyond commercialisation (Hochschild, 2010), advancing into the realm of self-commercialisation as the ego is wilfully branded.

The embedded creative, the counterpart to the free creative, is required also to be 'intrapreneurial', but this is an attitude geared towards the corporate environment and is well articulated in the notion of 'design thinking' that has been popularised in the corporate world through design companies such as IDEO. Designers in this mould are not designers per se, but abductive thinkers, notable for their capacities for flexibility and adaptability. The work that they perform is design-like rather than design. They are able to work in multidisciplinary teams and in fact can cross disciplines to drive innovation in a given firm or company. As a resource such practitioners are highly sought-after in industry and are typically highly mobile, lifelong learners with a seemingly insatiable and omnivorous appetite for cultural and social capital (Bennett, Savage, Silva, Warde, Gayo-Cal & Wright, 2010).

Those students who freelance during their studies and after graduating quickly learn that the industry is rapidly becoming deprofessionalised and are realising just how easily their labour can be exploited in the absence of unions and professional bodies. Designers are increasingly finding their work casualised and contractualised. As participants in what has been termed the 'gig economy', designers work on short-term projects bases as design entrepreneurs and consultants. It is not unusual for designers to juggle various jobs, to wear many hats in order to survive. They must pitch their concepts to 'the suits' and develop strategies to communicate their creative ideas to conservative people. More and more design students cannot enter the job market without first being put through gruelling internships that only the students with family support are able to endure. Young creatives must groom themselves to engage in what has been termed 'network sociality' well before they have graduated.

Creatives are attractive to potential employers and clients precisely because their flexible dispositions make them pleasing to employers and clients, reshaping and morphing themselves into whatever form will secure work and garner attention. In practical design teaching and professional courses especially, much pedagogical effort is expended on grooming students to 'hustle', an asset in the flexible labour market. In qualifications aimed at developing so-called creatives, much effort is put into facilitating a process whereby the student self-commodifies. Design students are taught to self-brand; to network; to showcase their work on digital platforms; to attend exhibitions, expos and book launches; to build intimate relationships that enhance their reputations and to be culturally fluent. Their socialities are increasingly reliant on networking (Wittel, 2001). They are enabled and encouraged to take the best parts of themselves – their expertise, personal styles, tastes and their personal identities – and to mould them not only into marketable products, but also into multifaceted brand experiences.

If it is the case that design students must be prepared to 'hustle' effectively in a gig economy as survivalists, they must also be prepared for the possibility of obtaining the much sought-after stable jobs as high-skilled, flexible workers in corporate environments. Although this demands a different skill set from the freelance designer-creative, or design consultant, the attitudes expected remain the same.

Design students are now taught early on in their careers to be self-reliant and self-promoting and pursue cultural distinction through styling of the self. This has been heightened by the digital revolution that places demands on creatives to be on call, have an up-to-date online presence, compete with their peers and work on demand. This need to prepare students to excel as vulnerable survivalists 'in industry' and on the peripherals means that the curriculum, or the hidden curriculum in the least, is increasingly arranged around the regime of insecure employment.

This has serious implications for citizenship education. Where the focus of design education may have traditionally centred on building competence in the vocational sense, preparing students for predictable and stable work, or for careers as professionals (depending on the discipline), that is no longer sufficient within the corporate world and outside of it. Nor is supplementing this by enriching students with appropriate cultural capitals, enough to prepare them for the trials of entrepreneurship. Designers must now self-identify as belonging to the special class – creatives – and have at their disposal a range of skills that allow them to survive in an aggressively competitive market. Contact with industry through various talks, professional practice modules focused on self-branding and intellectual property, portfolio evenings and a stream of self-branding design projects and portfolio presentations encourage students to self-commodify, self-promote and accept exploitation as a fact. Yet, despite their increasing vulnerability in the professional courses that are on offer, they are not taught about labour law, labour rights or how to protect themselves from exploitative employers and clients. In the pedagogy of entrepreneurship, design students are pitted against one another through assessment practices and institutional reward schemes that foreground competition, undermining potential solidarities between students.

The crime of socially responsibilised design: Reflections

So what can design educators and students do to counteract these global capitalist and neoliberal forces and the incursions of entrepreneurial thinking in the curriculum? I believe that it is imperative that community-engaged design projects and citizenship education in design must be seen by educators against the background of the dominance of entrepreneurial false consciousness. Design educators should reflect on the pervasive influence of the ideology of entrepreneurship on responsibilising the designer in relation to what is problematically termed the 'community'/'citizenship' and speculate on what steps they might take within their institutions to address the issues that I have outlined above.

In what follows below, I offer my perspective on the above in reflecting on the interdisciplinary project "Design for and with local communities". This project is hosted by the Faculty of Art, Design and Architecture (University of Johannesburg) and the Centre for Education Rights and Transformation (University of Johannesburg). It focuses undergraduate Graphic Design, Multimedia, Industrial Design and Architecture students on identifying problem ecologies in nearby Johannesburg communities (Fietas, Westbury, Kliptown) and working with activists on generating design solutions. The critical points below have been developed in my three years of teaching on the project and in each point (in italics) I propose a way forward:

Curricula obsessed with industry: Business as usual

Students come into citizenship and community projects entrepreneurially minded because they have been conditioned to think so in courses over-determined by the needs of industry and the market. In the mind of many students, community work forms a distraction from what is the real work of learning to be a designer and showcasing their expertise as 'creatives'. Students rarely include their group work and community work in their industry portfolios, which is strongly indicative of the irrelevance they consign to citizenship-oriented projects. *Critical citizenship projects should make students aware of the limitations of what is essentially design-for-profit, focusing students on use values, rather than profit values, promoted through design. At the same time as students might be made aware of the exploitation at the heart of capital accumulation, they might be made conscious of how they are themselves exploited in the workplace and the market as value adders through exposure to labour law and labour history, particularly as it pertains to design. As a student in our department remarked, there might be much to gain from comparing the subjectivities of designers to other kinds of workers – unlike workers who sell their labour, designers sell their identities. In this process of alienation it is the self that may be lost (Pakadi, 2017).*

Community work as charity and the perpetuation of middle-class arrogance

Students' view – that community design projects are a kind of charity preparing them for corporate outreach initiatives – propagates the view that communities are deficient and must be reformed culturally and attitudinally through the goodwill of the powerful. This often derives from untransformed, middle-class prejudice that many students hold about the poor and working class, linked to the students' background and family origin. The extent to which these views remain entrenched speaks to the failure of our curricula to teach critical thinking, ones that teach students why societies are structured the way they are. Changing this viewpoint (which in South Africa requires a racially transformative dimension) requires a concerted curriculum that would involve a component of critiquing entrepreneurial approaches that could be shown to be homologous to middle-class privilege. The middle-class character of the student bodies is itself problematic. We need more students living in marginalised communities engaging in citizenship. Imposing entrepreneurship and entrepreneurial identities onto communities through design ultimately reproduces existing dependencies while sustaining middle-class values of charity and elitist values of upper-class philanthropy, which in a South African context is racialised. *Critical design educators should advocate within their departments, schools and faculties a holistic approach to citizenship education that focuses on transforming the student habitus and making students aware of the class and racial biases in their outlook and curricula.*

Interrogating policy and position before entering the field of participation

Rather than addressing structural and policy problems in our teaching, we as designers and design educators, like many other privileged actors imbricated in the class structure, avoid confronting the realities of capitalist oppression. Instead of focusing our work on changing policy and examining our own privileged positions, we instead attempt to morally reform the vulnerable people with whom we are working in entrepreneurial terms. Psychologically, this constitutes a convenient process of displacement, pathologising, caricaturing and at times criminalising the community other.

Participatory design, human-centred design, user-centred design and action research give us as educators opportunities to critique policy and our own positions before we enter the field and to generate reflective forms of activist pedagogy. *Given the practical effects of design in the world, policy texts related to and impacting design (such as that related, for example, to economic development, environment, business regulations, human rights and so on) should be scrutinised in the classroom before students enter the field.*

Reporting on research as a process of colonisation and exploitation

At the very worst, community-engagement projects inflected with neoliberal values become outright exploitative of vulnerable subjects. Innovations are tested on the poor because they are uncomplaining targets of experimentation, easily giving consent in the hope of an undefined benefit. The community forms an effective backdrop in which to develop service-learning skills in which it secures no benefit, creating an exploitative pedagogical situation. Community work morally legitimises the work of participatory designers, giving their work greater credibility on the academic and publishing circuit. Rarely are design students in the position, given their transience as a population, to participate in long-term dialogical engagements with specific face-to-face communities. The short-term nature of many community design projects means that thorough and contextualised research, and genuine dialogical exchanges, cannot be undertaken. The attempt to build enduring and caring relationships with their collaborators is frustrated, lending itself to exploitation, where expert knowledge crowds out community-based knowledge. These issues are seldom reported on or raised by participants in community-engagement projects. *In lectures in this learning unit students are exposed to research paradigms related to 'research for' and 'research with' people, such as ethnography, action research, participatory action research and decolonial approaches, so that students understand, before they enter the field, the power dynamics at work in research practices.*

Responsibilisation is not enough

Although equality of exchange is often promoted in 'socially responsible' design projects, in reality there often exist many unequal power differentials that emerge on the ground between sponsors, designers, funders, institutions, community organisations and role players that are not reported on. In many ways the terms of a given project are set up undemocratically before it even commences. For example, it is taken as a given that the community member is a 'user', that the professional designer is a service provider, and that the funder must gain a return on its investment. In the process of stakeholder negotiation, community interests and problems might be side-lined. I have seen projects that uncritically and aggressively push onto communities the interests of corporate sponsors who have track records for violating human, labour and environmental regulations and are seeking new markets in communities. Community engagement is in some cases leveraged by universities simply to promote their brand value. In the worst cases, community work can become a form of greenwashing and whitewashing, so that values distorted by capitalism (such as entrepreneurship) come to be propagated under the cover of 'social responsibility', 'entrepreneurial action' and 'sustainability'. *Design educators and students need to analyse the bias and interests at work in the briefs with which they are working (the project frame), asking what institutions, private individuals, governments, businesses, politicians and so on stand to gain ideologically from their work in communities.*

The dangerous reach of what I term 'entrepreneurship ideology' in curricula and common-sense understanding of the world means that when students are confronted with design projects that are genuinely oriented to community, social justice, activism and critical citizenship, such as the project "Design for and with local communities" – projects that propose different ideas of activeness to those proffered by neoliberalism – students, out of habit, apply their entrepreneurial understandings to their experiences of citizenship and community. For me, this knee-jerk reaction to citizenship needs to be countered by consciously adopting *an activist approach to design research and design*, one where students work in partnership with social activists in oppressed communities to affect real social change. Before designers attempt to invent new systems to wicked problems of our present supercomplex world, they perhaps need to understand, in ideological terms, the nature of the issues and oppression in capitalist societies.

Conclusion

We might do well to remember that neoliberalism is not only a set of macro-economic and policy prescriptions aligned to advance capital. It is also a programme of reform aimed at responsibilising the citizenry, activating certain subjects (consumers, designers, communities) that take advantage of their market rights ('choice') to pursue their own selfish interests. Vitally, neoliberalism is a pedagogical programme made to *habitualise enterprising behaviours*. Neoliberalism appears to me as an attempt to do away with precisely the notion of critical citizenship and community associated with the public realm and replacing it with market subjectivities of hyper-individualism and consumption. We might note that entrepreneurship is not a new but a rehabilitated ideology, one that has always been linked to capitalist development and imperialist expansion.

My argument has always been that by adopting a sociological approach, critical design education can resist neoliberalism (Gray, 2014, 2015). Following this approach, design students will become more aware of their role as agents operating within a class system in a capitalist economy. This will provide apertures and develop critical tools to rethink their work. Only through this awareness of their class positionality will designers begin to see the ethical necessity of politicising and transforming their practices.

References

Baatjes, I., Baduza, U. & Sibiya, A.T. 2014. Building a transformative pedagogy in vocational education. In: S. Vally & E. Motala (Eds.). *Education, economy and society*. Pretoria: Unisa Press, 81–102.

Ball, S.J. 2013. *Foucault, Power and education*. London: Routledge.

Barnett, R. 2006. Graduate attributes in an age of uncertainty. In: P. Hager & S. Holland (Eds.). *Graduate attributes, learning and employability*. Dordrecht: Springer, 49–65.

Bennett, T., Savage, M., Silva, E., Warde, A., Gayo-Cal, M. & Wright, D. 2010. *Culture, class, distinction*. London: Routledge.

Bourdieu, P. 1990. *The logic of practice*. Vancouver: Stanford University Press.

Bowles, S. & Gintis, H. 1976. *Schooling in capitalist America: Educational reform and the contradictions of economic life*. London: Routledge and Kegan Paul.

Bowles, S. & Gintis, H. 2001. Schooling in capitalist America revisited. *Sociology of Education,* 75(1), 1–18. https://doi.org/10.2307/3090251

Chang, H.J. 2012. *23 things they don't tell you about capitalism.* New York: Bloomsbury.

Chimucheka, T. 2014. Entrepreneurship education in South Africa. *Mediterranean Journal of Social Sciences,* 5(2), 403–416. https://doi.org/10.5901/mjss.2014.v5n2p403

Crompton, R. 2008. *Class and stratification.* Cambridge: Polity.

Dilts, A. 2011. *From 'entrepreneur of the self' to 'care of the self': Neoliberal governmentality and Foucault's ethics.* Western Political Science Association 2010 Annual Meeting Paper. Available at https://papers.ssrn.com/sol3/papers.cfm?abstract_id=1580709 [Accessed 22 March 2017].

Du Gay, P. 2006. *Production of culture/cultures of production.* London: Sage.

Fairclough, N. 2008. *Language and globalisation.* London: Routledge.

Florida, R. 2014. *The rise of the creative class revisited: Revised and expanded.* New York, NY: Basic Books.

Gray, B. 2014. Design for development discourses and neoliberal values: Designer, innovation, community and sustainability. In: *Design with the Other 90%: Cumulus Johannesburg Conference Proceedings.* Johannesburg: Cumulus Johannesburg, 241–252.

Gray, B. 2015. Ethics in design and issues of social class – reflecting on the learning unit: Design and the construction of class distinction. Paper presented at the Design Educators Forum of South Africa Conference, Midrand Graduate Institute, 2–3 September.

Harvey, D. 2007. *A brief history of neoliberalism.* New York, NY: Oxford University Press.

Harvey, D. 2010. *The enigma of capital and the crises of capitalism.* Oxford: Oxford University Press.

Harvey, D. 2014. *Seventeen contradictions and the end of capitalism.* Oxford: Oxford University Press.

Haste, H. 2010. Citizenship education: A critical look at a contested field. In: L.R. Sherrod, J. Torney-Purta & C.A. Flanagan (Eds.). *Handbook of research in civic engagement in youth.* Hoboken, NJ: Wiley, 161–188. https://doi.org/10.1002/9780470767603.ch7

Hochschild, A. 2010. *The managed heart: Commercialisation of human feeling.* Berkeley, CA: University of California Press.

Jesselyn, M. & Mitchell, B. 2006. Entrepreneurship education in South Africa: A nationwide survey. *Education and Training,* 48(5), 348–359. https://doi.org/10.1108/00400910610677054

Kotkin, J. 2014. *The new class conflict.* New York, NY: Telos Press.

Laclau, E. & Mouffe, C. 2001. *Hegemony and socialist strategy: Towards a radical democratic politics.* London: Verso.

Leibowitz, B. 2012. Reflections on higher education and the public good. In: B. Leibowitz (Ed.). *Higher education for the public good: Views from the South.* Staffordshire: Trentham Books, 1–29. https://doi.org/10.18820/9781928357056/00

Marx, K. 2015. *Capital: A critique of political economy.* Moscow: Progress.

McRobbie, A. 2010. Reflections on feminism, immaterial labour and the post-fordist regime. *New Formations,* (70), 60–76.

Muller, J. 2000. *Reclaiming knowledge: Social theory, curriculum and education policy.* London: Routledge.

National Planning Commission. 2010. *National Development Plan: Vision for 2030.* Available at http://www.gov.za/sites/www.gov.za/files/devplan_2.pdf [Accessed 11 November 2016].

North, E. 2002. A decade of entrepreneurship education in South Africa. *South African Journal of Education,* 22(1), 24–27.

O'Connell, B., Favish, J. & Simpson, G. 2016. Community engagement. In: *South African higher education reviewed: 20 years of democracy.* Pretoria: CHE, 241–278.

Oxfam. 2016. *Oxfam briefing paper,* 18 January. Available at https://www.oxfam.org/sites/www.oxfam.org/files/file_attachments/bp210-economy-one-percent-tax-havens-180116-en_0.pdf [Accessed 12 November 2016].

Pakadi, K. 2017. Unpublished student review of a lecture presented by the author.

Papagiannis, G.J., Klees, S.J. & Bicketl, R.N. 1982. Toward a political economy of educational innovation. *Review of Educational Research,* 52(2), 245–290. https://doi.org/10.3102/00346543052002245

Piketty, T. 2014. *Capital in the twenty-first century.* Cambridge: Harvard University Press. https://doi.org/10.4159/9780674369542

SAQA (South African Qualifications Authority). 2000. *The National Qualifications Framework and Curriculum Development.* Available at http://www.saqa.org.za/docs/pol/2000/curriculum_dev.pdf [Accessed 10 November 2016].

Schumpeter, J.A. 1934. *The theory of economic development.* Cambridge: Harvard University Press.

Schumpeter, J.A. 2012. *Capitalism, socialism and democracy.* Second edition. London: Verso.

Siivonen, P. & Brunila, K. 2014. The making of entrepreneurial subjectivity in adult education. *Studies in Continuing Education,* 36(2), 160–172. https://doi.org/10.1080/0158037X.2014.904776

Singer, P. 1980. *Marx: A very short introduction.* Oxford: Oxford University Press.

Standing, G. 2011. *The precariat: The new dangerous class.* London: Bloomsbury.

Steen, M. 2011. Tensions in human-centred design. *CoDesign: International Journal of CoCreation in Design and the Arts,* 7, 45–60.

Tikly, L. 2003. Governmentality and the study of education policy in South Africa. *Journal of Education Policy,* 18(2), 161–174. https://doi.org/10.1080/0268093022000043074

Treat, J. 2014. On the use and abuse of education: Reflections on unemployment the 'skills gap' and 'zombie economics'. In: S. Vally & E. Motala (Eds.). *Education, economy and society.* Pretoria: Unisa Press, 171–189.

Wacquant, L. 2009. *Punishing the poor: The neoliberal government of social insecurity.* London: Duke University Press. https://doi.org/10.1215/9780822392255

Wacquant, L. 2012. Three steps to a historical anthropology of actually existing neoliberalism. *Caderno CRH,* 25(66), 505–518. https://doi.org/10.1590/S0103-49792012000300008

Wittel, A. 2001. Toward a network sociality. *Theory, Culture, Society,* 18(6), 51–76. https://doi.org/10.1177/026327601018006003

Creating Citizen Designers by Nurturing Design Thinking Skills through Experiential Learning

7

FATIMA CASSIM

Introduction

Katherine McCoy (2003: 2) presents designers with the following question:

> How can a heterogeneous society develop shared values and yet encourage cultural diversity and personal freedom? Design and design education are part of the problem and can be part of the answer. We cannot afford to be passive anymore. Designers must be good citizens and participate in the shaping of our government and society.

This excerpt is from a contribution by McCoy, a reputable American graphic designer and educator, to the book *Citizen designer: Perspectives on design responsibility* (Heller & Vienne, 2003). This book highlights the increasingly important role that designers play as a social and political force in society and as such, it questions and explores the morals and values that need to underpin professional design solutions. Even though the book was published over a decade ago, the call for increased accountability and responsibility from designers still holds true today, especially within a South African context. Two decades after democracy, the post-apartheid nation is in a state of flux with a palpable sense of compromised civic values such as tolerance, respect and justice. From an ideological perspective, all South African citizens now have an opportunity to cast their political votes; however, in terms of participation, the need remains to educate the population for more active and critical citizenship engagement on a day-to-day basis.

In light of the increased need for citizenship, the underpinning premise of this chapter is that citizen designers in South Africa should be educated to affirm McCoy's (2003: 2) belief that "[a]s designers, we could use our particular talents and skills to encourage others to wake up and participate as well". Accordingly, this chapter proposes on a theoretical level that experiential learning can help to instil abductive thinking skills and the practice of framing in communication design students to address complex design problems and, ultimately, to encourage critical citizenship among themselves and the people with and for whom they are designing (the extent of user engagement depends on the project). To this end, the chapter uses Dorst's (2011) argument, namely that abductive thinking

125

and the related act of framing are central to design thinking, as the point of departure. Even though Dorst's argument is situated in an organisational context, it is not restricted to it; therefore, his argument is extended to a design education context for the purposes of this chapter.

The chapter begins with a brief contextualisation of the role of design education towards critical citizenship. Thereafter, abductive thinking and framing are presented theoretically as the key elements of design thinking before considering the facilitation of framing in a South African student design project at a tertiary education level. The theoretical exploration in the chapter is approached from a design educator's perspective.[1] Furthermore, as the vantage point is design education towards critical citizenship, the discussion is guided by John Dewey's (1938) and Paulo Freire's (1970) seminal contributions to the discourse on critical pedagogy and more specifically on the role of experience in education. Three overarching tenets, namely the real world as the context of experience, the role and relationship between teachers and students and the experiential learning process (praxis) guide the discussion. The author recognises that there are numerous teaching strategies and methods over and above experiential learning that are employed for purposes of moral and critical citizenship education, such as co-operative learning, dialogic learning (discussion) and service learning (Schuitema, Ten Dam & Veugelers, 2008), but they are not the focus of this chapter.

The role of design education towards critical citizenship

The role of design towards citizenship is not unheard of. For example, design for democracy creates tools for government to ensure effective administration – the redesign of the Australian tax system (Golsby-Smith, 1996) and the design of America ballots and other electoral documents (Lausen, 2007) are examples of this. Visual design is also used to promote political parties and persuade voters in the run-up to an election – Obama's 2008 political marketing campaign illustrates this practice (Seidman, 2010). However, Weber's (2010: 9) criticism of state-commissioned design (as undervaluing citizenship through its top-down approach) recognises that design has a wider role to play because "design mediates the very same fundamental political questions as does citizenship". Essentially, contemporary design and citizenship operate out of a concern for justice, and this is evident in contemporary conceptions of each.

Contemporary notions of citizenship go beyond mere voting to include more widespread participation by citizens in their immediate environments with the intention of social change. Similarly, citizenship education also goes beyond its historical function of supporting homogenous state formation and "is now often expected to achieve a far more complex set of purposes which broadly reflect changing conceptions of what it means to be a good citizen" (Johnson & Morris, 2010: 77). One such purpose is to promote shared values with the aim of preparing citizens to live together despite their differences in national identity; another purpose of critical citizenship education is to "contribute to the promotion of social justice, social reconstruction and democracy" (Johnson & Morris, 2010: 77-78).

---

[1]   By approaching the chapter from a design educator's perspective, it is not the intention of the author to exclude the students' voices; their direct reflections have not been quoted because permission was not received to do so. However, consent was given by one group of students to publish their photographic documentation as well as a description of their toolkit that appears in this chapter.

While social change is usually predicated on social and economic transformation, the environment or the context in which critical citizenship plays out also needs to be introduced in the conversation in order for the aims of justice and social reconstruction to be advanced. As we are witnessing, without due consideration for environmental thinking and ethics, societies are facing challenging circumstances. For example, uninformed energy usage and animal poaching are two pertinent South African examples that hinder sustainable development. Hence, the notion of 'environmental citizenship' (Dobson, 2007) is also central to critical citizenship education owing to the aim of nurturing mindful and respectful behaviour among citizens in relation to their surroundings.

Although environmental citizenship is not the focus of this chapter, it informs the practical project that is used to illustrate the theoretical claim that is made for educating citizen designers in this chapter and therefore warrants a brief overview. Dobson (2007) argues that for environmental citizenship to take effect, a change in attitude that is underpinned by justice concerns is likely to bring about behaviour change in citizens and, accordingly, sustainable development in societies. According to him, environmental citizenship "involves the recognition that self-interested behaviour will not always protect or sustain public goods such as the environment" and that it "follows through the implications of the view that environmental responsibilities follow from environmental rights as a matter of natural justice" (Dobson, 2007: 80). Ultimately, the moral and ethical decisions that citizens make and the behaviour that they exhibit from a personal point of view have far-reaching public implications.

To this end, design has an increasingly important role to play in facilitating such an attitude, and by extension behavioural change among citizens, through its professional practice. The trajectory in design discourse in a post-industrial age supports this claim for the contribution of design to the common good. Design is no longer restricted to the creation of tangible products to support commercial gain. The term has broadened from its traditional focus on products towards the creation of systems, experiences (Buchanan, 1998) and even a culture of design (Julier, 2014). As such, the focus in design has shifted from material objects to the structuring of immaterial processes. This viewpoint is not to discredit the formal aspects of design, but it expands the reach of design beyond its traditional realms of practice, which are not only commercial, but also increasingly social in nature.

Concurrent to changes in design practice, design education cannot afford to be passive. Design as a social practice requires new ways of thinking and doing in order to address the complex nature of contemporary problems. Therefore, students need to be equipped with the necessary design thinking capabilities to tackle the problems with which they will be confronted in their professional practice. The sentiment that design education bears an increasing responsibility was voiced by Icograda,[2] the International Council of the Societies of Communication Design, through the publication of a design education manifesto in 2011. This new designation was adopted by the global member-based network to reflect the multidisciplinary nature of contemporary design without neglecting its historical visual communication stance.

---

[2]   Icograda has since been renamed Ico-D.

The design education manifesto recognises that "[n]ew opportunities and challenges confront the designer. Social, cultural, technological, environmental and economical challenges over the last decade have profoundly affected communication design education and practice" (Bennett & Rarig, 2011: 25). Like contemporary notions of citizenship, design for social change is not limited to social and economic development. As noted in the design education manifesto, there is also "a dire need for a more advanced ecological balance between human beings and their natural environments. This environmental challenge has brought about the need for more sustainable design materials, methods and outcomes" (Bennett & Rarig, 2011: 25). As a contributing author to the manifesto publication, Tunstall (2011: 133) picks up on the need for an ecological balance by her notion of "respectful design", which she defines as "something akin to the creation of preferred courses of action based on the intrinsic worth of all human, animal, mineral, fauna and flora and the treatment of them with dignity and regard". Accordingly, Tunstall (2011: 134) proposes that it is essential for "design education to focus on how students and staff exist ontologically, or 'be' in the world rather than solely how they see the world". This stance of being in the world resonates with what it means to be an active, critical citizen. Hence, since contemporary design is very broad in its application, it has become increasingly necessary to cultivate a specific attitude or mindset, namely design thinking, in students so that, irrespective of the medium in which they are working, they can work towards being citizen designers by making responsible decisions and imbuing their solutions with good values.

The core of design thinking: Abductive thinking and framing

The growing popularity of contemporary design extends beyond the confines of the design disciplines themselves. In particular, design thinking has become a buzzword and is increasingly making an appearance in innovation and business contexts (Brown, 2009; Martin, 2009). There has been criticism about design thinking being a fad or even a failure (Nussbaum, 2011) rather than a real opportunity, but its value extends beyond its current popularity; this is evident when reviewing design literature by the likes of Herbert Simon (1969) as well as Rittel and Webber (1984), who consider the relationship of design to complex or 'wicked' problems. The word 'wicked' is used to denote real-world problems that are complex and indeterminate in nature. With regard to the purpose of design, Buchanan (1992) extended the concept of wicked problems to the field of design by affirming that the purpose of design is to solve such wicked problems.

Accordingly, design methods to solve wicked problems have a long history (Bousbaci, 2008) and as Cross (2006: 1) indicates, there are "designerly ways of knowing" and doing that are inextricably linked to the practices of designers across different design disciplines. Owing to its broad scope and application in practice, there are challenges in defining design thinking to adequately cover its basic tenets, but both Cross (2006, 2011) and Lawson (2006) see it as comprising a series of human, cognitive acts. Kimbell (2011), in her consideration of design thinking, highlights design thinking as a cognitive style as one account of contemporary design thinking. Although Kimbell (2011) questions whether this account may limit design thinking to individual designers, she nonetheless acknowledges this cognitive focus in the discourse on design thinking.

The proliferation and application of design thinking as a mode of reasoning in other disciplines such as business, education and healthcare, for example, have stimulated research and discussion from within various design disciplines as well. For example, in the article titled "The core of 'design thinking' and its application", Dorst (2011: 522) puts forward a convincing argument about designers' reasoning skills. He explains that designers' specific way of reasoning – abduction – has value in that it differs from traditional forms of reasoning and thereby differentiates design from other disciplines. This is a widely held belief by key design theorists, in particular Cross (2011: 27), who acknowledges that "[s]everal theoretical arguments have been advanced in support of the view that design reasoning is different from the conventionally acknowledged forms of inductive and deductive reasoning".

From a Western perspective, two analytic forms of logic or reasoning – induction and deduction – have traditionally been favoured (Crouch & Pearce, 2012; Golsby-Smith, 2008) for their contribution to the so-called hard sciences in order to "predict and explain phenomena in the world" (Dorst, 2011: 523). Inductive reasoning facilitates discovery, typically in the natural and social science realms, because, according to Steen (2013: 17), when using an inductive mode of logic, "one starts with a series of observations and then speculates about a pattern". For deductive reasoning, "one starts with two or more premises and then draws a conclusion" (Steen, 2013: 17); therefore, this type of logic is employed for purposes of justification, often within a mathematical context.

Dorst (2011) refers to Roozenburg's description of pragmatic philosopher Charles Sanders Peirce's work to consider the following three variables in an equation in order to explain different types of reasoning: the what (thing), the how (working principles) and the result (value). It is the relationship between the first two variables, the 'what' and the 'how' in the equation, that ultimately determines the 'end result'. So, if one were to consider inductive and deductive reasoning using this equation, there are two known variables in the equation in both instances: in deduction, the 'what' and the 'how' are known and these variables allow for a safe prediction of results, whereas in induction, it is the 'how' that is the unknown variable (Dorst, 2011).

In contrast to induction and deduction as forms of reasoning, "abduction can be thought of as the argument to the best explanation. It is the hypothesis that makes the most sense given observed [phenomena] or data and based on prior experience" (Kolko, 2010: 20). This explanation indicates that abduction serves as a form of inference or, to describe it in Roger Martin's (2009: 68) words, the "logic of what might be". Although Martin's viewpoint captures the underpinning ethos of abductive thinking, it is too simplistic and therefore not entirely accurate (Kolko, 2010). Hence, it requires further elaboration.

Dorst (2011) provides a dual classification for abductive thinking, which he refers to as Abduction 1 and Abduction 2. Both forms of abduction share common ground in that there is an aspired result at the end (Dorst, 2011). However, Dorst (2011) argues that it is Abduction 2 in which designers need to be proficient. Abduction 2 involves less certainty than Abduction 1, because the aspired 'end result' is the only known variable at the onset of a design project. According to the afore-mentioned equation for reasoning, the 'what' and the 'how' both need to be developed during an abductive reasoning process. The aspired end result or value stems from the "desiderata" (Nelson & Stolterman, 2012: 107) or the intention of the client and is often detailed in a project brief. The emphasis on value creation resonates with design, as a service profession, where the outcome of the design process is a means of creating value and providing meaningful change (Nelson & Stolterman, 2012). Owing to the fact that designers' work always results in an outcome – be it a tangible product or an intangible system or experience – their abductive thinking is regarded as a form of "productive reasoning" (March, 1976, cited in Cross, 2011: 28). The outcome or end result of abductive reasoning, that is, the design process, resonates with Herbert Simon's (1969: 129) seminal definition of design that "[e]veryone designs who devises courses of action aimed at changing existing situations into preferred ones".

Cross (2011), who provides insights into the design ability and working processes of designers, states that abductive thinking, colloquially acknowledged as an 'intuitive' way of thinking, could be an inherent skill designers have or it can be nurtured by means of education. This leads to the recognition that there are different levels of design expertise – ranging from novice to expert (Cross, 2011) – and that designers move along the different levels by developing their own processes through which they become familiar with abductive ways of thinking. Irrespective of their training in different design disciplines, Cross (2011: 75) identifies three key strategic aspects of design thinking common among designers: "(1) taking a broad 'systems approach' to the problem, rather than accepting narrow problem criteria; (2) 'framing' the problem in a distinctive and sometimes rather personal way; and (3) designing from 'first principles'." The act of framing is considered for the purposes of this chapter.

The term 'framing' can be traced back to the work of Donald Schön (1983) and recurs in contemporary design literature (Cross, 2006, 2011; Dorst, 2011, 2015; Kolko, 2010; Lawson, 2006). Dorst (2011), for example, acknowledges the act of framing as one of the steps of the abduction process. A frame can be regarded as a point of view; hence, the act of framing refers to the creation of "a (novel) standpoint from which a problematic situation can be tackled" (Dorst, 2011: 525). Framing, or frame creation, is particular to design practice in that it helps the designer to read a situation in order to propose appropriate design solutions to address the criteria and aspired values necessitated by a given project. According to Dorst (2015), this stance facilitates 'frame innovation', the creation of new approaches to a given problem.

Steen (2013: 18) regards framing as an iterative process and in light of Dorst's equation of reasoning, defines it as "combinations of a result and a working principle". Steen (2013: 28) also notes that it is the move between the "problem-setting and solution-finding" that makes inherent the moral and ethical questions that designers need to consider as part of their process. Because design solutions are initiated and ultimately informed by abductive reasoning and framing, it follows that designers need to understand the social consequences and civic responsibility that come with such a practice.

Educating citizen designers: An overview of the student design project

Teaching students the core of design thinking more consciously requires new and/or improved ways of teaching. In light of this, an experiential education approach was employed for a design-for-development[3] project completed by final-year BA Information Design students at the University of Pretoria. The design students were tasked with designing a creative intervention in

---

[3]   'Design-for-development' is the term used as part of the Information Design course to denote design that has as its aim social development and/or transformation.

the form of an educational toolkit in order to cultivate environmental awareness and responsibility in young primary school learners in South Africa. The project was commissioned by the board of South African National Parks (SANParks) and the Information Design project brief was one component of a larger, interdisciplinary project involving the university's Fine Arts Division as well as the Drama Department.

The project brief

Pragmatically, the project brief necessitated that that the students' toolkits "consist of a number of educational activities (with a comprehensive set of instructions) that could take the form of a board game, performances or screenings at the schools, activities and so forth" (Cassim & Bowie, 2013: 2). Essentially, this requirement moved design education away from the modernist myth of design where form follows function and instead gave students an opportunity to learn first-hand that form follows content. Students had to work in groups of three for the project. Accordingly, the assessment was broken into two components: a group assessment as well as an individual assessment. The group assessment counted 70% of the final project mark and comprised the process documentation (a logbook to document the design process), the toolkit (identity and package) as well as the final, digital project presentation. The individual toolkit activity designed by the respective student as well as a peer assessment made up the remaining 30% of the final project mark. The peer assessment ensured that students assumed a specific role in their group to try to allow for an equal distribution of work; it also ensured increased accountability in each team.

To reiterate, the pedagogic aim was to develop abductive thinking and framing skills in students with a view towards nurturing citizen designers (that is, to nurture critical citizenship skills). To support these aims, the project brief highlighted the following key ideas of the overarching theme of design for development that pertained to the design division's component of the interdisciplinary project (Cassim & Bowie, 2013: 1):

Project intent is:
- Human-centred

Project strategy is:
- Interventionist – search for change and improvement in existing social and environmental conditions
- Relevant – focus on the real and immediate needs of people, immediate beneficial impact of design on lives of people and environment
- Accountable – need for concept to be understood, adopted and acted upon by users, sustainability of implementation

Project process is:
- Ethical – in terms of the process incorporating participation with potential users and in terms of its research orientation, through which issues of responsibility and accountability are addressed.

A project example

A group of nine fauna mascots that were made into puppets by the Fine Arts students formed part of a play that was scripted and performed by the university's Drama students for primary school learners on behalf of SANParks. Accordingly, each group of design students was assigned a mascot. The students had to "translate the physical puppet mascots into 2-dimensional characters to be used on all communication design material" (Cassim & Bowie, 2013: 2) and use the nature of their mascot as a point of departure for the educational focus of their toolkits. For example, Orla – a kingfisher who is passionate about saving water – was allocated to one group of students. Orla's role informed the overarching theme of this group's toolkit, namely to educate young learners to be responsible with water. The toolkit, as seen in Figure 1, was titled *Saving water with Orla* and was aimed at learners from Grade R to Grade 3. The students described their final project as follows:

> The structure of the toolkit follows a narrative story where Orla explores various aspects of water conservation. The book has five chapters with corresponding activities. The toolkit comprises of a carry bag, the storybook, 5 activity posters, 2 white board markers, one set of teacher goggles and a comprehensive teacher's guide to help the educator facilitate activities and clarify educational objectives. The program aims to provide the learners with a good foundation for learning to appreciate water and be careful about the way they live. The toolkit also strives to introduce a fun and valuable dimension to environmental education.

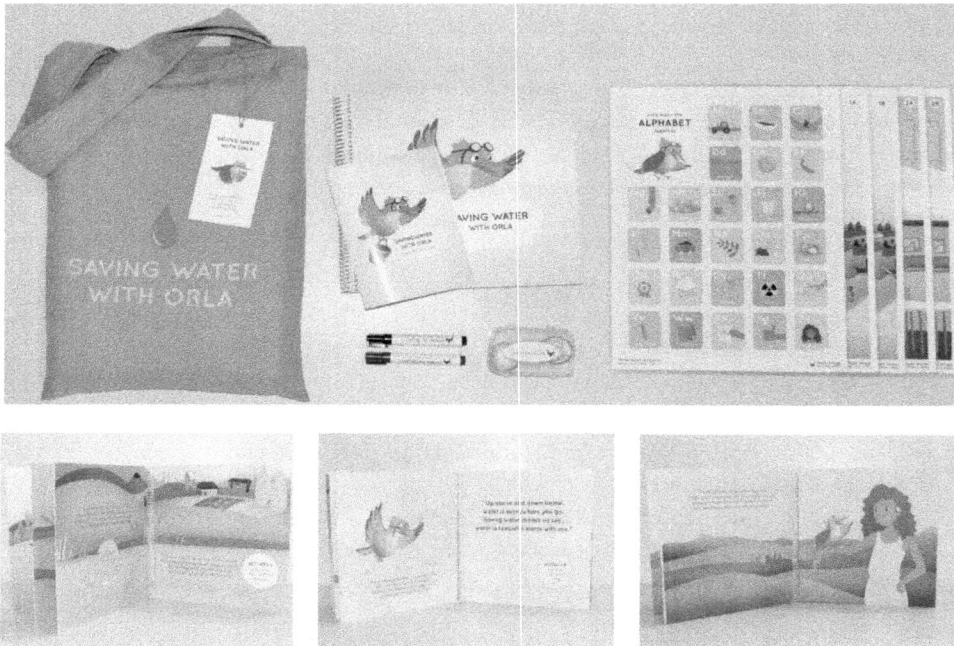

Figure 1 *Saving water with Orla* (Information Design student project 2013)

Experience is the best teacher: New frames of mind

The relationship between experience and education takes on many guises, such as action design and service learning, and is often aligned with practices at institutions of higher learning. Moon (2004) highlights the distinction between learning from experience and experiential learning. She asserts that all learning is dependent on experience, but experiential learning as a concept and/or practice is a formalised learning situation that draws on prior learning and constructs experience in a particular way so as to transform that experience into knowledge. It is necessary for the experience to fit the nature of the discipline and, more importantly, the profession in which students will practise. In addition, reflection must be a mandatory component of experiential learning.

With regard to the concept and nature of experiential learning, Beard and Wilson (2006: 17) acknowledge that "Dewey is arguably the foremost exponent of the use of experience for learning". Paulo Freire's contribution, which has shaped the nature of experiential education from a political and social activism point of view, is also commonly acknowledged (Beard & Wilson, 2006; Moon, 2004). Kolb (1984) has also made a significant contribution to the experiential learning discourse with his pragmatic model of experiential learning and authors such as Moon (2004) and Beard and Wilson (2006) continued the conversation to date. However, the recurring affirmation of Dewey's and Freire's historical influence and contribution to experiential learning informed the decision to draw primarily on their key texts and education philosophies for the purposes of this chapter. Furthermore, it is noteworthy that Freire's scholarship also informs citizenship education. For example, Johnson and Morris (2010: 78) recognise that "citizenship education in England is often linked to the work of Paolo Freire by scholars who promote more active forms of citizenship". For the purposes of this chapter, the following overarching tenets of experiential learning were considered in relation to the SANParks project:[4] (1) the real world as the context for experience, (2) the relationship between teacher and student and (3) the experiential learning process – praxis. The three tenets also serve as a structural guide for the following discussion.

The real world as the context for experience

Owing to the social/environmental nature of the SANParks project and the complexity of the design brief that called for multiple participants, the project necessitated engagement beyond the classroom. This is in keeping with Freire's (1970: 79) sentiment that education must comprise the "posing of the problems of human beings in their relations with the world". Experiential education is therefore valuable because it allows for circumstances that facilitate a critical consideration of reality, as experiences are based in the real world. A critical consideration of reality is important for design education, because students need to have first-hand experience of situations in order to be able to exercise abductive thinking and effectively frame the problems and situations that they are creatively tackling. Similarly, in terms of critical citizenship education, curricula manifestations should include nurturing "skills of critical and structural social analysis" as well as the "capacity to think holistically", to name a couple (Johnson & Morris, 2010: 90).

---

[4]   The discussion on experiential learning considers the SANParks project as a whole and is not restricted to Saving water with Orla, the one toolkit that is featured in this chapter as a project example.

At the onset of the project, the students were required to conduct research in their respective groups on their complex environmental topics such as recycling, water conservation, biodiversity and climate change. The target audience was primary school children, so not only did the design students have to conduct research about their topic, but they also had to better understand the age group as well as the teacher facilitators for whom they were designing. The fact that it was a client-driven project also meant that the students were accountable for their work to a larger extent. As such, the lecturers identified a school in a nearby Pretoria suburb where students would be taken to conduct primary research by engaging with learners and schoolteachers alike (there were three school visits during the three-week project period). In concurrence with Dewey's (1938: 40) statement that "experience does not occur in a vacuum", it was important that the learning scenarios were contingent on the specific educational needs as well as the local context of the project brief.

For the SANParks project, the decision to immerse the students in the real world at the school enabled them to not only understand, but also embrace external variables such as language and cultural differences that would impact on their designs. The school visits gave students an opportunity to prototype and test their toolkit activities with the end users and provided a better understanding of how the activities would fare in a real classroom setting. The placement of students in the real world had numerous pedagogic advantages. Firstly, it encouraged the design students to conduct primary research. Primary research is insightful for framing in that it encourages students to interrogate the status quo by asking relevant questions. Secondly, it also facilitated community engagement so that the design students could be taken out of their comfort zone and could engage with learners from different backgrounds and races; in this way, the real-world experience taught the students not to make assumptions about others and to engage directly with a diverse audience. Students were therefore encouraged to create a "community of enquiry" (Fisher, 2008: 195), where they recognised themselves as part of a larger network of citizens and not as lone creators. One could argue that this circumstance has the potential to make the humanist philosophy of *ubuntu* tangible owing to its focus on "allegiances and relations to one another" (Lange, 2011: 93). Immersion in the real world also introduced the students implicitly to participatory design methods such as those advocated by Sanders (2008).

The relationship between teacher and student

The traditional education that Freire and Dewey reacted against is teacher-centric and follows a linear, one-way communication model that makes students passive and complacent. In contrast, experiential education mimics contemporary design and creative processes in that it is iterative and cyclical and comprises more than one active participant or group. Owing to the multiple stakeholders involved in the project – lecturers, other students, client, schoolteachers and young learners – the design students did not only create their own frames, but also had to learn to work with multiple frames. More importantly, the students learnt that the design process is democratic and that all stakeholders have a significant role to play. This clearly highlights the citizenship underpinnings of the project in that students had an opportunity to understand that their design process and related actions have the collective power to shape their environments and communities.

During the project, the lecturers, as one group of stakeholders, adopted the role of facilitators. This meant that the students were given the freedom to explore and experience the project context and become familiar and confident with the design process while at the same time receiving continuing guidance from the lecturers. Such an arrangement sees students as unique individuals who need to be provided with the correct tools for dialogical encounters. Dialogue, according to Freire (1970: 91), has the ability to develop a "horizontal relationship of which mutual trust between the dialoguers is the logical consequence". In addition, Freire (1970: 97) asserted that dialogue facilitates "generative themes" among learners. Similarly, Dorst (2011: 528) also supports themes as a "sense-making tool, a form of capturing the underlying phenomenon one seeks to understand".

Therefore, by adopting the role of facilitators, the lecturers were able "to regulate the way the world 'enters into' the students" (Freire, 1970: 76) and to impress the concept of "respectful design" among students so that they too would act as facilitators rather than approaching their end users (and even their choice of materials for the toolkits) in a patronising manner. In addition, the students could be co-creators in knowledge as per Freire's (1970) suggestion. For design, this is essential because students ultimately proposed the desired result of their intention, that is the "not-yet-existing" (Nelson & Stolterman, 2012: 35), and provided innovative solutions to complex problems using abductive thinking.

The experiential learning process – praxis

Praxis is a key term in Freire's (1970: 79) work that is defined as "the action and reflection of men and women upon their world in order to transform it". For Freire, praxis makes increased critical consciousness and liberating action possible. Praxis is also one of the key elements of critical pedagogy that appears in the framework for critical citizenship education by Johnson and Morris (2010). Problem-posing education and experiential education therefore move from being mere action to being informed, responsible and ethical action coupled with reflection. This viewpoint is shared by Moon (1999), who indicates that reflection denotes a form of mental processing and goes beyond experience to provide context and meaning and ultimately results in the creation of embedded knowledge. It is this move from experiential/tacit knowledge to disciplinary/procedural design knowledge for design for development that was one of the pedagogic aims of the SANParks project.

For the duration of the project, the students were required to keep a logbook and reflect *in* action and *on* action. The intention was for the students to embody being reflective practitioners in the way that Donald Schön (1983) advocated. Schön's argument that professionals engage better with new situations because they think back to previous actions and experiences (and over time form a collection of images and actions) speaks to the continuity and quality of experiences for which Dewey (1938) argued. Therefore, it is not surprising to note that Schön's notion of a reflective practitioner was influenced by Dewey's philosophy on experience (Steen, 2013).

Following from the above, it can be argued that the students' experiences of framing during their training would support their professional trajectory from novice to expert designers. Although it is impossible at this stage to gauge the long-term benefits of this project for the students, their logbook entries certainly hint at how the students utilised prior knowledge in the attempt to frame the project initially and also how new knowledge was arrived at. Therefore, praxis resulted in considerable action and, more importantly, reflection. Reflection served as a tool for students to understand and articulate their project experience (including their feelings, emotions and learning curve) as well as their role as designers.

Project reflection and conclusion

At the end of the three-week project, all nine groups of design students were able to come up with a range of meaningful and exciting environmental education solutions. This viewpoint was shared by the client; SANParks representatives felt that the students successfully answered the brief and the solutions managed to surpass their expectations. The tangible toolkits, coupled with the students' individual written reflections, served as a useful measure to gauge the experience of the students against the pedagogic aims. In particular, the students' reflections were very valuable because they made the following elements visible, thereby indicating that from a pedagogic perspective, the project was clearly situated at the intersection of critical thinking and critical pedagogy (Johnson & Morris, 2010: 80): "skills of reasoning and logic", namely abductive thinking; "dialogue"; and "the discovery of 'new' knowledge" and approaches, such as framing.

A number of students made reference to the iterative design process in their reflections. Although none of the students referred to their mode of reasoning as abduction or to their acts of framing during the design process using these explicit, theoretical terms, the descriptions of their cognitive processes and their design methods aligned very closely with the design thinking concepts explained earlier in this chapter. Furthermore, the students' reflections point to the fact that, through their experience outside the classroom, they experienced deeper learning. The deeper learning relates to the way in which design students realised that at once they are designers as well as citizens and therefore their learning extended to grappling with the question of what it means to be a citizen designer. Students also mentioned the value of prototyping and the consequences of it could definitely be seen in the final toolkit activities that showed significant development from the initial conceptualisation phase of the project. Having said this, it should not go unnoticed that one of the shortcomings of the project was its duration. For the scope of the project, the three weeks proved too short to fully immerse the students in the real world. Theoretically, this resonates with the challenge by critical pedagogy of projects remaining at a small scale owing to Freire's "emphasis on local contextualisation as a vital element for his methods, which contrasts with the need to emancipate huge numbers of people from oppression" (Johnson & Morris, 2010: 82). More contact sessions at the school would have increased local contextualisation and allowed for more continuous testing, which would have aided additional refinement of the final toolkit activities. Nonetheless, the face-to-face primary research conducted by the students throughout the project certainly helped them to shape their final deliverables. The role of research in/for design is relevant to arguments to support and elevate practice-led research and although it is not the focus of this chapter, it warrants further exploration.

Many students acknowledged the project as being complex and challenging, but despite this, the learning curve of their experience was substantial. An interesting observation from the reflections was that in addition to being reflective, the students were actually reflexive too and as such, were able to better understand their role as citizen designers. Firstly, the students understood and appreciated the value of engaging with end users during the process. In this regard, the project seems to have instilled a practice of prototyping in students that will hopefully ensure the application of human- or citizen-centred design processes and solutions in subsequent projects. Secondly, some students commented on the fact that they had to work in groups; some valued working as a team and understood its advantages, while others felt that it hindered the design process. In future, this should be considered and where necessary, students should be openly encouraged to negotiate different frames when working in groups.

The chapter does not allow for a more in-depth and pragmatic discussion of the project's results, but it introduces on a theoretical level how the philosophy of experiential education is significant for design education, especially when design educators consider new learning environments for design thinking and, in addition, how to accommodate critical citizenship learning objectives in untraditional and/or creative ways in their curricula. If facilitated correctly, experiential education may be advantageous in design education to nurture the core of design thinking – abductive thinking and framing – in students, which may in turn help to nurture citizen designers. Furthermore, if experiential education is viewed as a social undertaking, it follows that such shifting education would allow students to each have an opportunity to propose innovative ideas and solutions for complex contemporary problems and to feel a responsibility towards their education, one another (Dewey, 1938) and the environment.

Acknowledgements

An earlier version of this chapter was presented at the Cumulus: What's on: Cultural diversity, social engagement and shifting education conference, held at the University of Aveiro, Aveiro, Portugal, in May 2014. The author is grateful to Anneli Bowie for facilitating the Information Design student project with her in 2013, to the Information Design students as well as the students and staff of Mogale Primary School in Mamelodi for their cooperation. The author also expresses her gratitude to SANParks, SANParks Honorary Rangers and Sanlam for providing financial support.

References

Beard, C. & Wilson, J.P. 2006. *Experiential learning: A best practice handbook for educators and trainers.* London: Kogan Page.

Bennett, A.G. & Rarig, A. 2011. Icograda Design Education Manifesto MMXI. In: A.G. Bennett & O. Vulpinari (Eds.). *Icograda Design Education Manifesto 2011.* Montréal: Icograda, 24–29.

Bousbaci, R. 2008. "Models of man" in design thinking: The "bounded rationality" episode. *Design Issues,* 24(4), 38–52. https://doi.org/10.1162/desi.2008.24.4.38

Brown, T. 2009. *Change by design: How design thinking transforms organizations and inspires innovation.* New York, NY: HarperCollins.

Buchanan, R. 1992. Wicked problems in design thinking. *Design Issues,* 8(2), 3–20. https://doi.org/10.2307/1511637

Buchanan, R. 1998. Branzi's dilemma: Design in contemporary culture. *Design Issues,* 14(1), 3–20. https://doi.org/10.2307/1511825

Cassim, F. & Bowie, A. 2013. Information design for environmental education. Information Design 400. Unpublished student brief.

Cross, N. 2006. *Designerly ways of knowing.* London: Springer-Verlag.

Cross, N. 2011. *Design thinking: Understanding how designers think and work.* Oxford: Berg. https://doi.org/10.5040/9781474293884

Crouch, C. & Pearce, J. 2012. *Doing research in design.* New York, NY: Bloomsbury. https://doi.org/10.5040/9781474294010

Dewey, J. 1938. *Experience and education.* New York, NY: Collier Books.

Dobson, A. 2007. Environmental citizenship: Towards sustainable development. *Sustainable Development,* 15, 276–285. https://doi.org/10.1002/sd.344

Dorst, K. 2011. The core of 'design thinking' and its application. *Design Studies,* 32(6), 521–532. https://doi.org/10.1016/j.destud.2011.07.006

Dorst, K. 2015. *Frame innovation: Create new thinking by design.* Cambridge, MA: The MIT Press.

Fisher, R. 2008. *Teaching thinking: Philosophical enquiry in the classroom.* Third edition. London: Continuum.

Freire, P. 1970. *Pedagogy of the oppressed.* Translated by M.B. Ramos. New York, NY: Bloomsbury.

Golsby-Smith, T. 1996. Fourth order design: A practical perspective. *Design Issues,* 12(1), 5–25. https://doi.org/10.2307/1511742

Golsby-Smith, T. 2008. The second road of thought. *Rotman,* Winter, 46–50. Available at http://karenhegmann.typepad.com/tellingthestory/files/rotmanwinter2008.pdf [Accessed 17 March 2014].

Heller, S. & Vienne, V. 2003. *Citizen designer: Perspectives on design responsibility.* New York, NY: Allworth Press.

Johnson, L. & Morris, P. 2010. Towards a framework for critical citizenship education. *The Curriculum Journal,* 21(1), 77–96. https://doi.org/10.1080/09585170903560444

Julier, G. 2014. *The culture of design.* Third edition. London: Sage. [Kindle e-book.]

Kimbell, L. 2011. Rethinking design thinking: Part 1. *Design and Culture,* 3(3), 285–306. https://doi.org/10.2752/175470811X13071166525216

Kolb, D. 1984. *Experiential learning: Experience as the source of learning and development.* London: Prentice Hall.

Kolko, J. 2010. Abductive thinking and sensemaking: The drivers of design synthesis. *Design Issues,* 26(1), 15–28. https://doi.org/10.1162/desi.2010.26.1.15

Lange, J. 2011. The change we seek: An African perspective. In: A.G. Bennett & O. Vulpinari (Eds.). *Icograda Design Education Manifesto 2011.* Montréal: Icograda, 90–95.

Lausen, M. 2007. *Design for democracy: Ballot and election design.* Chicago, IL: The University of Chicago Press. https://doi.org/10.7208/chicago/9780226470634.001.0001

Lawson, B. 2006. *How designers think: The design process demystified.* Fourth edition. Burlington: Architectural Press.

Martin, R. 2009. *The design of business*. Boston, MA: Harvard Business Press.

McCoy, K. 2003. Good citizenship: Design as a social and political force. In: S. Heller & V. Vienne (Eds.). *Citizen designer: Perspectives on design responsibility*. New York, NY: Allworth Press, 2–8.

Moon, J. 1999. *Reflection in learning and professional development*. London: Routledge Falmer.

Moon, J. 2004. *A handbook of reflective and experiential learning: Theory and practice*. New York, NY: Routledge.

Nelson, H.G. & Stolterman, E. 2012. *The design way: Intentional change in an unpredictable world. Foundations and fundamentals of design competence*. Second edition. Cambridge, MA: The MIT Press.

Nussbaum, B. 2011. Design thinking is a failed experiment: So what's next? *Fast Company blog*. Available at http://www.fastcodesign.com/1663558/design-thinking-is-a-failed-experiment-so-whats-next [Accessed 18 December 2014].

Rittel, H.J.W. & Webber, M.M. 1984. Planning problems are wicked problems. In: N. Cross (Ed.). *Developments in design methodology*. New York, NY: Wiley, 135–144.

Sanders, E. 2008. An evolving map of design practice. *Interactions,* 15(6), 13–17. https://doi.org/10.1145/1409040.1409043

Schön, D. 1983. *The reflective practitioner: How professionals think in action*. New York, NY: Basic Books.

Schuitema, J., Ten Dam, G. & Veugelers, W. 2008. Teaching strategies for moral education: A review. *Journal of Curriculum Studies*, 40(1), 69–89. https://doi.org/10.1080/00220270701294210

Seidman, S.A. 2010. Barack Obama's 2008 campaign for the US presidency and visual design. *Journal of Visual Literacy,* 29, 1–27. https://doi.org/10.1080/23796529.2010.11674671

Simon, H. 1969. *The sciences of the artificial*. Cambridge, MA: The MIT Press.

Steen, M. 2013. Co-design as a joint process of inquiry and imagination. *Design Issues*, 29(2), 16–28. https://doi.org/10.1162/DESI_a_00207

Tunstall, E. 2011. Respectful design: A proposed journey of design education. In: A.G. Bennett & O. Vulpinari (Eds.). *Icograda Design Education Manifesto 2011*. Montréal: Icograda, 132–134.

Weber, C. 2010. Introduction: Design and citizenship. *Citizenship Studies*, 14(1), 1–16. https://doi.org/10.1080/13621020903466233

Winschiers-Theophilus, H., Bidwell, N.J. & Blake, E. 2012. Community consensus: Design beyond participation. *Design Issues*, 28(3), 89–100. https://doi.org/10.1162/DESI_a_00164

Nurturing Critical Citizen Designers: Applying Strategic Models for Reflective Practice

TERENCE FENN AND JASON HOBBS

Introduction

Design at its best seeks to transform existing situations into preferred ones. In theory, then, design has the potential to deliver to humankind a more just, equitable and sustainable future. However, design as a distinct field of practice is in many ways ill-equipped to execute on this potential. For most of its short life as a taught academic discipline, the mainstream focus of design has been on what Muratovski (2016) refers to as the 'traditional' or 'apprenticeship' models, which focus on the visual and formal aesthetic shaping of products and technologies for human consumption. Here design is learnt through the imitation of the works of others, with the design teacher acting as 'master' technician and the student as the 'apprentice'. Positioning design as capable of disrupting the status quo of our current 'situations' is to assign to design an immense responsibility and power that, we believe, designers, academics and educators are only beginning to comprehend.

Critical to the premise of this chapter is that the potential of design to have a deep and meaningful impact on the planet and its communities is not assured, but rather an ideal intention that needs to be debated, critiqued and explicitly supported through new knowledge methods and techniques. Central to this notion is the societal role of the designer as the intermediator of the aspirational and direct needs of users of design solutions in the context of broader communities, future communities, business and other related organisations and structures. Accompanying this role, we believe, is a great responsibility that requires of designers firstly, a mature ability to reflect on the intentions and consequences of their actions, and secondly, the ability to conceptually manage the complexities that are the realities of a deep engagement with all these role players. These two responsibilities are not necessarily mutually exclusive. Therefore, the overarching theme that guides this theoretical positioning is the integration of notions of critical citizenship within human-centred design (HCD) practice and education and the new forms of criticality that this blend brings to design.

In this regard two novel design tools, the Firma Model and Experience-led Relationship Models (ExRMs), which we have designed and which our third- and fourth-year Interaction Design students applied in their own design projects, will be discussed. The intention behind both tools is to assist designers in managing complexity in terms of both problem framing and strategic thinking that emerge from a meaningful, designerly engagement with societal problems. However, before introducing these design tools, we provide a brief theoretical contextualisation of our approach to teaching design.

The role of critical citizenship in design education

Critical citizenship is a highly contested concept (Ruitenberg, 2015). In South African design circles, as is no doubt evident by the various chapters of this book, there are various interpretations of what critical citizenship may include. At a broad level, we define critical citizenship as a teleological desire for equitable and inclusive societies. For us the value of engaging with critical citizenship in design education is highly impactful, as critical citizenship provides numerous frameworks to help unpack the responsibility and roles that designers assume when they profess to design with or for others. Providing explicit frameworks for novice designers that articulate a social rationale for practice is an essential starting point in helping students to begin to develop their own design identity, regardless of whether they may agree or disagree with the frameworks provided.

To this point we contrast two interpretations of critical citizenship: 'citizenship-as-equality' (Ruitenberg, 2015) and 'affective citizenship' (Zembylas, 2015). Citizenship-as-equality recognises critical citizenship as fundamentally concerned with power relationships within a societal system (Ruitenberg, 2015) and includes both ensuring an equal distribution of rights within the system for citizens and the responsibilities and the ability of citizens to hold these powers to account. Of importance to our positioning of design as human-centric and participative (which we expand on in subsequent sections) is how citizenship-as-equality presupposes equality between human beings and that it seeks to verify this equality through actions (Ruitenberg, 2015). In this sense, citizenship-as-equality refers to the capacity of individuals to participate in public decisions and emphasises the capability of citizens to create and change the communities to which they belong (Zembylas, 2015), both of which present characteristics valued in participatory engagement in design.

In contrast, affective citizenship focuses on the emotional relationship that citizens are encouraged to experience in their relationship to 'others', the community or the state. These emotional relationships, Zembylas (2015) warns, while not necessarily so, can be 'monolithic notions' that may introduce cultural bias, particularly when applied uncritically in multicultural societies. As we will discuss later, the unquestioned application of aspects of critical theory to all societies and cultures is an example of well-intentioned affective citizenship introducing cultural bias into design practice.

Reframing design

While critical citizenship as a framework for acting in the world is of value to design (as no doubt it could be of value to business analysts, accountants and politicians!), design, as a unique disciplinary field of practice, has specific characteristics and ways of being understood that we believe need to be foregrounded if design is to deliver on its potential to create equitable and sustainable futures.

To deliver on this potential, design education must be radically reframed. This reframing (which we have seen emerging in many design schools, academic publications and case studies) emphasises design as a unique discipline distinct from the paradigms of science and the humanities.

Abductive logic and design thinking

Understanding how design differs from science and the humanities requires a brief description of how each paradigm approaches the generation of new knowledge.[1] Scientific thinking is typified by objective analytical enquiry (Owen, 2007), which aims to explain the *what is* of the natural world by applying deductive or inductive logic (Wendt, 2014). Deductive reasoning can be understood as formal logic with the frequently provided example: if A = B and B = C, then A must = C (Wendt, 2014). Inductive reasoning, on the other hand, is logic based on experiential observation of the world. In inductive reasoning, patterns that reoccur are regarded as representing a factual state – at least until the pattern breaks or a new one emerges. The humanities, in contrast, seeks to represent human experience (Owen, 2007; Wendt, 2015). As such, the humanities value subjective interpretation, imagination, commitment and a concern for social justice (Wendt, 2015).

Abductive logic has been recognised by many theorists (Cross, 2001; Kolko, 2010; Owen, 2007; Wendt, 2014) as the fundamental reasoning of design and that which distinguishes it from science and the humanities. While abductive logic applies scientific logic and the humanities effort to understand people's lived experiences and cultural patterns (Kolko, 2010), it is oriented towards the speculation of future states. So, while abductive reasoning begins from a framing of what is, its problem-solving orientation is extended beyond the purely indexical by utilising the subjective, experiential knowledge, intuition and creative solutioning (Cross, 2006) of the designer to 'dream' of new ways of putting things together (Kolko, 2010). Importantly, this creative thinking process is deeply embedded in 'making'. Here the designer considers the problem and solutions through embodied tangible engagements with the world (Owen, 2007; Wendt, 2015). While this type of thinking-through-making is commonplace in the humanities, in design the difference is that the 'creative dream solution' must still acknowledge and if necessary be evaluated in reference to its "cultural fit, appropriateness and effectiveness" (Owen, 2007: 21).

Although abductive logic utilises both scientific and humanities thinking, it should not be reduced to a simple hybrid. Abductive logic extends beyond using both science and the humanities in that it has a central pragmatic concern focused on action and transformation. In this sense, abductive logic is fallible in that it addresses future states, but also holds the potential to be very powerful, as it can transcend current states to create preferred ones.

Thomas Wendt (2014: 64) describes design thinking as "a method to help designers stay somewhere in the middle of purely intuitive thinking and purely analytical thinking". As such, design thinking can be considered to be an abstraction of the abductive reasoning process into a series of action-oriented phases that support (but do not ensure) creative problem solving. Many design companies,

---

[1] Other paradigms include medicine and law; however, their relationship to design thinking is fairly remote in terms of this discussion and they are therefore not included.

such as IDEO (Brown, 2008) and locally Terrestrial (2016) as well as educational institutes such as the Stanford University Institute of Design (2016) and the Southern Methodist University (Lorenzo, 2016), have sought to define design thinking for commercial application. This has led to a proliferation of representations of design thinking in model form; however, invariably all design thinking models share a number of phases that, although variously named, reflect the abductive thinking process. As illustrated in Figure 1, these phases typically include an exploration of a problem, a framing of that problem with a definition of one or more strategically oriented actions aimed at resolving the problem, the ideation of multiple concepts that reflect the strategy, the making of selected solutions to establish their effectiveness in the world and an evaluation of the thinking and solutioning. Importantly, these phases, while often represented as a linear sequence of actions, are in practice highly iterative, as the designer recognises and develops preferred and alternative courses of action through cycles of learning. In the generic model below, each phase has been mapped to the various types of thinking that we consider to be most essential. This mapping indicates the integrated reflective modes of contemplation required in abductive thinking.

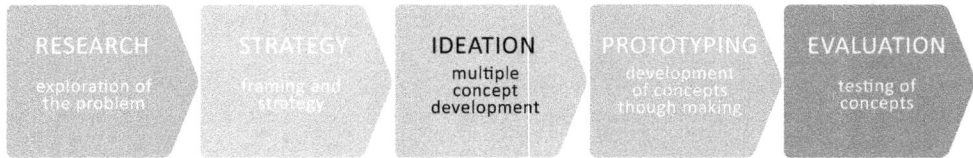

Figure 1   Generic model showing the typical phases of design thinking

Design thinking does not presuppose any particular level of complexity in terms of problem solutioning for its effective application. It can be applied in non-complex craft-based design activities (such as the creative design of a new teapot as well as to highly complex and indeterminate problems (such as those that we will describe in relation to HCD).

Human-centred design and complexity

We believe that HCD is best understood as a philosophical approach to design that encapsulates a variety of distinct modes of engagement with the people affected by problems and their subsequent solutions. At a very foundational level, IDEO's 'three lenses of HCD' (2015) provides a framework for HCD that describes how, in order to ensure the likelihood of successful design solutions, designers need to address issues related to people's needs (desirability), business sustainability (viability) and technological feasibility. Ensuring that design research and solutions account for what is desirable, viable and feasible is not unique to HCD. What distinguishes HCD from other design approaches (such as engineering design or advertising) is that in HCD viability and feasibility are always considered as enablers of the core design focus on desirability: Human need always takes centre stage.

How human need is addressed in HCD takes the form of a range of methodological approaches that are often very different in the degree to which they engage with people. For example, contextual design (Steen, 2011) engages users primarily through interviews and observational methods with a clear separation between design research and user; while co-design (Steen, 2011), in contrast, views the design researcher and the participants as equally valuable members of the design team, each contributing their particular skills and knowledge in a participatory manner.

While the intention of this discussion of HCD is to be introductory in nature, what is important to our narrative is that in practising design thinking within the philosophical positioning of HCD, the likelihood of encountering complexity during problem framing is high, as societal problems tend to present as wicked problems (Buchannan, 1992; Rittel & Webber, 1973), often with no clear understanding of how they should be understood or resolved. While complexity is not unique to HCD, we suggest that in contrast to the 'apprenticeship model' for design education, HCD introduces a requirement for understanding the nature of and engaging with complexity that traditional forms of design education do not.

Our experience of teaching students to explore complex problems embedded in social reality (in order to engage with human need and in so doing meaningfully construct for themselves a framing of the design problem and subsequent strategic and designerly interventions) has been a valuable approach for facilitating the growth of reflective and critical design practitioners. However, what we have found to be of growing concern is that although design is already much altered, it is in a state of transition, where notions of criticality in design have not shifted from a culturally specific 'affective citizenship' approach to one that encompasses and is relevant to the emancipatory ethos of a shared desire for a better future, which HCD embodies.

What does criticality mean in design education?

Over the last decade, South African design education has been affected by this reframing of the discipline, as described previously. In South Africa, design has begun to distinguish itself from an overtly humanities-influenced culture of practice to one that addresses the unique paradigmatic identity of design.[2] To a large degree, the humanities, due to the long association of design with fine arts, have had a major influence on how, and to what end, criticality has been employed in tertiary design education. In the humanities, criticality (as taught in fields such as critical and literary theory) is considered as a set of normative values to which a social system should aspire to achieve certain ends (such as social justice). As the humanities are concerned with interpreting the human experience of the world (Owen, 2007; Wendt, 2014), criticality is often applied to problematise unequitable power relationships in the world. However, design in its modern offering has a problematic legacy strongly linked to capitalistic consumption, development and nationalism (Fry, 2009). The need for reflective critique has long been apparent and in many design schools critical theory has served this purpose.

However, criticality is always value-laden and never neutral. A basic grasp of sociology implies that what is most important for one group of people is not necessary transferable to a different group, and equally so, the judgement criteria of what is of value should never be approached as being universal.

---

[2] This can be contrasted with the Indian experience, where design has been historically associated with the more scientific pursuits of aeronautics and engineering within the Indian Institutes of Technology.

So while many of the values embedded in critical thinking may be considered laudable, what requires careful consideration in design (particularly when designers engage with participants in a culture different to their own) is the extent to which the critical theory is transferable between the designers' own culture and that of the community for which they are professing to mediate, and to what extent it may negate the community's own values and agency. Critical theories continue to bring much value to design, but it is our contention that in design, when applied as a seemingly unquestioned moral compass (Dunne & Raby, 2013), critical theory can be problematic.

Furthermore, critical theory, while critical of the hegemony of Western modernity, could be argued to only hold relevance in its relationship to modernity. At worst, critical theory perpetuates the very cultural value system that it seeks to dismantle and at best it represents a very selective cultural viewpoint. The result of this is that many students (and many of the people for whom we design) without a European orientation are 'told' what 'good' values are without any consideration for their cultural, ethical or moral background. While a seeming counterargument to this point is that many of the values communicated through critical theory are enshrined in the South African Constitution, the difference, while minimal, is immense, because constitutional values are a negotiated vision for a shared society, as opposed to a set of mandatory values.

Another related point regarding the influence of humanities thinking on design is that of the dominant role that the designed product has tended to play in design curricula (Brown, 2007) and indeed societal conceptualisations of design and designers. The relationship between design and the designed product is closely associated with the notion of apprenticeship design education and is typically focused on the aesthetic value of the final solution. Regarding the value of design as summative and embedded in the generated solution deprives the discipline of many of its most fundamental and powerful attributes. The value of strong aesthetic consideration and product crafting is indisputable; however, design has much to offer beyond product design. Furthermore, criticality in design is often limited to the scope of the designed product (Buchanan, 1992). This includes the critique of design products, for example advertisements that objectify women as well as the creation of design products that create awareness of or comment on social concerns.[3] Therefore, while designers and advocacy groups such as Adbusters (2016) have long utilised design products and mediums to problematise and critically reflect on societal concerns, applying criticality through its modes of consumption (which often requires an informed and knowledgeable comprehension of the discipline) tends to limit the role of design (and designers) in critically engaging with the role of the discipline in affecting the world in an actionable manner.

Applying critical theory as a default approach to criticality perpetuates the role of design as a purely responsive set of activities to strategic direction rather than as an active agent capable of generating strategic intent. In this sense, critical theory articulates a viewpoint that design has been 'captured by capitalism' and that the only form of defiance is to use capitalism's own forms of media against itself. It is our argument that a fixation on product as the subject of criticality in design limits the role of

---

[3]   See Dunne and Raby (2013) for numerous examples of critical design.

criticality in design and, to an extent, entrenches a conceptualisation of design as overly object- or product-oriented, which over the last decade has been challenged.

To substantiate this point, we draw a strong parallel with Richard Buchanan's (1992) warning of the limiting dangers of product 'categorisation' in design. Categorisation, Buchanan (1992) states, is a fixation on certain categories of design outcome (artefact, schema or pattern) that negate, due to their pervasiveness, the allowances for any alternative solutions to exist. These categorical responses are often embedded in products that appear to resolve particular types of problems. For example, cars solve the problem of transport and chairs solve the problem of a place to sit.

Many of these categorical responses have emerged over time and in relation to particular cultural needs and preferences and have also demonstrated their effectiveness (and will no doubt continue to do so). Nonetheless, many of the current categorical responses, their causational logic and contexts are no longer valid and/or they no longer adequately resolve the problem for which they were conceived (for example, the personal-use, privately owned motor vehicle may no longer be regarded as an effective solution to transporting the world's population). Therefore, Buchanan (1992) cautions that as designers we can no longer assume that our existing approaches to problem solutions can resolve the range of problems we are called upon to resolve. This is not to say that our existing design solutions are redundant, but rather that they should be treated with caution (and critically assessed) and applied when merited.

The logical extension of this argument, as put forward by a range of design theorists, including Buchanan (1992), Krippendorff (2007), Van der Merwe (2010), Sanders and Stappers (2008), Hassenzahl (2010) and McCarthy and Wright (2004), is that developing plausible solutions (and, we are arguing, just and equitable solutions too) to design problems involves an engaged understanding of the societal context from which the problem emerges. As approaches, both HCD and critical citizenship speak directly to this need.

Design in this positioning is an inherently phenomenological/pragmatic field of practice, one in which praxis is always constructed through situated contexts (Buchanan, 1992; Van der Merwe, 2010) and in relationship to the ability of technology[4] to extend the human experience. In this sense, praxis extends beyond exploring human need and contexts (in order to establish what must be made to enable better experiences) and further asks to what extent an "understanding of human life is embodied in the prevailing technical arrangements" (Feenburg, 1991, cited in Dunne & Raby, 2013: 34). Therefore, the design activities involved in identifying the problems that ought to be solved, the repercussions of resolving (or not resolving) these problems and the mode in which these problems are solved require criticality as a fundamental skill. Criticality, when practised in a phenomenological sense, however, does not have any easy fall-back to a set of shared and documented values, such as may be found in critical theory. Instead, these values, as with other aspects of what is learnt and which emerge through engagement with the problem ecology in HCD, are local, subjective and evasive and are revealed through exploration, analysis and synthesis.

---

4   Where technology is considered to be the introduction of the artificial into situated contexts.

In this pragmatic framing of design, we see HCD and design thinking as valuable philosophies and processes for approaching and managing this emergent complexity in terms of both the why-to-design and the what-to-design. Positioning design education within an HCD thinking framework, however, is not without its challenges. Working with societal complexity is in itself an often difficult and confusing process that requires particular abilities that are not typically taught in undergraduate design education. Design traditionally tends to prioritise the ideation, prototyping and evaluation phases of the design thinking process. The research and strategy phases are particularly neglected in undergraduate teaching, tending either towards the un-complex imitation of existing products or resolved within the design brief from a lecturer where the strategic resolution is implied.

However, applying HCD in a meaningful way in students' design projects that either resembles or simulates the expectation of professional practice, more often than not, ensures that design students are confronted with wicked problems and therefore there is an emphasis for them to engage with all the phases of the design thinking process. We believe that if students are expected to learn how to resolve complex problems in an authentic human-centric manner capable of realising a just and equitable future for all, they should be prepared to do so.

Imbedded in the meditative role of the designer in the HCD thinking process is the need to make decisions that impact on other role players in the problem ecology. These decisions, often undertaken in conditions of uncertainty, define what will be. These decisions are never value-neutral and will always impose some form of power. We believe that the responsibility for making these types of decisions needs to be supported, particularly when facilitating the educational growth of novice designers. To this purpose, we position citizenship-as-equality with its emphasis on participation and citizens' capability as a critical framework with HCD thinking providing the pragmatic logic and designerly structure for the critical reflection.

Tackling complexity in design education

In the remainder of this chapter we discuss two specific tools and their related methods. These are the Firma Model (Hobbs & Fenn, 2015) and ExRMs (Fenn & Hobbs, 2017), both of which we created and have used in our teaching practice to support students in their HCD thinking process. Both tools present visual models that assist students in synthesising data into manageable and meaningful insights, but in addition, and specifically in relation to the theme of this chapter, require students to engage critically with their own process of knowledge construction in the formation of design strategy. While we have primarily applied these models with Interaction Design students, we believe that they are discipline-neutral and applicable in any design project that involves framing wicked problems in a human-centric manner.

We use the term 'design strategy' here to refer to a conceptual plan to achieve one or more objectives under uncertain conditions, where reflecting on the 'diagnosis and critique' of a social context presents a hypothesis of where and how change can occur. Both the Firma Model and ExRMs are designed with the objective of supporting students in developing their own design strategy, but importantly, it is expected that the strategy will be reflective of the contexts they address. Embedded in both models are suggestions firstly, as to what type of data/information the research methods should generate and secondly, how this research data/information can be modelled to inform strategic decision making. Neither tools require a particular research method, although in the description we will refer to techniques that we have found to be particularly effective. Lastly, both the Firma Model and ExRMs can be used in unison, as we describe, or as stand-alone tools in combination with other research and strategic tools.

The Firma Model

The Firma Model (Hobbs & Fenn, 2015) is a meta-framework for research, strategy and critique in HCD. As shown in Figure 2, the Firma Model provides a set of generic content categories through which to explore specific problem contexts.[5] The Firma Model tool was designed to:

- assist the design student in the determination of a problem ecology;
- allow for speculative consideration of how these areas should be amended and transformed; and
- form the basis for a critical reflection on the impact of a design on the societal context of the problem.

The areas of concern identified in the Firma Model follow and are categorised into immediate, contextual and paradigmatic concerns.

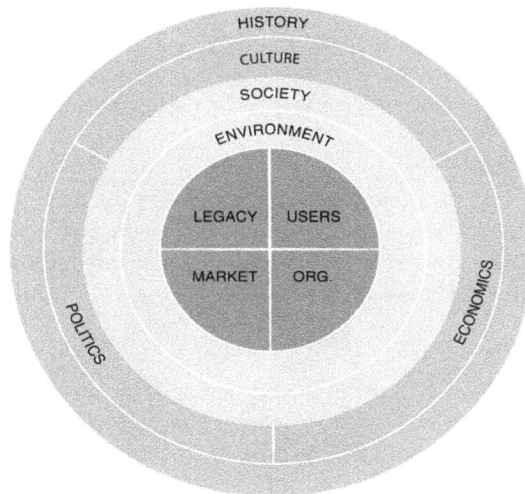

Figure 2   The Firma Model

Immediate concerns present the most direct influences on design problems, namely the needs, opportunities and limitations presented by clients, 'value-chain' stakeholders, competitors and end users. Immediate concerns occur within specific sectors, industries and marketplaces. Immediate concerns tend to address factors most commonly associated with how HCD is practised in

---

5   Problem contexts, problem ecologies and problem framing are terms widely used (often interchangeably) to describe the contexts within which wicked problems emerge. For more on this topic, see Rittel and Webber (1973), Cross (2006), Dorst (2015) and Fenn and Hobbs (2012).

commercial design contexts (namely that 'good' design creates value for users and business in a way that improves on or negates competitors). Existing models such as IDEO's three lenses of HCD (particularly desirability and feasibility) and Collis and Rukstad's Strategic Sweet Spot (2008) informed our selection of the categories presented in the immediate areas of concern. Paradigmatic concerns, which sit on the outermost rings of the Firma Model, present the broadest influences on problem ecologies, as they span places, markets and sectors. Paradigmatic concerns are often where power structures and macrostructural relationships play out. In terms of critical reflection, histories, cultures and economics allow for understandings of 'oppression' and 'injustices' (Johnson & Morris, 2010). Contextual concerns occupy the rings between paradigmatic and immediate concerns, as they are the result of the bottom-up forces generated through the activities of immediate concerns as well as the top-down forces of macrostructural paradigms. The contextual areas of concern are influenced by IDEO's viability lens of HCD. In the Firma Model, we address viability as concerned firstly with environmental contexts (including both natural and technological) and secondly with the cultural background that orientates acceptable social practice.

Immediate areas of concern include:
- The organisation (Org): the business or organisational entity that commissions the design project
- Users: the people affected by the design problem
- Market (the marketplace): relates to existing approaches to resolving the design problem or aspects of it, including competitor solutions, the supply chain of products and services and other immediately affected organisations
- Legacy: of the organisation, users and marketplace in relation to the problem in question.

Contextual areas of concern include:
- Environment: the context of use, spaces and places where the problem occurs. In the model, environment includes both natural and artificial environments. Environment for design is a key concern, as it is the material placement of any existing and future technologies.
- Society: the societal context in which the concerns of the immediate and paradigmatic play out.

Paradigmatic areas of concern include:
- Economics: the macro- and micro-economic forces that affect or are affected by the problem ecology
- Politics: both the broad framework of governance and the interpersonal relationships that affect decision making
- Culture: the beliefs, norms, values and behaviours of a society at large; the interplay of cultures within a society and sub-cultures as they relate to the problem ecology[6]
- History: the broad historical context (and possibly contended views thereof) that inform and contextualise a specific problem ecology.

---

[6] Arguably, the difference between society and culture can be subjective. In our framing, we see society as more local (as in South African society versus African cultural practice). However, we acknowledge that this is a semantic decision and that culture, for example Afrikaans culture, could pre-inform South African society.

While we present these concerns within the immediate, contextual and paradigmatic typology, we believe the essential point of the Firma Model is to address problem ecologies as systemic, interrelated networks where aspects of one concern may bear influence on all the other areas of concern.

In use, students would apply the Firma Model categories to guide their research interventions and then map emergent data and insights into the model. As stated earlier, the research can take many different and multiple forms. For example, our students have used the Firma Model applying only secondary research as well as with secondary, explorative and generative methods together on other occasions. Often, particularly for more involved senior work, we encourage students to use the model iteratively, whereby starting with secondary research they continue to build the data saturation through a number of research interventions over time. To this point, we caution that while we present the model in the circular format presented in Figure 2, in the execution of the model, for ease of use, we often encourage students to use other formats to visually represent data (for example, see Figure 3).

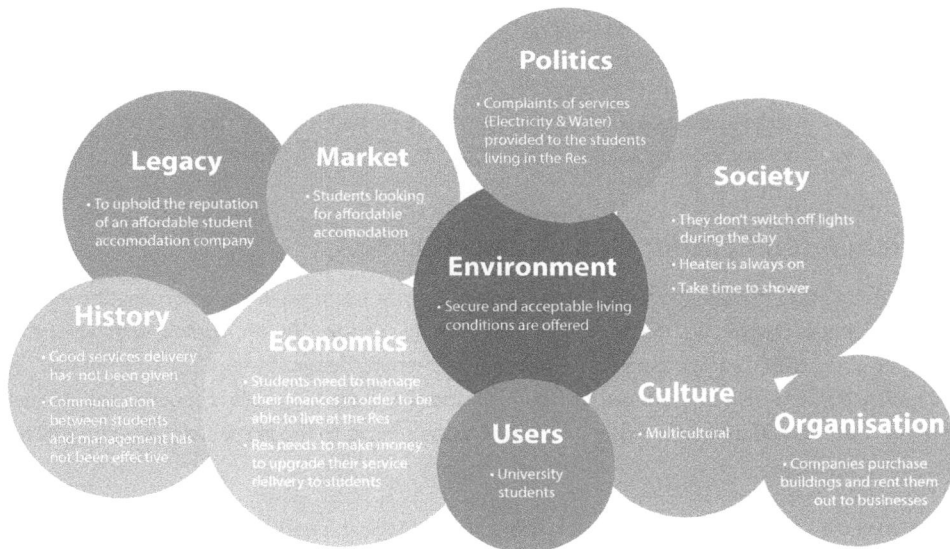

Figure 3   Example of a student's Firma Model

In design research, applying the model to guide exploration is effective for numerous reasons. Firstly, it ensures that complex problems are framed in a rigorous and holistic manner. Using the model's categories ensures that to a large degree many of the influences and phenomena that may affect the problem are identified and considered.

Secondly, the model acts against students fixating on resolving design problems purely in response to the needs of business and end users, and, as such, acknowledges the needs of broader society, the environment, economy and so on.

Thirdly, as the model is visual, when filled with research data it acts as a communication tool that allows viewers such as lecturers, fellow designers and community members to quickly grasp the details of the research and subsequently promotes dialogue and suggestions in a way that data captured on an Excel sheet, for instance, cannot. A visual representation of the data is, in our experience, highly beneficial in assisting students to identify key areas of concern within the problem ecology that require and can be resolved by a design intervention, and therefore the model assists in articulating the why, what and how of the design strategy.

Lastly (and perhaps the major benefit of developing a visual, systemic interpretation of a problem ecology), it allows the student to speculate about possible ways of resolving the problem in a critically reflective and often participatory manner. In a cognitive mode that shares many similarities with critical design (Dunne & Raby, 2013) students can envision transformation, but can also envision impact and effect within a specific societal placement. This critical reflection is not a top-down, morally driven judgement, but is rather deeply embedded in, and emergent from, the lived experience of the people who inhabit the problem ecology. In the research phase of applying the Firma Model, problems are treated as outputs of a systemic network in operation. In the speculation phase of use, this concept is in many ways reversed to attempt to determine how actions send change back into the other areas of concern.

While here we are largely addressing the application of the Firma Model for design practice, it is also a useful tool for critiquing existing solutions in terms of their systemic impact.

Experience-led Relationship Models (ExRMs)

In its design and conceptualisation, the Firma Model is a meta-framework for describing the various systemic influences that impact the framing of a problematic ecology. When working within an HCD framework, as described earlier, there is an emphasis on orienting design strategy from the perspective of human needs. ExRMs (as modelled in Figure 4) address these particular concerns and as such principally relate to and extend the users' concerns as they relate to the immediate areas of concern in the Firma Model.

ExRMs describe a relationship between users' psychological needs and a set of reciprocal 'experience drivers' that any subsequent design solution should embody to fulfil the users' emotional needs and psychological motivations. In this model, both the users' psychological needs and the experience drivers are contextualised by a set of coherent actions that reflect the strategic intent of a hypothesised design solution. The fundamental logic of ExRMs is that they ensure a synthetic continuum in which research insights gained from (user) research and strategic thinking contribute explicitly to the ideation of final design solutions. For us this is a critical concern. In our experience working with design students, ensuring that final design products reflect research findings in a meaningful and effective manner is one of the hardest abilities to learn. For students, ExRMs provide a framework that assists them in communicating and reflecting their strategic thinking in a manner that purposefully relates research insights to solution thinking.

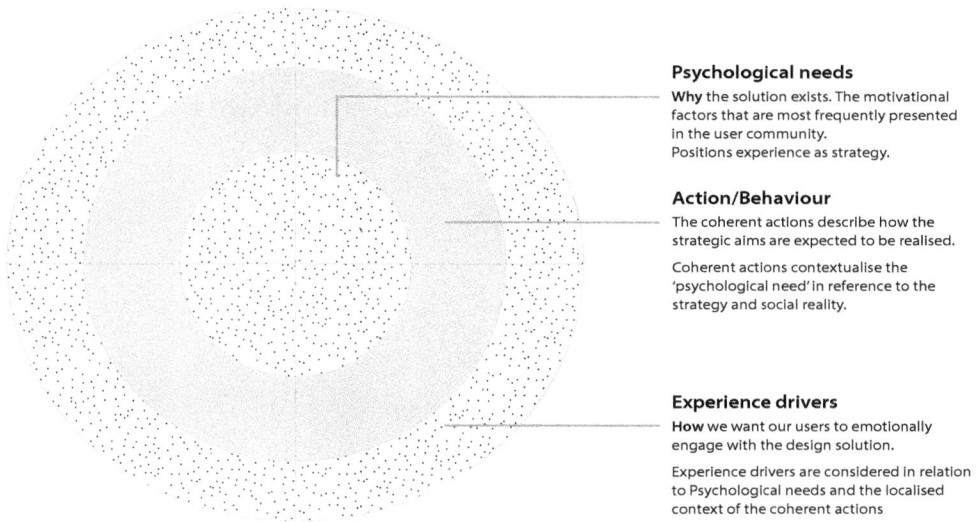

Psychological needs

Why the solution exists. The motivational factors that are most frequently presented in the user community.
Positions experience as strategy.

Action/Behaviour

The coherent actions describe how the strategic aims are expected to be realised.

Coherent actions contextualise the 'psychological need' in reference to the strategy and social reality.

Experience drivers

How we want our users to emotionally engage with the design solution.

Experience drivers are considered in relation to Psychological needs and the localised context of the coherent actions

Note Although the quadrants of the template suggest four Psychological needs, Actions and Experience driver categories, this is only illustrative. The number of categories may vary as per the particular results of the design research.

Figure 4   The template for creating Experience-led Relationship Models

The design of ExRMs was conceived of in reference to a number of theoretical positions from the disciplines of experience design and business strategy. The focus of experience design (Hassenzahl, 2010, Wright & McCarthy, 2010) is on curating the emotional engagement that users generate when encountering and using technology. Essentially, 'experience' here is understood as the naturally occurring inner narrative that is constantly present in our human mind when engaging with the world. Experience can be either positive or negative and is our emotional response to situated engagement. The intention of experience design is to ensure, as far as possible, that users' engagement with designed solutions is appropriately positive. The psychological drivers ring of the ExRM template describes the emotional reactions that the designer intends the user to experience when interacting with the solution. In design fields that emphasise a strong engagement with experience design, such as user-experience design and service design, much has been written (Garrett, 2010; Rogers, Sharp & Preece, 2015; Unger & Chandler, 2009; Wilson, 2010) about the need to curate positive experiences; however, in these accounts, what counts as an appropriate experience is often elusive (McCarthy & Wright, 2004) and is often described in generic terms such as 'fun', 'surprise' or 'delight'.

While a 'felt' account of experience as embodied in the designed solution is of value, Wright and McCarthy (2010) and Hassenzahl (2010) argue that these felt experience factors should be contemplated in response to the lived experiences of users. In this positioning of experience, which in the ExRM resides in the innermost ring (psychological needs), an 'appropriate' emotional engagement is one that emerges through an exploration of the larger life needs of users.

Applying an activity theory framing (Hassenzahl, 2010), 'life needs' are understood as the motivational goals that orientate activity and action (Hassenzahl, 2010). In design research, uncovering the larger motivational goals of users requires an enquiry into why and to what end users perform the activities that they enact. In our teaching, we have found it useful to provide students with Hassenzahl's categorisation (based on Sheldon *et al.*'s list) of the ten most commonly occurring psychological needs that, when fulfilled, equate to a positive life experience. These needs are (Hassenzahl, 2010: 44):

- Autonomy/Independence
- Competence/Effectance
- Relatedness/Belongingness
- Self-actualisation/Meaning
- Security/Control
- Money/Luxury
- Influence/Popularity
- Physical thriving/Bodily
- Self-esteem/Self-respect
- Pleasure/Stimulation.

Typically, within user research, a range (but not all) of the ten categories will emerge, which form the basis of the psychological needs category ring. For example, an investigation into rural farmers may result in the need for autonomy/independence, competence/effectance and money/luxury, while an exploration of high school children doing homework may generate self-actualisation/meaning, pleasure/stimulation and relatedness/belonging.

As the psychological needs presented in Hassenzahl's categories are intentionally broad, the middle ring of the ExRM, actions/behaviour, provides a contextualising orientation. For example, security/control could have many diverse interpretations that range from physical threat all the way to maintaining order in one's life. Relating the selected psychological need to action therefore implies the manner in which the psychological need should be considered in the scope of providing the correct emotional engagement of the solution.

How the actions/behaviours ring is conceptualised extends beyond only addressing issues of contextualisation to also include a specific articulation of design strategy. To guide the creation of the strategic drivers that inform the actions/behaviour ring, we utilise strategy theorist Richard Rumelt's (2011: 77) three kernels of strategy, which are described in the following steps:

1. A diagnosis that defines or explains the nature of the challenge
2. A guiding policy for dealing with the challenge
3. Coherent actions designed to carry out the guiding policy.

The 'diagnosis' refers back to the framing of the problem at hand. To this end, the Firma Model (when applied in the strategic thinking phase that addresses which problems are most requiring and capable of resolution) fulfils this aspect of the kernel. The 'guiding policy' is informed by the 'diagnosis' and is the outcome of the synthetic resolution of the complexities of desirability, viability and feasibility. The 'guiding policy' in essence describes the transformation that needs to occur in the existing system and what the 'preferred' effects of this transition will be. The 'coherent actions' describe a set of conditions, which must occur, in order for the transformation to take place.

The coherent actions created using Rumelt's three kernels of strategy become in ExRMs the content of the actions/behaviours ring and as such are the contextualising factors that locate the psychological needs and, collectively with the psychological needs, inform the experience drivers. ExRMs ensure that psychological motivations become the reason for being of the design solution and they orientate experience as strategy.

Figures 5 to 9 show examples of how a third-year design student developed an ExRM. Figure 5 shows how the student amalgamated Rumelt's three kernels of strategy with psychological needs to determine suitable coherent drivers. The student's ExRM, in Figure 8, demonstrates the conceptual orientation linking the emotional drivers (responsible, connected, respect[ed]) with the psychological drivers (effectance, influence, competence) within the situated contexts of the coherent actions. This conceptual link can be exemplified, for example, in the relationship between:

- the psychological driver: influence;
- the cohesive action: the creation of a student residence forum; and
- the emotional driver: relatedness.

'Influence' as a concept could have enumerable interpretations; however, the cohesive driver locates the interpretation of influence within a particular context, namely that of the need of students to have a united voice. Therefore, the experience driver, relatedness, speaks to the specific need of the students to feel 'united' and 'heard'.

[Users]

Res Students are falling behind on school work

because of their need for security, competence and control **has not been met.**

This is because

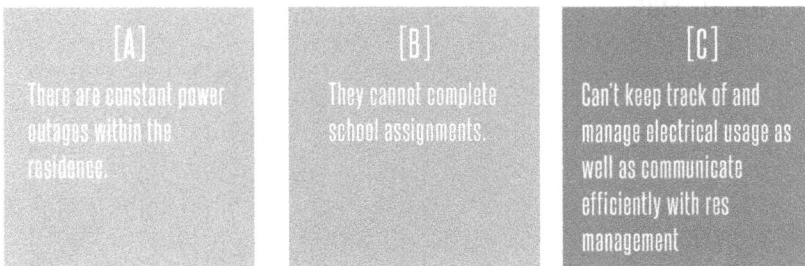

[A]	[B]	[C]
There are constant power outages within the residence.	They cannot complete school assignments.	Can't keep track of and manage electrical usage as well as communicate efficiently with res management

Figure 5   The problem definition, the psychological needs that are in deficit and the resulting impact on the university residence students

155

By updating the systems used and providing a direct communication channel as well as providing a way of keeping track of water & electricity usage,

[Users]
Res students will achieve security, competence and control

And thus they will complete their assignments on time, be able to communicate with management in case of an emergency or complaint, as well as keep track of usage within the residence.

Figure 6   The guiding policy for resolving the users' problems and the expected benefit of such action

By providing a more efficient system, an effective communication channel to management as well as a system to keep track of usage,

[Users]
Res students will achieve security, competence and control

If we provide

[A] An updated system for the water and electricity service

[B] a better communication channel to res management

[C] and a way to track electrical usage

Figure 7   The coherent drivers that the student identified as capable of supporting the guiding policy of the strategy

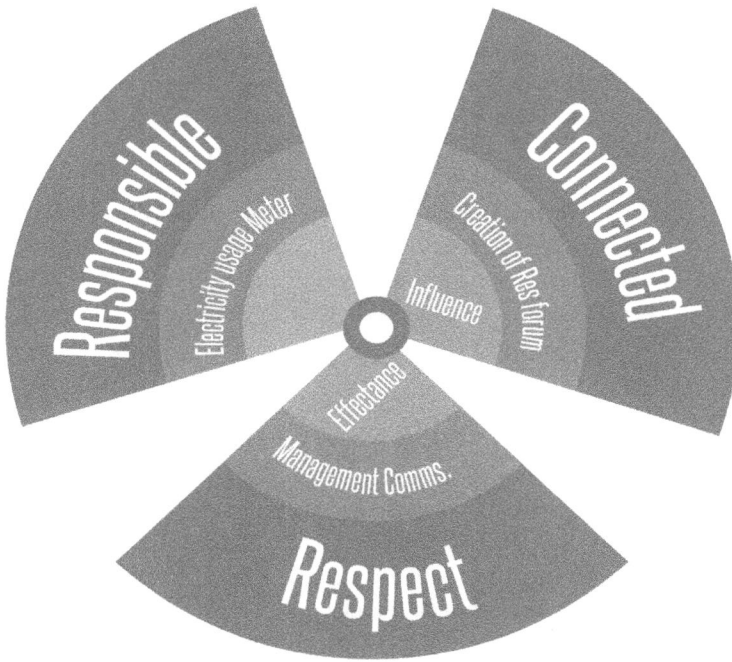

Figure 8   The student's Experience-led Relationship Model

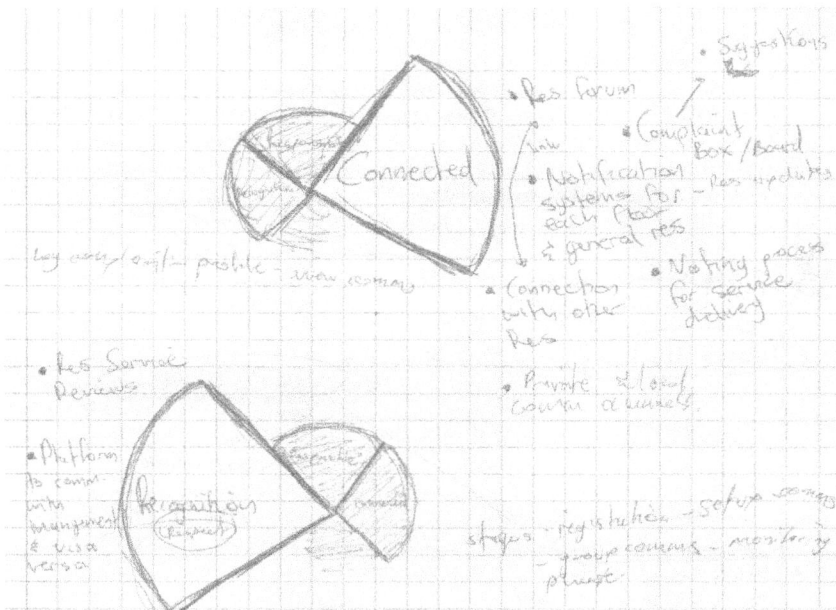

Figure 9   Example of student ideation in reference to specific experience drivers

Conclusion

Introducing students to complex societal problems and assisting them in decision making (and thereby, hopefully, producing effective solutions that speak to the real needs of people) are a central concern that aims to ensure that students are capable of critically reflecting on their roles as critical citizen designers and thereby contribute effectively with and in society.

In this chapter we have provided various frameworks that explore this concern and approaches to guiding students through the often problematic process of critical decision making in the context of complex societal design problems. To this end, we first provided a brief framing of criticality in which we argued that the changing nature of design education requires a new version of critical practice. While this argument is of a theoretical nature, we use it as a conceptual backdrop within which we have placed our two design tools.

As described in the relevant sections, both the Firma Model and ExRMs provide frameworks to assist students in engaging with their research practice to generate design strategy. Design strategy is an abductive act that requires critical and reflective thought on the side of the practitioner to "theorise the journey from the present to possible futures" (Wright, 2010, cited in Dunne & Raby, 2013: 44) and is, in a sense, the explicit articulation of the designers' decision making. Both models enable students to frame an account of the contextual, societal system in which the problem they seek to address is located.

By framing problem ecologies using these tools, students can engage with design as an effective agent of systemic change within a phenomenological construct of their own devising, which allows them to orientate their criticality in a manner that is participatory, empathetic and effective in delivering the just, equitable and sustainable futures we desire.

References

Adbusters. 2016. Available at http://www.adbusters.org [Accessed 15 January 2017].

Brown, T. 2008. Design thinking. *Harvard Business Review*, June, 84–95.

Buchanan, R. 1992. Wicked problems. *Design Issues,* 8(2), 5–21. https://doi.org/10.2307/1511637

Collis, D. & Rukstad, M. 2008. Can you say what your strategy is? *Harvard Business Review*, April, 1–9.

Cross, N. 2001. Designerly ways of knowing: Design discipline versus design science. *Design Issues,* 17(3), 49–55. https://doi.org/10.1162/074793601750357196

Cross, N. 2006. *Designerly ways of knowing.* London: Springer-Verlag.

Dorst, K. 2015. *Frame innovation: Create new thinking by design.* Cambridge, MA: The MIT Press.

Dunne, A. & Raby, F. 2013. *Speculative everything: Design fiction and social dreaming.* Cambridge, MA: The MIT Press.

Fenn, T. & Hobbs, J. 2012. The information architecture of transdisciplinary design practice: Rethinking Nathan Shedroff's continuum of understanding. In: *Proceedings of the 2nd International Conference on Design, Development and Research Design*. Cape Town: Cape Peninsula University of Technology, 1–16. https://doi.org/10.1007/978-981-10-3521-0_45

Fenn, T. & Hobbs, J. 2017. Conceiving and applying relationship models for design strategy. Paper delivered at ICORD 1, the 6th International Conference of Research into Design, 10–12 January, Guwahati.

Fry, T. 2009. *Design futuring: Sustainability, ethics and new practice.* Oxford: Berg. https://doi.org/10.5040/9781350036079

Garrett, J. 2010. *The elements of user experience design.* Berkley, CA: New Riders.

Hassenzahl, M. 2010. *Experience design: Technology for all the right reasons.* San Rafael: Morgan & Claypool.

Hobbs, J. & Fenn, T. 2015. The Firma Model: A meta-framework for design research, strategy and critique. In: L. Collina, L. Galluzzo & A. Meroni (Eds.). *Proceedings of the Cumulus Conference, Milano 2015: The Virtuous Circle: Design Culture and Experimentation.* Milan: McGraw–Hill, 271–284.

IDEO. 2015. *The field guide to human-centered design.* Available at https://www.ideo.com/us/post/design-kit [Accessed 20 April 2016].

Johnson, L. & Morris, P. 2010. Towards a framework for critical citizenship education. *The Curriculum Journal,* 21(1):77–96. https://doi.org/10.1080/09585170903560444

Kolko, J. 2010. Abductive thinking and sensemaking: The drivers of design synthesis. *Design Issues,* 26(1), 15–28. https://doi.org/10.1162/desi.2010.26.1.15

Krippendorf, K. 2007. Design: An oxymoron? In: R. Michel (Ed.). *Design research now.* Basel: Birkhauser Verlag AG, 67–81. https://doi.org/10.1007/978-3-7643-8472-2_5

Lorenzo, D. 2016. Why higher education needs design thinking. *Co. Design.* Available at https://www.fastcodesign.com/3066293/designing-women/why-higher-education-needs-design-thinking-right-now [Accessed 15 January 2017].

McCarthy, J. & Wright, P. 2004. *Technology as experience.* Cambridge, MA: The MIT Press.

Muratovski, G. 2016. *Research for designers: A guide to method and practice.* London: Sage.

Owen, C. 2007. Design thinking: Notes on its nature and use. *Design Research Quarterly,* 2(1), 16–27.

Rittel, H. & Webber, M. 1973. Dilemmas in a general theory of planning. *Policy Sciences,* (4), 155–169. https://doi.org/10.1007/BF01405730

Rogers, Y., Sharp H. & Preece, J. 2015. *Interaction design: Beyond human-computer interaction.* Fourth edition. Chichester: Wiley.

Ruitenberg, C. 2015. The practice of equality: A critical understanding of democratic citizenship education. *Democracy & Education,* 23(1), Article 2. Available at http://democracyeducationjour- nal.org/home/val23/iss1/2 [Accessed 15 January 2017].

Rumelt, R. 2011. *Good strategy bad strategy: The difference and why it matters.* New York, NY: Crown Business.

Sanders, E. & Stappers, P. 2008. Co-creation and the new landscapes of design. *CoDesign: International Journal of CoCreation in Design and the Arts,* 4(1), 5–18.

Stanford University Institute of Design. 2016. *Welcome to the virtual crash course in design thinking.* Available at http://dschool.stanford.edu/dgift [Accessed 15 January 2017].

Steen, M. 2011. Tensions in human-centred design. *CoDesign: International Journal of CoCreation in Design and the Arts,* 7(1), 45–60.

Terrestrial. 2016. Available at http://trstrl.com [Accessed 15 December 2016].

Unger, R. & Chandler, C. 2009. *A project guide to UX Design: For user experience designers in the field or in the making.* Berkley, CA: New Riders.

Van der Merwe, J. 2010. A natural death is announced. *Design Issues,* 26(3), 6–17. https://doi.org/10.1162/DESI_a_00025

Wendt, T. 2014. *Design for Dasien.* Self-published.

Wilson, C. 2010. *User experience design remastered.* Burlington, MA: Morgan Kaufman.

Wright, P. & McCarthy, J. 2010. *Experience-centered design: Designers, users, communities in dialogue.* San Rafael: Morgan & Claypool.

Zembylas, M. 2015. Exploring the implications of citizenship-as-equality in critical citizenship education. *Democracy & Education,* 23(1), 1–6.

Learning to Act on Courageous Convictions: Developing a Critical Citizenship Module for Undergraduate Design and Branding Students

9

Anika van den Berg

Introduction

Our planet and our collective history have always flourished on the initiatives of brave individuals who were willing to take a stand, take responsibility, partner with others and serve unselfishly. Each generation relies on its own peers to make their contributions. Critical citizenship education is more than a theory and reaches far beyond the conventional parameters of academic inquiry. Laura Johnson and Paul Morris's (2010) framework for critical citizenship education taps into the complexity and richness of this theoretical landscape. Critical citizenship entails a complex interaction between the knowledge, skills, values and dispositions necessary to engage with the ideological, social, personal and practical areas of citizenship (Johnson & Morris, 2010).

I encountered critical citizenship through the Master's in Art Education programme at Stellenbosch University in 2014. The focus of the programme on citizenship and social justice was unlike any topic covered during my school and undergraduate education. Two years after completing the master's degree in Art Education, I was approached by the Vega School[1] (where I was teaching at the time) to develop a new module that would run across a few of their degrees and on multiple campuses. This chapter is a reflection on the ideas and literature that inspired the Active Citizenship module, in conversation with the feedback received from the lecturers who taught this module and the students who took this module over the past two years.

At the outset this chapter unpacks the necessity of critical citizenship education, particularly in the South African context. Our current climate of volatile politics, constant technological advances and unprecedented global inequalities is fertile ground for leadership and innovation to manifest. There

---

[1]   Vega School was formed in 1999 in anticipation of the shift in the global paradigm away from conventional marketing and advertising toward a synchronous cohesion of design, branding and business. Vega School is an educational brand of The Independent Institute of Education (Pty) Ltd, which is registered with the Department of Higher Education and Training as a private higher education institution. Students can attend certificate, baccalaureate, honours and master's programmes (Vega School, n.d.).

are ample theories by South African and international authors that could guide educators in the field of critical citizenship. I then touch on the writing of Maxine Greene (1995a, 1995b, 2013), which is particularly stimulating, as are the socio-cultural view of learning (Lave & Wenger, 1998) and the situative framework for experiential learning (Fenwick, 2001). These theories guide educators to move beyond theoretical knowledge into the unknown and unpredictable convergence of information, abilities, beliefs and character (Johnson & Morris, 2010). Once we understand why critical citizenship is relevant and how such an abstract topic can be taught, we might start pondering on what we will actually teach. In the last section I combine various theoretical perspectives on compassion, postmodernism, ethnicity, multidimensional citizenship and media construction that formed the academic foundation of the Active Citizenship module. These theoretical perspectives could be helpful for those wishing to develop critical citizenship courses. I emphasise the value of open discussion that enables educators and students to recognise imperial ideologies in their thinking and to see how the media shapes their connections with their communities.

The teaching of critical citizenship cannot be reduced to purely the transformation of knowledge, but is about transforming students and their impact on their world. People vary in their awareness of and engagement with pressing global challenges and can be emancipated towards a greater sense of compassion to engage with the suffering of others in a "thoughtful, active and personal" manner (Cogan & Kubow, 1997: 1).

A need for critical citizenship education

We are "living in the age of 'supercomplexity' in which the world is increasingly unknowable, disruptive, unequal and disturbing" (McMillan, 2015: n.p.). South Africans are bombarded with heated debates and complex issues regarding "poverty, inequality, democracy, justice, responsibility and restitution" (McMillan, 2015: n.p.). We navigate a complex landscape of unpredictable politics, rapid technological advancement and unprecedented inequalities. Complexity and uncertainty make room for innovation and leadership. This is the moment when young South Africans should "engage actively in shaping the country" and establishing their own legacy for future generations (Matola, 2014: n.p.). South African youths are once again becoming vocal about their convictions, "demanding greater social justice in higher education" in the form of student protest movements (Badat, 2016: 15). Students are actively participating in public affairs, but the results may not be sustainable. Critical citizenship education could provide a framework of hope for students in South Africa.

Johnson and Morris (2010: 90) list the "ability to imagine a better world" as one of the key engagement skills in critical citizenship education. Instead of feeding off the energy of demands, power, violence and rebellion, impactful change often follows sacrifices, compassion, selflessness and connection. Critical citizenship education relies on the disposition that each of us should be "willing to learn with others" (Johnson & Morris, 2010: 90); not merely focusing on our own interests, but considering the interests of others as well. Yusef Waghid (professor of Philosophy of Education at Stellenbosch University) contends that "citizenship education initiatives in South Africa need to promote a sense of compassion" towards taking "seriously the suffering of others" (Waghid, 2004: 525). Critical citizenship is therefore not about selfish actions, but instead about using resources on behalf of others and recognising the needs of others. Waghid (2004: 525) holds that compassion is the "precondition of genuine educational transformation". According to Johnson and Morris (2010: 77), citizenship education promotes "a common set of shared values which prepare young people to live together in diverse societies". There is therefore an emphasis on what we have in 'common', what we 'share' and how we 'live together'. There lies significance in feeling affection from strangers because it "widens out the boundaries of our being and unites all living things" (Matola, 2014: n.p.); this could be the result of active citizenship education.

Citizenship education is not a matter of knowledge transfer from one individual mind to another. Instead, it implies "the emancipation and transformation of students ... toward a better society" (Johnson & Morris, 2010: 92). Such education becomes meaningful when it is interdisciplinary and interactive (Johnson & Morris, 2010), when it ignites minds to "be responsive to, and responsible for, the world in which we live" (McMillan, 2015: n.p.). During the past 20 years, educational transformation discourse had constantly surfaced in South African political and public conversations. Most of these conversations deal with the political aspect of transformation: "the 'decolonisation of the university', the social composition of academic staff, institutional culture, the inadequacy of state funding of higher education, the level and escalation of tuition fees, student debt and the question of free higher education" (Badat, 2016: 19). These are important conversations to have.

Educators and institutions may respond to this need for critical citizenship education in differing ways based on values, mandate and field of expertise. Vega School briefed the development of the Active Citizenship module in an attempt to translate its core values into interactive and interdisciplinary academic content. These values include: "brands with meaning add value to how people live their lives" and "an organisation is responsible for its every decision and action" (Vega School, n.d.: n.p.). Adding 'meaning' and 'value' and being a 'responsible' organisation are intangible and largely an intrinsic characteristics that do not translate easily into academic content. The development of the Active Citizenship module required innovation and this module was met with varying degrees of enthusiasm by lecturers and students across the Vega campuses.

Principles of critical citizenship

At the core of critical citizenship education lays the connection between individuals and their communities. Stereotypes and generalisations about people often alienate people, who cultivate a sense of fear, entitlement or division. In this section I delve into the social nature of learning that allows abstract topics such as critical citizenship to be taught. Learning is more than a set of tasks; it is a "set of relationships over time" (Lave & Wenger, 1998: 2).

Educational philosopher, social activist and teacher Maxine Greene shares valuable insights throughout her many publications. Many of her texts are based on the arts, the expansion of knowledge, participation, conversation and relationships – cornerstones of critical citizenship education. Greene (2013) places emphasis on the fact that education should help individuals recognise the connections between themselves and their communities. In *Releasing the imagination* she theorises the "social imagination of students" as their ability to hope and to engage with potential in their midst (Greene, 1995b: 5). This hope in potential resonates with Johnson and Morris's (2010: 90) "ability to imagine a better world"; it is a hope that looks beyond current suffering and self-gratification. Hope towards change rests on long-term vision, community awareness and "non-mainstream writings and ideas in addition to dominant discourses" (Johnson & Morris, 2010: 90). The "social imagination" is activated when the boundaries of valid and appropriate knowledge are expanded towards active learning through dialogue and participation (Greene, 1995b: 5). Active learning is initiated when educators prompt students to ask more questions, develop their own reasoning and learn to converse in diverse groups (Greene, 1995b).

This resonates with me as an educator, but also as a human being. It is easy for educators and students to accept their thoughts, generalisations and stereotypes as universally applicable. I have seen that it can take as little as one conversation with someone completely other than yourself to shatter a solid stereotype. Maxine Greene (1995a) identifies with traditional educators who experience discomfort and powerlessness when they free students to discover meaning on their own terms. Nevertheless, she encourages educators to persist despite discomfort in order to foster individual growth: relational capabilities, inventiveness, problem solving and zeal for living (Greene, 1995a). Critical citizenship emphasises what we have in "common", what we "share" and how we "live together" (Johnson & Morris, 2010: 77). It is not about being activists who stand up for their own rights to the detriment of others, about alienation, exclusion or power; critical citizenship is about connection, community and solidarity. Education can enable students to grow, find their voices in the public domain and learn to see themselves as participants in their communities (Greene, 1995a).

Humans are social beings, designed to function interdependently in communities. Socio-cultural views on learning assume that "learning is social" (Lave & Wenger, 1998: 1). Learning is not a task in which students participate, but a "set of relationships over time" (Lave & Wenger, 1998: 2). Communal learning does not necessarily refer to our traditional understanding of group work (doing work in groups), but to the class environment as a whole; the dynamic relationship between students and their appreciation of one another's unique perspectives and contributions. It cannot be contained in a set of assignments, but takes the form of a foundation on which tasks are designed and explained. Educators can strive to implement these principles in class by allowing diverging answers and open-ended reasoning, which develop students' skills to think critically, reflectively and interdependently. Lave and Wenger's (1998) socio-cultural view of learning as well as Greene's perspective on active learning can be applied in conjunction with the situative framework of experiential learning. This framework holds that educators assist students in becoming dynamic participants in a specific community by exposing them to authentic situations that contain "rich, multifaceted problems" for students to identify and unravel (Fenwick, 2001: 52). Group tasks that force students to work and socialise outside of their comfortable group of friends naturally create such authentic situations. Furthermore, multifaceted tasks that require decision making and time management also provide effective learning opportunities. One of the aims of the Active Citizenship module was to leave students with impressions of "togetherness, solidarity and collaboration" that encourage "positive risk taking and inquiry in learning environments" as stated by Fenwick (2001: 37).

Encouraged students address their stereotypes and develop their reasoning through questioning and conversations in diverse groups. This is pivotal for critical citizenship because connection, community and solidarity can only be cultivated in environments where people have compassion for one another. The value of shared learning environments that require togetherness and collaboration is important. The theories in this section shape the concept of critical citizenship and challenge notions of education.

Navigating a complex landscape

Critical citizenship moves beyond the facts of inequality, politics and environmental concerns into the lesser-tread territory of compassion, empathy and active problem solving. The theoretical perspectives in the following section informed the Active Citizenship module and can be used in conjunction with subject-related content in a variety of design courses. Cogan and Kubow (1997) provide a functional model of four interwoven dimensions of citizenship used in the Active Citizenship to evaluate and execute citizenship interventions. From this stable starting point, the section picks up a number of multifaceted conversations on topics of representation in the media, cultural imperialism, postmodernism and the new wave of youth activism: slacktivism.

Theoretical perspectives

Multidimensional citizenship and globalisation

On a surface level, many students might be aware of some of the economic, environmental, social and ethical issues prevalent in their vicinity, but a module on critical citizenship should challenge them to engage with these topics "in a manner that is thoughtful, active, personal" and committed "to the common good" (Cogan & Kubow, 1997: 1). "Active citizenship" is compassionate towards fellow humans, responsive to injustice (McMillan, 2015) and therefore multidimensional (Cogan & Kubow, 1997). Cogan and Kubow's (1997) theory of multidimensional citizenship distinguishes between four interconnected dimensions of citizenship that can be used to evaluate case studies and active citizenship interventions. Educators can instill in students "both a sense of self and of local history, and a connection to the kinds of knowledge that can enable them to understand the complexity of the global" (McMillan, 2015: n.p.).

The personal dimension relates to the personal capacity for commitment and critical thought, sensitivity to interpersonal differences and the ability to resolve conflict and problems in a "cooperative and non-violent" manner (Cogan & Kubow, 1997: 37). The social dimension acknowledges that we are part of a community; citizens need to interact with others and make our decisions with full cognisance of the rights and needs of our fellow citizens (Cogan & Kubow, 1997). The spatial dimension stresses the fact that we are all "members of several overlapping communities" (from local to global) and that current challenges "transcend national boundaries and will require multinational solutions" (Cogan & Kubow, 1997: 39). Citizens need to be able to negotiate the interplay between being rooted in local culture and immersed in a global village (Cogan & Kubow, 1997). In terms of the temporal dimension, citizens should be able to gain a deep-rootedness and understanding from the past, learning from it and considering its shortfalls (Cogan & Kubow, 1997). At the same time we are aware that "we are stewards of the future" who are "called upon to balance our readiness to explore and innovate with respect for the knowledge and values that constitute our heritage" (Cogan & Kubow, 1997: 39).

These four dimensions are in reality interwoven, but can be analysed separately to evaluate whether an intervention is comprehensive and sustainable. Courses on critical citizenship can lead students to notice global trends, some of which must be monitored, while others ought to be encouraged (Cogan & Kubow, 1997). It is not useful to remain aloof towards issues such as a widening economic gap, environmental deterioration, deforestation and the effect of technology on our privacy (Cogan & Kubow, 1997). The media is a powerful civilising force that affects all aspects of social, personal and political life. Critical citizenship education should reframe students' current understanding of the media's contribution to globalisation. It is crucial that we aim to develop an understanding of active citizenship and its relevance to the future of our nation and our globe. O'Shaughnessy and Stadler (2012) argue that globalisation and the media can affect the afore-mentioned global issues as well as our sense of responsibility, in both positive and negative ways. Although globalisation spreads information and turns us into a global village, cultural imperialism and media homogenisation have several detrimental effects (O'Shaughnessy & Stadler, 2012). One of the lecturers of the Active Citizenship module used prominent social media case studies such as A21 and Kony (2012) to offer "insights on narrative shaping and media representation" in order to highlight "appeals to subjective virtue-signaling, social media manipulation, theories of reinforcement, as well as selective exposure" (Kony, 2012: n.p.)

Representation and ethnicity

Our perceived reality has been mediated through the media apparatus. We are often deluded by media representations to regard these as a 'window on the world' rather than a social construction (O'Shaughnessy & Stadler, 2012). Media theorist Stuart Hall (1997) explains that media representations give meaning to the people or events that are portrayed. Studies on representation are then concerned with "measuring that gap between ... the true meaning of an event or an object and how it is presented in the media" (Hall, 1997: n.p.). Young people are spending increasing amounts of their time consuming social media, virtual reality, series, films and reality television. These exposures impact the subconscious mind. The Active Citizenship module increases students' awareness of the media they consume and the effect it has on their relationship with themselves and their fellow citizens. Vega School emphasises the importance of "the human imagination, in creativity and its power to impact what people think, feel and do" (Vega School, n.d.: n.p.) and thus equips students in design, brand and media industries with tools such as media studies and semiotic analysis to uncover ethnic stereotypes and power structures embedded in development discourse. Citizenship discourse is useful for addressing imperial ideologies and cultures.

Cultural imperialism is the term used to describe the common instances where the cultural and media products of one community infiltrate and dominate the cultural and media products of another (this includes their fashions, music, films, vocabulary, humour and social practices) (O'Shaughnessy & Stadler, 2012). Cultural imperialism imitates historical imperialism in the sense that it provides a 'benchmark' for local productions and dominates traditional cultures with Western ideologies (O'Shaughnessy & Stadler, 2012). Stereotypes, 'othering' and binary oppositions were established through imperialism, but these residual discourses remain part of our collective vocabulary through media repetition. Students should be made aware of racial stereotypes and social power structures embedded in films, series and music videos because these sources also affect how we conduct ourselves as citizens. Western activists, missionaries and philanthropists throughout history have approached indigenous communities through this imperial lens that devalues local culture and difference. For example, Cogan and Kubow's (1997) attributes of citizenship represent Euro-American values such as rights, obligations (tax, obeying laws and military duty) and national identity. Western activists often extend these values over non-Western cultures, failing to acknowledge that other parts of the world would prioritise family and human relationships, moral aspects or religion and spirituality in matters of citizenship (Cogan & Kubow, 1997).

An awareness of ethnic power structures and imperial ideologies is particularly important to South African youths and should be included in critical citizenship curricula. The current wave of student protests contests a "deeply embedded culture of whiteness" in "historically white universities" that has stifled true transformation towards inclusion, respect and affirmation of different cultures (Badat, 2016: 7). Rhodes University's former vice-chancellor, Dr Saleem Badat (2016: 10), holds that white students tend to feel "at home" and thrive at university, "largely oblivious to the association of the current cultures with power, privilege, and advantage". On the other hand, less affluent black students "tend to experience the environments and cultures of the historically white universities as discomforting, alienating, disempowering, and exclusionary" (Badat, 2016: 10). According to Badat (2016: 10), "[t]o imagine that South Africa is a 'rainbow nation' is to seriously confuse aspirations with realities". This is no easy topic to discuss in class; it should be approached with caution, courage and much grace. Educators should create safe spaces where students can discuss and come to terms with these complexities in order to emancipate and transform students so that they can "live together in diverse societies" (Johnson & Morris, 2010: 77).

Bhattacharyya (2004: 22) explains that any help afforded by active citizens should affirm "human variation" and therefore resist "developmental imposition from above". Any development may be driven from the understanding that shared identity and norms (solidarity) are essential to communities and that the primary purpose of aid is to promote the capacity to change, create and define (agency) (Bhattacharyya, 2004). Citizens often remain complacent because of the binary 'us and them' mentality that disregards the challenges and problems of others. The most liberating and sustainable creative solutions seldom emerge out of official projects and briefs, "but rather as a manifestation of passion, enthusiasm and commitment to a cause" where the designer allowed the agenda to be set by the community (Fell & De Villiers, 2012: n.p.). One of the Active Citizenship lecturers faced a challenge that may resonate with other critical citizenship educators: "I sometimes struggled to keep my students interested; some of them are just too privileged and entitled to care", while "some care too much and fall victim to their emotional kneejerk reactions." Another lecturer highlighted a "need to shift our students from being highly engrossed social-media slacktivists to hands-on design-thinking professionals who embrace compassion, empathy and generosity"

Postmodernism and slacktivism

We live in a postmodern era. Students are part of the most informed generation with almost any kind of knowledge at their fingertips (O'Shaughnessy & Stadler, 2012). "Knowingness" is a phenomenon of a postmodern society in which people are bombarded with information to such an extent that they start to embrace "non-rational modes of knowledge" and submit to a "passive uncertainty"

(O'Shaughnessy & Stadler, 2012: 449). Knowledge (and media studies) uncovers social and media constructions, which often makes people cynical and mistrusting when they become aware of power structures. Knowledge has the power to make us more aware of others, but O'Shaughnessy and Stadler (2012) argue that it tends to lead to cynicism and powerlessness. This powerlessness stems from the realisation that "corporate powers are too strong to resist", "injustices are too overwhelming to react to" and people sometimes become ultimately uncertain who to follow or believe (O'Shaughnessy & Stadler, 2012: 449). The authors argue that all the above-mentioned factors lead people, especially youths, to "indulge in humour, wit and pleasure" as an easy escape from the uncertainties and suffering in the world (O'Shaughnessy & Stadler, 2012: 449). The danger of this type of postmodern cycle is that it could lead to denial of material reality and injustice as a result of ultimate uncertainty and media construction (O'Shaughnessy & Stadler, 2012).

These concerning outcomes stand in direct contrast to critical citizenship. According to Waghid (2004: 536), a "compassionate person pays greater attention to those who suffer and are oppressed and less attention to his or her self-interest". Waghid (2004: 539) invites educators to "cultivate compassion as an appropriate response to the situation of others". It was difficult to include this cultivation of compassion into the Active Citizenship module. Some students may more readily relate to this type of content and see the value in developing compassion, while others might have no context or time for these conversations. I received diverging student feedback on the Active Citizenship module. One student found the module "at times very difficult to grasp and understand, but definitely interesting", and another mentioned "I don't particularly enjoy critical thinking but I know it is necessary to have this module". On the other side of the spectrum, a student commented that the "topics are boring and not fun to work through", while another concluded "I don't think it's a very useful module".

The rise of the internet and social media poses another threat to active critical citizenship: slacktivism. 'Slacktivism' is defined as activities that require little effort (such as online sharing, liking and reposting) and that are "more effective in making the participants feel good about themselves" than in making any tangible difference to the stated cause (Skoric, 2012: 77). This new form of youth activism does not pose significant financial or personal commitments or risks and "typically do not require the participants to confront socially entrenched norms and practices" (Skoric, 2012: 78). Skoric (2012: 83) contends that the benefits of slacktivism are that such campaigns can reach large audiences, maintain top-of-mind awareness and "lower the barriers to entry for participation". On the other hand, he raises a few valid concerns regarding the dangers of slacktivism, such as the fact that simplified online engagement "may divert people from helping the same cause in more productive ways" (Skoric, 2012: 85). Moreover, within an active citizenship module there should be concern about the lack of connection among the members of online social movements (Skoric, 2012), which affirms Waghid's (2004: 535–536) emphasis on "mutual respect, warmth, friendship, trust, self-respect, dignity, generosity and compassion" towards fellow citizens.

There are times when the task of critical citizenship education seems insurmountable. Is it even fully possible to instil in students "both a sense of self and of local history, and a connection to the kinds of knowledge that can enable them to understand the complexity of the global" (McMillan, 2015: n.p.)? This is not the type of subject matter that can be covered in a single course, by a single lecturer or even within a single year. The aim of this chapter is to inspire educators to see themselves as cogs in a greater cycle of education for life and to create safe spaces for open discussions in which students are provided with the opportunity to recognise imperial ideologies in their own context and where they are confronted with the impact of media representations on how they connect with people. The postmodern era has delivered spectacular achievements in technological innovation, which also pose a threat in that it could lead to denial of material reality and injustice (O'Shaughnessy & Stadler, 2012). Despite the fact that technology 'connects' us more than any preceding generation, we run the risk of neglecting deep, meaningful and empathetic relationships.

Teaching active citizenship

Active citizenship requires an understanding of the relationship between local and global issues. Each of us belong to a number of "overlapping communities" (from local to global), which exposes why current challenges "transcend national boundaries and will require multinational solutions" (Cogan & Kubow, 1997: 39). In the Active Citizenship module, current circulating case studies were used to stir up class discussions about the value of being rooted in a local culture in relation to globalisation and homogenisation (cf. Cogan & Kubow, 1997). The conversations were often complex, fragmented and roused mixed responses from my students. Some students and lecturers reacted in similar ways; reactions ranged from disinterest to passion, from anxiety to guilt and conflict and even understanding. These kinds of conversations are often taxing on both educator and student, but they can be immensely influential in the lives of students.

The case studies in the module ranged from election campaigns, blood drives, food banks and non-profit organisations to design, leadership and citizenship competitions such as Lead SA (www.leadsa.co.za) and Your Street (www.yourstreetchallenge.org). There were three case studies that particularly intrigued students and invited the most polarised responses. The first is the American Kony 2012 campaign that launched a short documentary film aiming to "make an obscure war criminal famous" (Invisible Children, 2014: n.p.). The documentary was viewed 100 million times in its first week, which made it the "fastest growing viral video of all time and resulted in unprecedented international action to end Africa's longest running conflict" (Invisible Children, 2014: n.p.). However, an ongoing debate continues as to whether the media hype of Kony 2012 is an accurate reflection of the impact it made on the 'invisible children', kidnapping and war in Uganda. Many lecturers found that students identified this campaign as a prime example of slacktivism because of its social media foundations, unprecedented following and controversial impact. This new form of youth activism is mainly based on social media presence and trends, but does not require financial or personal involvement, which often leads to unmet aims and destitute situations despite significant budgets, awareness and marketing (Skoric, 2012).

On the other hand, there were two case studies that gained students' respect across campuses, namely A21 and Unashamedly Ethical. A21 is a multinational non-profit organisation founded by Christine and Nick Caine, which "exists to abolish injustice in the 21st century" (A21, c2017: n.p.). A21 focuses on global human trafficking and its strategies include "raising awareness, preventing future trafficking, taking legal action, and providing rehabilitation services to survivors" (Caine, c2017: n.p.). Students in the Active Citizenship module commended A21 for its social media presence as well as its understanding of human trafficking as a multinational problem that requires multinational solutions (*cf.* Cogan & Kubow, 1997). Unashamedly Ethical is a South African anti-corruption organisation founded by Graham Power (Unashamedly Ethical, c2017). The organisation confronts "corruption and injustice through co-ordinated, targeted and impactful advocacy and campaigns to advance ethical behaviour" (Unashamedly Ethical, c2017: n.p.). Unashamedly Ethical has partnered with committed individuals and organisations globally "who support each other" and who are kept accountable "through an independent ombudsperson" (Unashamedly Ethical, c2017: n.p.). The Active Citizenship module relies on essay-based questions that require students to measure these, and other, organisations against the prescribed theories in the module (explained above) and many found that A21 and Unashamedly Ethical served as prime examples of most principles.

Lave and Wenger (1998: 2) remind educators that learning is not a task in which students participate, but a "set of relationships over time". This statement does not discredit reading articles, analysing case studies and completing worksheets, but these kinds of tasks are complemented with relational real-world situations. The situative framework of experiential learning holds that students can become role players in communities when they are exposed to real situations that contain "rich, multifaceted problems" for students to recognise and investigate (Fenwick, 2001: 52). In research on existing citizenship modules, two prominent ways in which citizenship can be activated was found. The first is through realistic ideation and problem solving, such as Design Indaba's Your Street Challenge, which encourages creatives and designers to think about urban challenges in new ways (Fell & De Villiers, 2012). While vast amounts of pressing issues shared on social media can make us feel powerlessness in the face of such immense suffering, Your Street challenges participants to start with "what is right in front of you: your street" (Fell & De Villiers, 2012: n.p.). Your Street provides an appropriate and practical platform on which the Active Citizenship module engages students in critical citizenship. Creativity can be used to improve people's lives and address the most pressing social needs around us (Fell & De Villiers, 2012).

Some of the reflective tasks and group activities in Active Citizenship module dare students to look beyond themselves and their lack of resources (time, money or skills) to recognise their own capacity (through compassion and generosity) to make a tangible difference in the lives of others. Social change starts with empathy and is driven by the willingness to serve with passion. It is for this reason that value was placed on the practical component of the module. However, this emphasis was not necessarily placed by other lecturers teaching the module on other campuses and this could be why some students perceived the module as lacking impact and purpose.

An ideal second activation of the Active Citizenship module would take the form of compulsory community service in engagement with under-served or marginalised people in partnership with an existing non-profit organisation. Educators as well as students should discover causes and people with which they connect on a personal level. This could include a wide range of activities such as assisting the elderly, developing literacy, helping with animal rescue, empowering people with disabilities or volunteering for a river clean-up.. A compulsory community service component has not yet been included in the module, but the Active Citizenship module can still lead students to discover their passions and interests and mobilise them to take the first step in that direction.

Critical citizenship education is complex, but not an unattainable process. One lecturer, class or subject cannot contain this topic. Nevertheless, educators could make an effort to introduce students to critical citizenship, expose them to citizenship theories and case studies and encourage them to practise critical citizenship. Creativity, compassion and the willingness to serve are powerful tools to improve people's lives and address the most pressing social needs around us.

Conclusion

Johnson and Morris (2010: 90) mention the willingness "to learn with others" as one of the key dispositions of critical citizenship. To my understanding, that does not only refer to students learning among one another, but also to educators learning with students and community workers learning with communities. Critical citizenship education uses practical reasoning as the building blocks of earnest affection, generosity and concern for others.

This chapter contains my experiences with critical citizenship education: from my master's degree, to research on citizenship modules and programmes, the development of an Active Citizenship module for Vega School and feedback by lecturers and students across multiple campuses and, finally, to my reflection on the experience. I believe that the ultimate goal of critical citizenship education is to activate citizenship: to prompt realistic ideation and problem solving and bridge the gap between theoretical compassion and practical implementation. My hope is that this collection of conversations on critical citizenship leads to reflection on one's place within communities, to develop independent critical thinking as well as collective critical thinking and to gain the courage to act on courageous convictions (*cf.* Johnson & Morris, 2010).

We inhabit this earth together and life truly resides in what we have in common, what we share and how we live together. Critical citizens develop the skill to "imagine a better world" (Johnson & Morris, 2010: 90).

References

A21. c2017. Available at www.a21.org [Accessed 24 January 2017].

Badat, S. 2016. *Deciphering the meanings, and explaining the South African higher education student protests of 2015–16.* Available at http://www.sahistory.org.za/archive/deciphering-meanings-and-explaining-south-african-higher-education-student-protests-2015-16 [Accessed 14 November 2016].

Bhattacharyya, J. 2004. Theorizing community development. *Journal of the Community Development Society,* 34(2), 5–34. https://doi.org/10.1080/15575330409490110

Caine, C. 2017. *A21.* Available at http://christinecaine.com/content/a21/gjqtnc [Accessed 24 January 2017].

Challenging Media. 2016. Representation & the media: Featuring Stuart Hall. *YouTube.* Available at https://www.youtube.com/watch?v=aTzMsPqssOY [Accessed 19 June 2016].

Cogan, J.J. & Kubow, P.K. 1997. *Multidimensional citizenship: Educational policy for the twenty-first century.* Final report of the citizenship education study project. Tokyo: Sasakawa Peace Foundation. Available at http://digitalcommons.unomaha.edu/cgi/viewcontent.cgi?article=1005&context=slceinternational [Accessed 15 March 2016].

Fell, S.J. & De Villiers, D. 2012. Breaking out of the silo and onto the street. *Design Indaba*, 12 September. Available at http://www.designindaba.com/articles/design-indaba-news/breaking-out-silo-and-street [Accessed 25 March 2016].

Fenwick, T. 2001. *Experiential learning: A theoretical critique from five perspectives.* Available at http://blackboard.liu.se/webapps/portal/frameset.jsp?tab=courses&url=/bin/common/course.pl?course_id=_1575_1 [Accessed 24 May 2014].

Greene, M. 1995a. Art and imagination: Reclaiming the sense of possibility. *The Phi Delta Kappan*, 76(5), 378–382.

Greene, M. 1995b. *Releasing the imagination.* San Francisco, CA: Jossey-Bass.

Greene, M. 2013. The turning of the leaves: Expanding our vision for the arts in education. *Harvard Educational Review*, 83(1), 251–253. https://doi.org/10.17763/haer.83.1.j3k4055083178g5k

Hall, S. 1997. *Representation and the media* [transcript]. Media Education Foundation. Available at http://www.mediaed.org/transcripts/Stuart-Hall-Representation-and-the-Media-Transcript.pdf [Accessed 15 March 2017].

Invisible Children. 2014. Available at https://invisiblechildren.com/kony-2012/ [Accessed 24 January 2017].

Johnson, L. & Morris, P. 2010. Towards a framework for critical citizenship education. *Curriculum Journal*, 21(1), 77–96. https://doi.org/10.1080/09585170903560444

Kony. 2012. Available at https://www.youtube.com/watch?v=Y4MnpzG5Sqc [Accessed 1 February 2018].

Lave, J. & Wenger, E. 1998. *Communities of practice.* Available at http://199.87.225.219/facultydevelopment/tla/documents/CommunityofPractice.pdf [Accessed 24 May 2014].

Matola, M.M. 2014. *Active citizenship and its role in changing the South African brand reality.* Available at www.sanews.gov.za/features/active-citizenship-and-its-role-changing-south-african-brand-reality [Accessed 14 December 2016].

McMillan, J. 2015. Developing civic-minded university graduates. *University World News*. Available at http://www.universityworldnews.com/article.php?story=20150121144528579 [Accessed 25 March 2016].

O'Shaughnessy, M. & Stadler, J. 2012. *Media and society.* Fifth edition. Oxford: Oxford University Press.

Skoric, M.M. 2012. What is slack about slacktivism? *Methodological and Conceptual Issues in Cyber Activism Research.* Singapore: National University of Singapore, 7, 77–92.

Unashamedly Ethical. c2017. *About us.* Available at http://unashamedlyethical.com/about-3/ [Accessed 24 January 2017].

Vega School. N.d. *Who we are.* Available at https://www.vegaschool.com/Pages/About-Us.aspx [Accessed 6 February 2018].

Waghid, Y. 2004. Compassion, citizenship and education in South Africa: An opportunity for transformation? *International Review of Education*, 50(5/6), 525–542. https://doi.org/10.1007/s11159-004-4638-3

Lessons on Critical Citizenship from a 'Non-citizen'

AMOLLO AMBOLE

Introduction

Traditionally, the design profession has been associated with the promotion of wanton consumerism. And rightfully so, given the fact that designers are taught to make products and services attractive enough to seduce consumers into buying them. As Papanek (1984: ix) describes it: "Never before in history have grown men sat down and seriously designed electric hairbrushes, rhinestone-covered file boxes, and mink carpeting for bathrooms, and then drawn up elaborate plans to make and sell these gadgets to millions of people."

However, this is not the whole truth about design; there are designers who promote responsible consumerism by using design methods to bring about social change. For example, Manzini (2014: n.p.) has for many years promoted design for social innovation by insisting that "designers have to facilitate the convergence of different partners toward shared ideas and potential solutions". In the same vein, other designers have promoted design as a method for achieving solutions towards environmental and social sustainability (Cipolla & Bartholo, 2014; Vezzoli, Delfino & Ambole, 2014). To do this effectively, these designers have to be critical and question their own design profession. This is no easy task, because it involves challenging the consumerist approaches that are the very foundation of today's unjust capitalist systems.

In this chapter, I challenge unjust systems by first exposing how I have benefitted and suffered from such structures. I see this as a necessary step towards questioning other people's position; very much like removing the proverbial plank in my own eye, before pointing out the speck in someone else's.

Am I a critical citizen?

Critical citizenship is a concept with which I have dealt for a long time without even knowing I was doing so. Let me start from the beginning. Or rather, a beginning that is of interest to the topic at hand. I, at the age of 32, having lived and worked all my life in Kenya, became restless and started

173

looking for a university abroad at which to do my PhD. Naturally, I turned to the internet and pored through webpage after webpage of scholarship offers. I also wrote to a number of professors I found online, asking them if I could study with them. Most did not reply to my e-mails, but I did get a reply from the Department of Visual Arts at Stellenbosch University. This was encouraging and it piqued my interest in Stellenbosch, even though at the time I could not possibly afford the finances needed to support my studies there.

Eventually, I did end up at Stellenbosch University, but not in the Department of Visual Arts; as fate would have it, I joined the School of Public Leadership instead, because my scholarship terms required that I register at that school. Even though both my undergraduate and my master's degrees were in design, I was excited about the prospects of expanding my design research by working on development and sustainability issues at the School of Public Leadership. This is the opportunity that my scholarship, titled Transdisciplinary Training for Resource Efficiency and Climate Change Adaptation in Africa (TRECCAfrica), offered me.

In hindsight, I was setting myself up for a big challenge by doing a PhD in public and development management instead of in design or art, which is was what I was familiar with. The scholarship terms further required me to relocate to South Africa and reside in Stellenbosch for up to four years. These major changes in my research, and life as a whole, opened up new opportunities and challenges as well.

The challenges I faced during my stay at Stellenbosch and in doing my PhD led me to critically look at my research and consider my position as a foreigner and a researcher. In doing so, I became a critical citizen able to analyse my own position and context, with the aim of contributing to "changing structures, assumptions, identities, attitudes and power relations" (De Andreotti, 2014: n.p.). In this chapter, I take a look back at my research experience, which at the time seemed to be constantly falling apart, thereby turning me to deep introspection, which is what eventually helped me to complete my studies successfully.

The first unique attribute about my story is my 'outsiderness', given that I am not a South African. My three-year stint at Stellenbosch does not qualify me as an expert on the complex South African condition that is strongly shaped by racial identities. I am therefore a foreigner looking in. A second unique attribute of my story is my 'blackness', which allowed me to find resonance with the post-apartheid black consciousness that is so pervasive in Stellenbosch – a consciousness that allowed me some limited degree of 'insiderness' and identification with the social injustices and racial inequalities that are still so rife in South Africa.

This insider–outsider complexity grants me the self-reflexivity to define my "understandings, specific positions, and approaches" (Gentles, Jack, Nicholas & McKibbon, 2014: n.p.) with the hope that I will encourage design students and their teachers to critically reflect on how research roles and duties help to perpetuate or change unjust systems. As affirmed by De Andreotti (2014), critical citizenship is about changing the status quo from the inside to the outside, not the other way round.

Context: The South African condition

I have already issued a caveat that I am no expert on matters South African. So, I will provide an incomplete picture, like someone looking into a vast room through a key hole. I take courage, though, in the belief that "all knowledge is partial and incomplete" (De Andreotti, 2006: 49), as we construct it in our contexts, cultures and experiences. More importantly, acknowledging incompleteness offers the flexibility and agility to change when we are presented with new knowledge (Ambole, Swilling & M'Rithaa, 2016). So, it might be that years from now, others will poke holes into my account of South Africa; an outcome that is quite acceptable and even welcome in the scholarly quest for refined knowledge.

South Africa is a vast, beautiful country with a serious inequality problem. Nowhere is this inequality more stark than in urban settlement patterns that are still defined by the segregationist planning approaches of the apartheid government: Poor, inadequately serviced informal settlements are inhabited mostly by black people, while most white people live in rich, well-serviced neighbourhoods (Groenewald, Huchzermeyer, Kornienko, Tredoux, Rubin & Raposo, 2013). This is no different in the town of Stellenbosch, which is in fact regarded as the birthplace of apartheid. More specifically, Stellenbosch University, having been established in 1874 and being the oldest Afrikaans-language university in South Africa, is considered as the "bedrock for the formulation of the policy of apartheid" (Fransman, 2015: n.p.).

During my stay in Stellenbosch, thanks to my scholarship, I was able to live in a well-serviced neighbourhood and enjoyed the elitist lifestyle of wine tasting and fine food for which Stellenbosch is well known. In the beginning, I justified my privilege as a result of my own hard work and ingenuity, which had led me to win a prestigious scholarship. Such justification is what De Andreotti (2014) refers to as 'soft citizenship', in which privilege is seen as a result of one's own effort and resourcefulness. However, with time, I acknowledged that I was (in ways that I am not fully aware of, even now) a beneficiary of an unjust system that had favoured my position.

That unjust system was driven by hegemonic Western financial systems, which funded my scholarship through several layers of funding platforms. Specifically, I received my scholarship through my university in Kenya, which was part of a consortium of African universities that were funded by the Intra-ACP mobility programme. The Intra-ACP is in turn funded with support from the European Commission. The aim of Intra-ACP is to promote exchanges between higher education institutions in Africa, the Caribbean and the Pacific.

These funding platforms are not too dissimilar from the ancestral generations that shield white South Africans from the violent unjust systems that bequeathed them their wealth and privilege; they have no lived memory of the violence, just as I have no lived memory of the oppressive economic structures of the West that bequeathed me my scholarship. Similarly, there are many black South Africans who now enjoy privileges that can easily be traced back to an unjust apartheid system. In this regard, there are those who accuse the current ANC government that has ruled post-apartheid South Africa since 1994 of perpetuating a neo-apartheid system.

What this means is that even though inequality (in South Africa and in the world in general) has so far had racial dimensions, it is not enough to 'redistribute' wealth to black people. There has to be a concerted and continual effort to challenge power relations between the haves and have nots. In my own small way, I am challenging those relations by questioning my own position of privilege, which resulted in feelings of guilt, internal conflict and helplessness. These problems are described as potential results of becoming a critical citizen (De Andreotti, 2014). In the same way, Costandius and Rosochacki (2012) describe the guilt that some of their white students from Stellenbosch University reported feeling during their community engagement with black secondary school learners from Kayamandi township, a formal settlement that is adjacent to Enkanini informal settlement, where I carried out my research. Despite my growing feeling of guilt over my scholarship that privileged me over others, I took full advantage of it and made the best of my stay in Stellenbosch.

Co-production: Enkanini informal settlement, Stellenbosch

In early 2011, a group of Stellenbosch University postgraduate students from the School of Public Leadership started a community-engagement research process in Enkanini. I joined this group in late 2012. Enkanini is a poorly serviced informal settlement with a population of over 4 000 residents sharing 80 communal toilet blocks and a few water points. Most houses in the settlement are self-built shacks made of corrugated iron sheets supported by wooden frames. A large part of the settlement is unelectrified, so most residents use candles and kerosene lamps to light their homes. A few residents connect illegally to the electricity grid (Ambole, 2016; Wessels, 2015).

Our general aim in engaging with Enkanini residents was to co-produce infrastructure interventions. Indeed, we managed to co-produce three pilot interventions on sanitation (in which I was directly involved) as well as on waste management and household energy (Keller, 2012; Von der Heyde, 2014). An early reflection on the pilot interventions led to the articulation of the concept of incremental urbanism as a "tentative framework for initiating micro-scale actions towards larger-scale, longer-term upgrading objectives" (Swilling, Tavener-Smith, Keller, Von der Heyde & Wessels, 2013: n.p).

The unplanned and fragmented development of informal settlements lends itself to an incremental upgrading approach: Through incremental processes, informal settlement residents can participate in the building of their own settlement. The challenge here is in providing public services, such as sanitation, that traditionally require large-scale technical installations, and are therefore difficult to provide in a fragmented approach.

Service co-production

The incremental provision of infrastructure in informal settlements is anchored on community participation. In Brazil, the involvement of informal settlement dwellers in providing sanitation in the informal settlements (favelas) is taken for granted by practitioners (Nance, 2013). Unlike other civil engineers, the engineers working in favelas see participation in sanitation as a necessity in condominial sewerage construction. Condominial systems use smaller pipes that can be installed in shallow sewers in existing settlements, precluding the need for massive excavations or relocations. As such, condominial sewerage can be installed using a fragmented approach. The successes of condominial sewerage in Brazil is attributed largely to user participation (Nance, 2013). Critics of this kind of community participation argue that it can become coercive (Bartram, Charles, Evans, O'Hanlon & Pedley, 2012) or entrench negative relations of patronage and brokerage that are rife in informal settlements (De Wit & Berner, 2009).

Such participation also begs the question as to why informal settlement dwellers should be burdened with the responsibilities of the state, yet other residents in formal areas are provided with such services, often at a very affordable price. The reality, though, is that states, mostly in the global South, have not delivered adequate services to many of their citizens, hence the need to find alternative means to provide these essential services to informal settlement dwellers. Participation as an alternative means for delivering services can further become an opportunity for community members to empower themselves and gain political influence (Mitlin, 2008). As such, co-producing interventions in informal settlements is not merely about providing affordable technology; it is a complex socio-technical process.

Co-producing the social with the technical

In our research on sanitation in Enkanini, we proposed a low-cost, low-flush technology that, on paper, could easily be installed in phases in selected parts of the settlement. The installation of the technology was to be funded through the National Research Foundation of South Africa and the Water Research Commission of South Africa.

The installation of the sanitation system took place in early 2013 and included five shared pour-flush toilets connected to an anaerobic digester via simplified sewerage, installed in Section E of Enkanini. Following the installation, we, the researchers, facilitated the formation of a co-operative by five Enkanini co-researchers who were also users of the installed toilets. The idea was that the co-operative would manage the toilets by collecting charges from 20 users for the maintenance and repair of the toilets. Such co-operatives are common in informal settlements in Kenya and Pakistan (Ambole, 2016).

Initially, the users agreed to pay for the convenience of a toilet near their homes, as opposed to using free municipality toilets that were far from their homes. However, a large number of users later declined to participate in the intervention because they did not want to continue making payments. The sanitation co-operative we helped form also failed and was disbanded in 2014 over serious financial disagreements between the researchers and the co-researchers. So, despite having provided a seemingly sound technology, our research group was unable to deliver a long-term social solution to the sanitation challenge in Enkanini.

Knowledge co-production?

Apart from the sanitation technology installed in Enkanini, we also intended to co-produce social knowledge with Enkanini residents. In my own capacity as a researcher, I did produce knowledge, but it would be presumptuous to say that it is knowledge that is socially relevant to an Enkanini resident.

From my research, I was able to publish one journal article focusing on my role as a design ethnographer in the Enkanini case. My aim in that role was to provide …

> … an alternative design narrative, in which the designer participates in a multidisciplinary process and therefore has to take on other roles (as a design ethnographer); has to be flexible and agile in order to contribute to the technological and social innovation objectives of complex collaborative undertakings; and has to cede control over the design process. Other complex problems facing the world today could benefit from such an open-ended, flexible design approach. (Ambole et al., 2016: 83)

The open-endedness for which we advocate in the paper cited above resonates closely with the call for a commitment towards diversity while also searching for shared values; meaning that we need to acknowledge our differences in our quest to find some shared space where we can co-produce better futures.

I must admit, though, that my publication was largely for my own benefit as an academic. As argued by Beebeejaun, Durose, Rees, Richardson and Richardson (2014: n.p.), researchers and the researched are indeed "distinct groups with competing claims to knowledge", which results in power asymmetries that are visible in the embedded knowledge hierarchy of the expert versus the layperson. Nevertheless, efforts have to be made to challenge these asymmetries in the quest for democratic knowledge (Beebeejaun et al., 2014). To remedy this asymmetry, I am currently pursuing options of how to co-publish non-academic outputs such as community-produced maps, prototypes and films in my future research. By co-publishing these outputs with community members, the co-produced knowledge will be rightfully attributed to all those who own it.

Voice

The importance of voice is in its expression of power: Those who have a voice feel empowered because their concerns can be taken care of (Evans, 2007). In community research with disadvantaged groups, researchers tend to have a privileged voice, especially in processes that are researcher-driven. Consequently, there are greater calls for participatory processes that enhance marginalised voices in research (Beebeejaun et al., 2014). For my study in Enkanini, I became interested in voice when it became increasingly obvious that we researchers had a dominant voice in the sanitation intervention. It is important to question voice, because along with notions of power and difference, voice is central for critical citizenship education (De Andreotti, 2006).

Text-based language

One focus group discussion (FGD) that I organised in October 2013 was particularly interesting, as it brought to the fore the advantaged voice of researchers over that of Enkanini residents. The residents present in this FGD were contracted as co-researchers and had worked in the sanitation intervention for a couple of months at the time. The intention of the discussion was to deliberate on a brief for a short film that would showcase the sanitation intervention and its achievements and possibly attract further funding for the intervention. As such, the researchers were keen to articulate the direness of the sanitation situation in Enkanini, as demonstrated by the following statements by two researchers during the discussion:

> Researcher A: … 85% of households are still using buckets at night, for its safety reasons, and during the day about 60% of households are still using buckets for convenience reasons.

> Researcher B: There's 72 people per toilet, but that's not taking into account whether it's working, whether it's overflowing …

The Enkanini co-researchers, on the other hand, were not able to articulate the sanitation story, yet it is they who experienced it on a daily basis. During the discussion, they often veered off topic and referred to other challenges in Enkanini, such as healthcare and housing:

> Enkanini co-researcher 1: In Enkanini the real issue was the first issue of the toilet because we still need even the clinics here, mhm, we still need even the housing …

By expressing other concerns beyond the sanitation issue, the co-researchers were providing a more nuanced and holistic view of Enkanini's challenges, while the researchers rigidly stuck to their specific research focus on sanitation. Researchers also tended to dominate the conversation, which was conducted not only in English, but also in an academic approach that was an advantage to the researchers. In this regard, the language and tone of the FGD were not conducive to active engagement between the academic and non-academic participants (Ambole, 2016). As the facilitator of the FGD, I take responsibility for reproducing the rift between science and society in my quest to fulfil my research objectives.

Beyond-text language

A more engaging approach was in the drawing exercises I used in other FGDs to elicit ideas from the participants. Drawing provided symbolism, thereby offering metaphors for discussing the sensitive issue of sanitation (Figure 1). Drawing further challenged our dominant form of expression as researchers in a way that opened opportunities for shifting power relationships and possibly stimulating a change of ethos (Beebeejaun et al., 2014).

In my thematic analyses of the drawings produced by Enkanini residents, I found rich evidence of their in-depth understanding, which I was not able to capture in conversations with residents. For example, residents expressed gendered perspectives (of women as primary caregivers in the household) and Xhosa belief systems (about the proper disposal of used bath water) in their depiction of water use (Ambole, 2016). The drawings therefore helped the participants to articulate their individual perspectives without necessarily using rational argumentation methods. In the ensuing reviews of their drawings, the discussions were enriched, as the drawings served the role of boundary objects (cf. Gibbons, 2005).

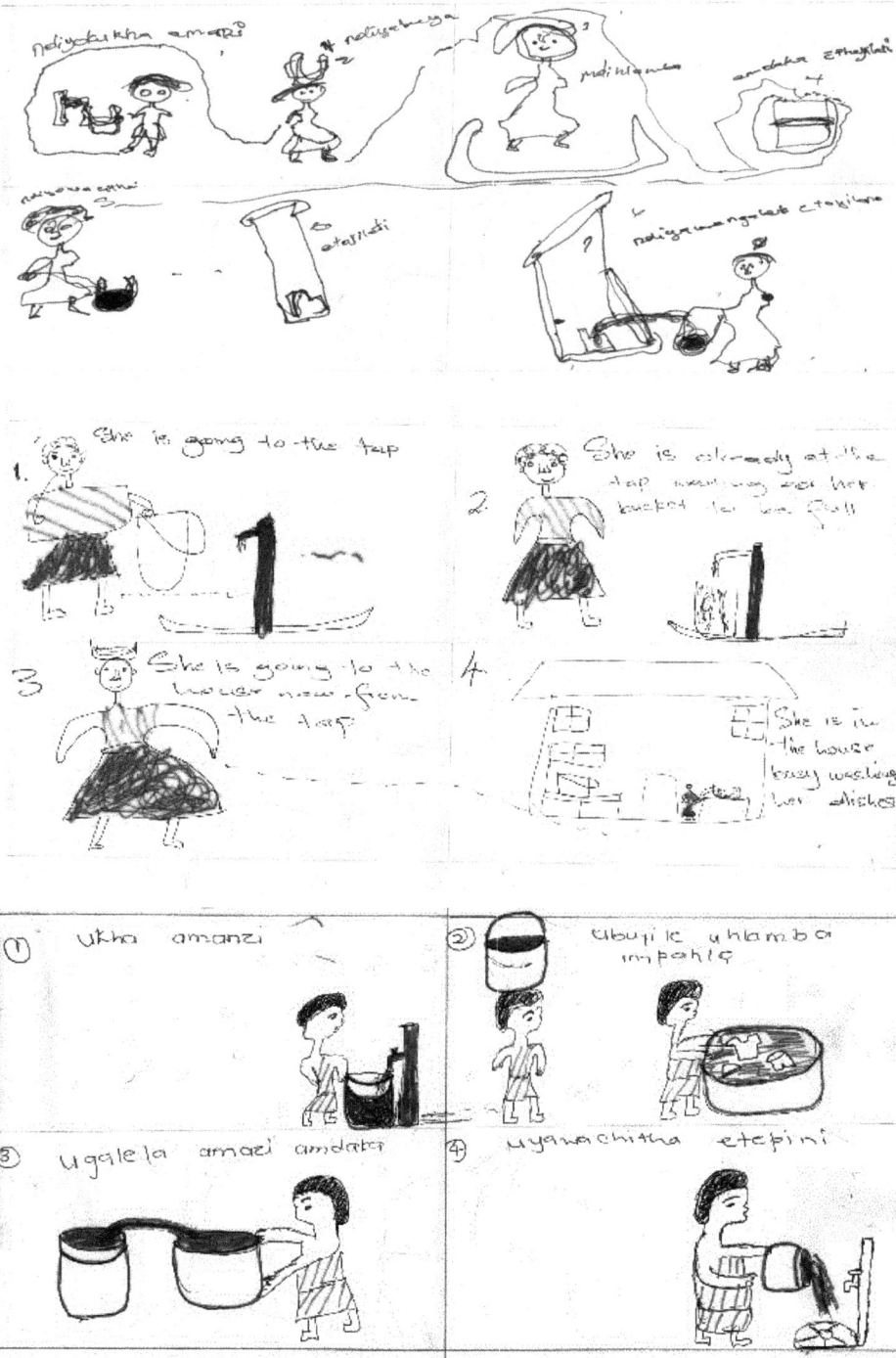

Figure 1   Cartoon strip drawings by Enkanini residents participating in the FGD

Voice translations and filters

Interestingly, the resulting film from the FGD film brief does not depict the contentions I identified in the FGD. Titled "Enkanini Sanitation Co-op",[1] the film provides a fair representation of the co-researchers' voices, who clearly articulated the sanitation problem in the settlement. Such clarity in the four-minute film was achieved through professional editing techniques that mask the messy production process of the actual filming, which took several hours.

Similarly, a more comprehensive film on our work in Enkanini[2] shows cleverly produced snippets of our work that are pieced together to tell an endearing three-minute story. The finesse of the film gives me chills, because I now take the position of the 'subject'; my one-hour interview, which I fumbled through, is reduced to the best few minutes of the conversation. The chills I get from this short film come from my discomfort in being 'cleaned up'.

In a longer version of the film,[3] I comment on my discomfort with being associated with white researchers by being referred to as *abelungu* (white people) along with the other researchers during a visit to the settlement. This comment is juxtaposed with that of another researcher, who admits that white researchers are often seen as leeches who come into the community to fulfil selfish ends. The two comments, though negative, come off as positive by showing that we are self-aware researchers.

During a viewing of the film in a workshop I attended recently, a Xhosa-speaking researcher asked why we mistranslated the word 'Enkanini' as meaning 'Taken by force' and even used it as the title of the film. In the film, I further reinforced this error by confidently voicing that Enkanini means 'Taken by force', in reference to the invasion of the land by residents from the neighbouring Kayamandi. Google Translator translates Enkanini as 'The stubbornness', as was confirmed by the Xhosa researcher in question. The bone of contention for me is that we, as researchers in a well-resourced university, did not bother to get an accurate translation. For the most part, we in fact relied on Enkanini co-researchers to provide translations, as we engaged in Enkanini on too regular a basis to afford a professional interpreter at all times. In the very least, though, we should have ensured that we use the correct translation of the word 'Enkanini'. Our poor translations pointed to a bigger problem, which was that our community-engagement research did not have any Xhosa-speaking researchers who would have been able to better translate not just the Xhosa language, but also our research concepts.

The two films are therefore, in many ways, a depiction of how messy research processes are filtered through analysis methods to arrive at 'clean' findings. In addition, it is a depiction of how participants' voices can be framed to fit into research or project agendas. As argued by Max-Neef (2005), scientists have a tendency to reduce their findings to rationalistic approximations that hide the intuitive and often messy process they used to arrive at those findings.

---

[1] Enkanini Sanitation Co-op: https://vimeo.com/103213666
[2] Enkanini: Taken by Force (short version): https://vimeo.com/164426384
[3] Enkanini: Taken by Force: https://vimeo.com/164419981

Reflection

As the contentions between researchers and co-researchers unfolded in the sanitation intervention, I found it increasingly difficult to write up my thesis. I wanted to write about all the problems that we were facing, but, as I was part of the problem, I was not able to see the theoretical significance of the work that we were doing. To make it worse, I found little support within the research group because the engaged approach of our research weighed heavily on all of us. I felt very much like one of Costandius and Rosochacki's (2012: n.p.) undergraduate students who reported that their work in the township made them feel like a tourist exploring and judging a foreign country "without the adequate knowledge to do so". The irony was that as a PhD researcher, I was supposed to be knowledgeable or at least capable of finding the knowledge I lacked.

The easy way out would be to avoid doing community-engagement research in the first place. But then that would preclude any form of meaningful dialogue between diverse worldviews. What is required therefore is a search for knowledge production and a strong learning component to ensure that students are not merely doing charity work, or worse still, falling into crises with which they cannot deal (Costandius & Rosochacki, 2012).

In my case, I later found motivation to work through my personal crises by talking about my research experiences. In this regard, I presented my preliminary findings at several international conferences and research workshops. These settings outside of the Enkanini research context provided me with a chance for reflection and for finding theoretical significance in my work. More importantly, I received critical feedback from a wide range of scholars.

Self-reflexivity or self-indulgence?

I have used an active voice in this chapter in order to articulate my agency in my PhD research process, as opposed to merely being an observer. My aim therefore in this chapter was to highlight my positionality by critiquing my race, citizenship and personal experiences in South Africa, while also pointing to my theoretical and ideological stance. I take cues from researchers such as Berger (2015), who uses an active voice to express the movement from the position of an outsider to an insider during the course of study. To demonstrate her insiderness, Berger reflects on her personal experience as a remarried woman and immigrant conducting research on migration and remarriage. Alternatively, she demonstrates her outsiderness by reflecting on research with legal representatives whose situation was not relatable to her own (Berger, 2015).

Berger (2015) further asserts that research is never free of the biases, assumptions and personality of the researcher. Reflexivity therefore allows researchers to acknowledge that their decisions and actions have an impact on the meaning and context of the investigation. Nevertheless, there is need for "balance between [a] researcher's own experience and that of the participants" (Berger, 2015: n.p.). This can be achieved by using logs and repeated reviews and seeking peer consultation. In keeping logs, for example, the researcher should record conversations verbatim as well as document the interpretations of those conversations. These entries can then be reviewed later to offer a new lens and identify researcher influences. Identifying one's own influence in research makes it possible to avoid "a patronizing stance and [to maximise] the opportunity for participants to impact the process and outcome of research" (Berger, 2015: n.p.).

So, while it may appear to have been self-indulgent of me to talk about myself in this chapter, it was in fact humbling, because I exposed my vulnerability in my research. Exposing oneself in this way is a rewarding experience, because it opens opportunity for learning (Gersema, 2015). It also opens opportunities for further dialogue on the issues I have raised concerning my research experience. For example, it would be research-worthy to further explore ways to either revive the Enkanini sanitation co-operative, or to find another socially innovative model of self-management by Enkanini residents.

Conclusion

My intention was in no way to disparage any of the other researchers or participants in the research, because, just like me, they faced challenges and had to find ways of dealing with them. Neither did I intend to belittle the privileges accorded to me that have enabled me to rise to my current position in life. In the same vein, I do not expect other privileged persons to blindly give up their positions in life. Critical citizenship, however, demands of them, as of me, that we be mindful and continue searching for ways to change the unjust systems around us. This of course starts by first identifying such systems. In this chapter, I have pointed at the skewed economies of the West that support exclusionary funding platforms such as the one from which I benefitted. A more vivid example of an unjust system is the apartheid system of governance (and vestiges of it) in South Africa. By identifying ourselves with such systems we can change them from the inside out. More importantly, underprivileged persons have a role to play in co-creating spaces where their voices can be heard so that their rights as citizens are addressed.

References

Ambole, L.A. 2016. Understanding co-production through sanitation intervention case studies in South Africa. PhD dissertation. Stellenbosch: Stellenbosch University.

Ambole, L.A., Swilling, M. & M'Rithaa, M.K. 2016. Designing for informal contexts: A case study of Enkanini sanitation intervention. *International Journal of Design*, 10(3), 75–84.

Bartram, J., Charles, K., Evans, B., O'Hanlon, L. & Pedley, S. 2012. Commentary on community-led total sanitation and human rights: Should the right to community-wide health be won at the cost of individual rights? *Journal of Water and Health*, 10(4), 499–503. https://doi.org/10.2166/wh.2012.205

Beebeejaun, Y., Durose, C., Rees, J., Richardson, J. & Richardson, L. 2014. 'Beyond text': Exploring ethos and method in co-producing research with communities. *Community Development Journal*, 49(1), 37–53. https://doi.org/10.1093/cdj/bst008

Berger, R. 2015. Now I see it, now I don't: Researcher's position and reflexivity in qualitative research. *Qualitative Research*, 15(2), 219–234. https://doi.org/10.1177/1468794112468475

Cipolla, C. & Bartholo, R. 2014. Empathy or inclusion: A dialogical approach to socially responsible design. *International Journal of Design*, 8(2), 87–100.

Costandius, E. & Rosochacki, S. 2012. Educating for a plural democracy and citizenship: A report on practice. *Perspectives in Education*, 30(3), 13–20.

De Andreotti, V.O. 2006. Soft versus critical global citizenship education. *Policy & Practice: A Development Education Review*, 3, 40–51.

De Wit, J. & Berner, E. 2009. Progressive patronage? Municipalities, NGOs, CBOs and the limits to slum dwellers' empowerment. *Development and Change*, 40(5), 927–947. https://doi.org/10.1111/j.1467-7660.2009.01589.x

Evans, S.D. 2007. Youth sense of community: Voice and power in community contexts. *Journal of Community Psychology*, 35(6), 693–709. https://doi.org/10.1002/jcop.20173

Fransman, M. 2015. Stellenbosch was bedrock of apartheid. *Politicsweb*. Available at http://www.politicsweb.co.za/politics/stellenbosch-was-bedrock-of-apartheid--marius-fran [Accessed 18 February 2017].

Gentles, S.J., Jack, S.M., Nicholas, D.B. & McKibbon, K. 2014. Critical approach to reflexivity in grounded theory. *The Qualitative Report*, 19(44), 1–14.

Gersema, E. 2015. How to reap the rewards of failure. *USC News*. Available at https://news.usc.edu/85448/how-to-reap-the-rewards-of-failure/ [Accessed 18 February 2017].

Gibbons, M. 2005. Engagement with the community: The emergence of a new social contract between society and science. Paper presented at the Griffith University Community Engagement Workshop, 4 March, South Bank campus, Queensland.

Groenewald, L., Huchzermeyer, M., Kornienko, K., Tredoux, M., Rubin, M. & Raposo, I. 2013. Breaking down the binary: Meanings of informal settlements in southern African cities. In: S. Bekker & L. Fourchard (Eds.). *Governing cities in Africa: Politics and policies*. Cape Town: HSRC Press, 93–115.

Keller, A. 2012. Conceptualising a sustainable energy solution for in situ informal settlement upgrading. MA thesis. Stellenbosch: Stellenbosch University.

Manzini, E. 2014. Making things happen: Social innovation and design. *Design Issues*, 30(1), 57–66. https://doi.org/10.1162/DESI_a_00248

Max-Neef, M.A. 2005. Foundations of transdisciplinarity. *Ecological Economics*, 53(1), 5–16. https://doi.org/10.1016/j.ecolecon.2005.01.014

Mitlin, D. 2008. With and beyond the state: Co-production as a route to political influence, power and transformation for grassroots organizations. *Environment and Urbanization*, 20(2), 339–360. https://doi.org/10.1177/0956247808096117

Nance, E. 2013. *Engineers and communities: Transforming sanitation in contemporary Brazil*. Plymouth: Lexington Books.

Papanek, V. 1984. *Design for the real world: Human ecology and social change*. Second edition. Chicago, IL: Academy Chicago.

Swilling, M., Tavener-Smith, L., Keller, A., Von der Heyde, V. & Wessels, B. 2013. *Rethinking incremental urbanism: Co-production of incremental informal settlement upgrading strategies. Pursuing partnership-based approaches to incremental upgrading in South Africa*. Johannesburg: Jacana.

Vezzoli, C., Delfino, E. & Ambole, L.A. 2014. System design for sustainable energy for all: A new challenging role for design to foster sustainable development. *FORMakademisk*, 7(3), 1–27. https://doi.org/10-7577/formakademisk.791

Von der Heyde, V. 2014. Towards a sustainable incremental waste management system in Enkanini: A transdisciplinary case study. MA thesis. Stellenbosch: Stellenbosch University.

Wessels, B.S. 2015. Turning points: Exploring power transitions in an incremental upgrading process in Enkanini, Stellenbosch. MA thesis. Stellenbosch: Stellenbosch University.

Design and its Education in 'Post' South African Society: A Way Forward

11

KAROLIEN PEROLD-BULL

Introduction

In the context of South Africa, transformation is a loaded concept. During the aftermath of apartheid, it has come to signify the change necessary to right the wrongs of the past. Despite the extreme complexity involved in the negotiation of this kind of change, the dominant transformation discourse seems to rely on dualistic logic. The popular belief seems to be that the inequality spawned by colonialism and consequent apartheid can be remedied by humans' strategic plans and interventions to ensure social justice in South African society. As argued by Max Price and Russell Ally, transformation is predominantly "about reconciliation, redress, affirmative action to achieve equity, academic support programmes to counter the effects of schooling deficits and ultimately the incorporation of those previously disadvantaged into the economic and power structures of society" (2016: n.p.). Within this ideological frame of reference, the notion of critical citizenship, i.e. the ability of humans to take part in everyday life based on a "common set of shared values (e.g. tolerance, human rights and democracy)" (Johnson & Morris, 2010: 77–78), has gained strength, and education considered as a process of emancipation driven by humans has been dominantly regarded as an effective medium to help drive the realisation of democratic ideals.

Critical citizenship education has been implemented in a variety of forms in South African educational curricula since the end of apartheid in 1994. The past two years' student protests[1] at South African higher education institutions have, however, made it clear that the ideals of social justice embodied by critical citizenship education seem to remain but a utopian vision in the distant

---

[1]   Throughout the course of 2015 and 2016, fallism has gained strength as a formal ideological construct. It has been described as "an institutional critique against the residue of the colonial and neo-colonial order" (Kasibe, 2015: n.p.). Examples of activist movements adhering to the philosophy of fallism include #RhodesMustFall at the University of Cape Town, #StelliesMustFall at Stellenbosch University as well as #FeesMustFall and #EndOutsourcing on a national level.

future. Despite numerous attempts towards transformation, for many the everyday experiences of higher education in South Africa remain a struggle fuelled by difference and opposition (Murris, 2016; Shay & Peseta, 2016). This seems to indicate that our approach to and methods in negotiating change have not been effective in producing the desired results. It would seem that working towards productive change from an individualised perspective of problem solving, that is, with the same logic that bred difference in the past, is counterproductive. It would seem that we need a different logic to think with.

In contrast to the linear, teleological interpretation of transformation related above, Rosi Braidotti (2011), in using the ideas of Gilles Deleuze and Félix Guattari, argues that any process of affirmative change necessitates a process of disidentification. Instead of thinking and acting from rationally predetermined perspectives privileging human agency, transformation "involve[s] a radical repositioning on the part of the knowing subject" (Braidotti, 2011: n.p.). Such a disidentification implies the creation of neither a single counter-identity (as modernists would have had it), nor a multitude of equally valid counter-identities (as postmodernists would have supposed) (Dolphijn & Van der Tuin, 2012), but rather attempts to simultaneously acknowledge and resist that which is given, thereby "push[ing] towards qualitatively stronger de-territorializations" (Dolphijn & Van der Tuin, 2012: 99). Transformation, so understood, can only sprout from the active acknowledgement of the mutual dependence of all beings – human, animal and earth – on one another (Braidotti, 2013). It is therefore through acknowledgement of our posthuman condition, Braidotti (2013) argues, that productive change can flow.

This chapter will consequently aim to provide a theoretical exploration of the notion of design and its concomitant education from posthuman perspectives. I will argue for an ontological shift in terms of how we think about design, how we do design and how we ultimately negotiate design in the realm of education. In this way, I hope to challenge and extend the anthropocentric tendencies within the notion of critical citizenship education and propose a theoretical foundation for a possible way forward in the field of South African design education.

Thinking about design ontologically

According to Arturo Escobar, "every tool and technology is ontological is the sense that, however humbly or minutely, it inaugurates a set of rituals, ways of doing, and modes of being" (2012: 35). In this sense, it can be argued that "the designed [always] goes on designing" (Willis, 2006: 93). Ontological design, then, functions in circular fashion: We encounter the designed in the world, we use it and make it our own, and then, in our use of it, we change and adapt it to be encountered in turn (Willis, 2006). One could argue that ontological design has therefore brought humanity to where it currently is, and, as we are all aware, cultural and political conflict as well as impeding environmental disaster is a harsh reality. Given the circularity of ontological design one can, however, simultaneously argue that ontological design also holds the power to affect some kind of positive future change. In this section I will map the working of the power of design understood ontologically by critically taking the local historical context of South Africa, as well as the global context into account. This will be done in order to provide insight into a relevant theoretical foundation for South African design in its current form.

One could argue that colonialists, in bringing the technologies of industrial Europe to Africa, ontologically designed South Africa in their image through processes of actualisation (Deleuze & Guattari, 1987). The actual should here be understood as constituting the realm where latent potential – that is possibility for change (or what Deleuze and Guattari refer to as the virtual) – is momentarily stopped in its tracks, resulting in the materialisation of "functional structures or substances" (Bonta & Protevi, 2004: 49) whose properties, in turn, become "the object of representational thought [but] occlude the intensities which gave rise to them" (Bonta & Protevi, 2004: 101). Actualisation therefore constitutes "the (problematic and problematising) relationship between what is and what could be" (Brassett & Marenko, 2015: 18), while representation, although an active part of the process, keeps us from gaining access to the immanent properties that could result in any form of qualitative change, that is, any form of true innovation and/or creation (Bonta & Protevi, 2004). Through the difficult process of doing and thinking the unknown, what has not been doable and thinkable before can therefore come into being. It would hence seem that, in this light, design not simply embodies processes of problem solving. Even problem finding would seem to limit its scope. Thinking of design as "possibility creation" (Brassett & Marenko, 2015: 20) is perhaps more apt.

Given the value tied to concrete form – its embodiment of objectivity and truth – within the humanism that characterised colonialism and consequent apartheid in South Africa, the notion of design, however, came to be strongly associated with the representational fields of industrial and visual communication or graphic design. Whereas, as briefly touched on earlier, representation most certainly forms part of design, design – understood as a process of actualisation – is not wholly representational (Escobar, 2012). Taking this aspect of design into consideration, it could therefore be argued that graphic design during colonial and apartheid times, being a thoroughly Eurocentric endeavour, harnessed the productive capacity of ontological design to, through representational communication, hide possibilities for thinking outside binary logic while promoting a humanist mode of being as the only valued option.

After the fall of apartheid, design has been consciously put to work in the reconstruction of a socially just citizenry (Slack, 2015, cited in Simanowitz, 2015), but 20 years along the line it has become clear that the nation's good intentions have most often been hijacked by their very own old habits. As Susan Buck-Morss (2008: 3) says, "[t]hat [we] seem [un]able to get beyond the hyphenated present is symptomatic of our times". In this light, Escobar (2012: 26) argues that while the aim of the post-discourses (postmodernism, post-colonialism, post-structuralism, post-apartheid, etc.) has predominantly been to unsettle dualisms, it has perhaps "dissolve[d] too much (structures, identity, foundations, essences, universals, naturalized histories) [and] has [consequently] not been so effective in reconstruction". These discourses have perhaps focused too strongly on affecting change by working with difference as sameness instead of accessing the productive force, or *potentia*,[2] that comes from working with difference in itself (Stagoll, 2010). Deleuze's notion of difference in itself refers to the "particularity or 'singularity' of each individual thing, moment, perception or conception. Such difference is *internal* to a thing or event … [and a product of] the singular, and the unique circumstances of its production" (Stagoll, 2010: 75–76). In contrast, when considering difference as sameness, difference "is understood in terms of resemblance, identity, opposition and analogy, the kinds of relations used to determine groupings of things" (Stagoll, 2010: 75). The old habit of dualistic logic still has a stronghold on South African design practices. In using representation to illustrate and/or embody the intended outcomes of a nation united in diversity, design practice ironically relies on, and hence perpetuates, the very divisions characteristic of apartheid South Africa. These divisions are then, through processes of ontological design, appropriated locally, but in relation to active global forces, and consequently, as stated by Achille Mbembe, "what looks like a negative moment … a moment when new antagonisms emerge while old ones remain unresolved" (2015) is currently experienced in South African society. This has been corroborated by Dina Zoe Belluigi, who states that "[n]ationally, both neo-liberal and social justice discourses have emerged, evidencing a tension between transformation as more responsive to the demands of the global economy, or as sensitive to the diverse social, historical and cultural needs of the country" (2014: 351).

Advanced capitalism has had a tremendous impact on the global socio-political landscape. It has been responsible for developing what Ian Buchanan (2015), *ala* Deleuze and Guattari, refers to as schizo-society. Buchanan (2014, cited in Olivier, 2014) is of the opinion that this is the kind of society in which we currently live – a society characterised by internal contradictions, where "the absurd is simply 'how things are'". He further elaborates by saying that …

> … the central problem today is that the false and the true can sit side by side without raising so much as a single eyebrow. Not because the line of distinction between the false and the true has been irrevocably blurred … but rather because the false and the true are given an equal footing in today's society. We have entered an age that requires us to 'hold two [or more, I would add] opposed ideas in the mind at the same time, and still retain the ability to function'. (Buchanan, 2014, cited in Olivier, 2014, n.p.)

The digital information communication networks within which we function these days play a crucial part in the design of our schizo-society. It allows an immense amount of information to constantly be produced. It also allows this information to circulate at an ever-increasing speed and this results in our attention becoming severely fragmented (Moulier Boutang, 2011). "This extraction of 'attention'", jan jagodzinski (2010: 2) argues, "becomes a productive value for capital in the way it seeks the distributive 'presence' of the (interactive) viewer". Our ability to see how, in the words of Hugh Crawford (2015: 98), "'things' hook onto each other in some form of sympathy" is being dissolved by designer capitalism[3] (jagodzinski, 2010). Images do not function as mere vessels of meaning anymore, but, in its increasing occupation of digital screens, "have changed our perceptions

---

[2] In Latin there are two terms to refer to power. Potestas (or pouvoir in French) refers to "power as restrictive or coercive … [and] focuses on the management of civil society and its institutions", while potentia (puissance in French) refers to "power as empowering and productive … [and focuses] on the transformative experimentation with new arts of existence and ethical relations" (Braidotti, 2011: n.p.).

[3] "Designer capitalism", according to jagodzinski (2010: 21), "trades on the capture of affect through screen media to establish a particular sensorium for its own ends".

of 'reality' through the modulation of speeds and intensities [that] they create in the affective flows of our bodies" (jagodzinski, 2010: 14–15). Jacques Derrida (2002, cited in jagodzinski, 2010: 2) describes the "vanishing gap that exists between the actual construction of the image and its virtual reception through the imperative of 'live' transmissions" in using the terms "artifactuality" and "actuvirtuality". We consequently become unhinged, feeling at the mercy of a world spinning much too quickly for us to have any control and then hastily reach towards technological consumption (that which caused our anxiety in the first place) to ironically ease our anxiety. This is a clear symptom of what can be described as cognitive capitalism (Moulier Boutang, 2011), and is a great force in the ontological design of current realities. In the local context of South Africa, these capitalist forces are most certainly contributing to keeping felt justice always out of reach.

Affirmative design praxis

In order to affect any form of productive change, we have to acknowledge our own position within our situated context (Braidotti, 2016). We have to acknowledge how we have been designed and contribute to ontologically designing the world in multidimensional ways. Such designing involves the complex interplay of global as well as local forces. Globally we are living in the age of the Anthropocene,[4] a geological era that has taken shape because of ontological dualism as a defining feature of dominant global ideology and because "[r]epresentationalism, metaphysical individualism, and humanism work hand in hand, holding this worldview in place", as argued by Karen Barad (2007: 134). In the context of South Africa, this has been manifested in colonialism and later apartheid, both of which have demonstrated that an ontology based on dualistic logic can have disastrous effects because of "the ways in which such divides are treated culturally, particularly the hierarchies established between the pairs of each binary, and the social, ecological, and political consequences of such hierarchies" (Escobar, 2012: 24). Braidotti's argument that we are "bound negatively by shared vulnerability, the guilt of ancestral communal violence, or the melancholia of unpayable ontological debts" (2013: 101) resonates strongly in our local context. Despite having officially made space for differences to exist on an equal level, South Africa is still in the process of dealing with the social and political, material as well as affective consequences of such hierarchies today. This may be explained, in part, because of dualistic logic being so strongly ingrained in our society's conscience on an ontological level. To work towards productive change with the same logic that has bred difference in the past is, as mentioned earlier, counterintuitive. In our current situated context, it has, for example, led to numerous processes intended to affect positive change resulting in re-essentialising and reinvigorating difference (Braidotti, 2013; Thiele, 2014). Critical citizenship education, for example, has run this risk.

---

[4] The Anthropocene refers to the geological epoch where human life is having significant impacts on the earth in a geological sense (Chakrabarty, 2009). Heather Davis and Etienne Turpin (2015: 7) extend the description of the Anthropocene by arguing that "the devastation that characterizes the Anthropocene is not simply the result of activities undertaken by the species Homo sapiens; instead, these effects derive from a particular nexus of epistemic, technological, social and political economic coalescences figured in the contemporary reality of petrocapitalism. This petrocapitalism represents the heightened hierarchical relations of humans, the continued violence of white supremacy, colonialism, patriarchy, heterosexism and ableism, all of which exacerbate and subtend the violence that has been inflicted upon the non-human world".

Whereas citizenship education "contributes to the promotion of social justice, social reconstruction and democracy" (Johnson & Morris, 2010: 78), the addition of the term 'critical' brings ideas related to "critical thinking" and "critical pedagogy" to bear on the concept (Johnson & Morris, 2010: 80). Critical citizenship education is therefore strongly built on the foundation of Paolo Freire's anti-colonial approach to education, and according to Michel Serres (1998, cited in Dolphijn & Van der Tuin, 2012: 98), "[a]n idea opposed to another idea is always the same idea, albeit affected by the negative sign. The more you oppose one another, the more you remain in the same framework of thought". It can therefore be argued that critical citizenship education in post-apartheid South Africa, in seeking emancipation from a position of inequality, can affirm the dependence of those to be emancipated on the emancipators (i.e. the teachers), so ironically keeping inequality in place (Lewis, 2013). Situated within the context of global capitalism, such perpetuation of inequality through critical citizenship education can be further strengthened in that …

> … learning becomes part of the cycles of exchange and commodification – a constant mode of adaptability to the needs of markets. Learning ceases to be an act of potential interruption, disruption, and dissensus and instead becomes a mechanism of integration or exclusion from the marketization of the life world. (Lewis, 2013: 62)

In light of the above, a relevant philosophical foundation for considering design and its education in the South African context where a great need for transformation and justice exists could be Spinozist monism and relational ontology.

> The Spinozist switch to a monistic political ontology stresses processes, vital politics and non-deterministic evolutionary theories. Politically, the emphasis falls accordingly on the micro-politics of relations, as a posthumanist ethics that traces transversal connections among material and symbolic, concrete and discursive, lines or forces. The focus is on the force and autonomy of affect and the logistics of its actualization. (Braidotti, 2013: 95)

From this perspective, there can be no such thing as a Designer or Educator, nor a field of Design or Education (note the capitalisation), as this would presume an all-powerful ability of humans to direct life as we know it. Monism rather assumes that all matter, human and non-human, animate and inanimate, exists on the same level and in flat, mutual interdependence. Disciplinary boundaries necessarily need to become fluid and Designers and Educators need to constantly engage in conscious processes of disidentification in order to start seeing their role in the world in a more relational light (Braidotti, 2011, 2013). Instead of Design and Education acting as mediators between reality and our understanding thereof, design and education (note the lack of capitalisation this time), rather, should actively be concerned with forging connections between all aspects of and in life (Barad, 2003). Design and education need to challenge the representational nature of its practice and become performative. As stated by Barad (2007: 49):

> Performative approaches call into question representationalism's claim that there are representations, on the one hand, and ontologically separate entities awaiting representation, on the other, and focus inquiry on the practices or performances of representing, as well as the productive effects of those practices and the conditions for their efficacy.

Performative design and education hence cannot merely respond to the world through processes of reflection, thereby simply perpetuating what already is, but "[l]ike the diffraction patterns illuminating the indefinite nature of boundaries – displaying shadows in 'light' regions and bright spots in 'dark' regions" (Barad, 2007: 135) – should articulate both poles of ontological dualisms as inherently part of one another. This renders design and its education as innately ethical as, in constantly embodying the process of becoming through the strategic relations it forges with others, it remains accountable for how the boundaries between previous ontological dualisms such as nature/culture, self/other and body/mind are dynamically moulded (Barad, 2007). This implies that "[e]pistemology, ontology, and ethics [become] inseparable. Matters of fact, matters of concern, and matters of care are shot through with one another" (Barad, 2012, cited in Dolphijn & Van der Tuin, 2012: 69).

The notions of knowing and being are so rendered as inherently entwined and both, in their mutual entanglement, are material in nature. It is only through our active doing within the world that we can come to know (Barad, 2007). In the South African context, this would imply that design and its education cannot be considered as media that humans can put to service in working towards social justice, as is often the case in critical citizenship education for designers. A monistic grounding to design education, a performative, material-discursive understanding, would suggest that design and its education, in being "think-practiced" (Thiele, 2014: 202), are inherently just activities. As Kathrin Thiele argues (2014: 202),

> ... it matters deeply to all political agendas how we theorize – and this is how we imagine in the deepest sense – 'differences', 'otherness' or 'the commons'. Thinking is an active force with-in-of this world, and in view of the above quest my argument wants to stress that I see the urge to think-practice this world differently.

In this light, it is important to note that theorising design and its education is done from the perspective of humans, and even though the theoretical ideas held might be inherently post-anthropocentric, a human vantage point cannot be denied. Critical posthumanism, therefore – as embodying accountability "for the role we play in the differential constitution and differential positioning of the human among other creatures (both living and non-living)" (Barad, 2007: 136) – can be a suitable overarching theoretical framework for design and its education. Theorised from this perspective, design and its education become activities aimed at enhancing humans' ability to relate (Braidotti, 2016). In order to do this, we as design educators need to position ourselves in such ways that allow assemblages that are conducive to the issues that are being addressed to form without pre-empting or trying to engineer what those assemblages should be and what they should do (Braidotti, 2016). An important part of such positioning, according to Jacques Rancière, would be to assume equality as an initial axiom from which to engage in processes of education.

In his book *The ignorant schoolmaster* (1999), Rancière conceptualises the notion of universal teaching as central to democratic education. These ideas can be useful with regard to design education understood from a posthuman perspective in the context of post-apartheid South Africa. Universal teaching, Rancière (2000, cited in Guénoun, Kavanagh & Lapidus, 2000: 3) holds, can only be initiated in "affirm[ing] equality as an axiom, as an assumption, and not as a goal". Therefore, instead of actively working to teach students how to be good citizens, design educators should aim to design situations where students will not merely be directed to act upon a given context, but will have to actively 'think-practice' and resist their situated socio-political contexts. Gert Biesta (2010: 150) argues, "[i]t is not, therefore, that education needs to make individuals ready for democratic politics; it is rather that through engagement in democratic politics political subjectivity [can be] engendered". The teacher's role, hence, is not to emancipate his/her students, but rather to call students to make themselves visible, to make their voices heard, and to assert their individual presence in the current distribution of the sensible (Rancière, 1999).

Where critical citizenship is committed to act "against injustice and oppression" (Johnson & Morris, 2010: 90), so upholding binary logic, posthuman design and its education aim to act *within* injustice and oppression, so embodying monism. Design educators and students alike should turn their skin inside out and become amoeba-like structures that roll through life slowly, softly and steadily (Latour, 2008), so becoming vulnerable in exposing themselves to be maximally affected by the world around them. Through intimately feeling all the nooks and crannies, all the tiny details of life intensely, we, and hence design and its education, should be able to position ourselves in ways that can facilitate empathic relationality (Braidotti, 2016). Through this kind of relationality, the other can be allowed to become part of us, so enabling the actualisation of the potential we constantly try to dream of in our idealistic visions for the new South Africa, but are never quite able to grasp before it, in fact, becomes. In this sense, Barad (2012, cited in Dolphijn & Van der Tuin, 2012: 69) notes that "differentiating is not about Othering, separating, but on the contrary, about making connections and commitments."

Whereas critical citizenship education relies on processes of "[i]nformed, responsible and ethical action and reflection" (Johnson & Morris, 2010: 90), posthuman design and its education functions diffractively, implying that we will only ever be able to make sense of the world through our intra-action with it. Within Barad's agential realist framework, intra-action differs significantly from interaction. Whereas interaction refers to the relationship between pre-existing, individual agencies, intra-action "signifies the mutual constitution of entangled agencies" (Barad, 2007: 33). The resulting diffraction pattern consequently "maps where the *effects* of differences appear" (Haraway, 1992, cited in Barad, 2007: 72), rather than representing the objects or cause of the interference (or difference) like reflection would. In actively intra-acting with the world, things will therefore not only become intelligible; they will also materialise. Things will come to matter in both senses of the word, as matter and meaning cannot be severed (Barad, 2007).

Whereas critical citizenship education aims towards acquiring the "ability to imagine a better world" (Johnson & Morris, 2010: 90), posthuman design and its education aim to act affirmatively in the present by actively resisting the present. Design education can so be posited as active critique of the world, but a critique that does not imply negation. Critique, in this sense, embodies creativity; it becomes a way of expressing negation as affirmation (Braidotti, 2016). Posthuman design and its education aim to modulate differences in a non-dialectical manner, so positing negation as a mode of connection (Braidotti, 2016). Design education aimed at affecting productive future change can therefore be put forth as the transformation of negative passions into positive ones or, put differently, the practice of affirmative politics.

On a pragmatic level, turning negative passions into positive ones in the context of South African design education would imply accounting for its situated position from the perspective of abundance rather than lack (Braidotti, 2016). We do not lack critical citizenship in South African society, for example, but rather have an abundance of energy in that the nation is hungry for change. What may seem like the re-essentialising of difference along racial and economic lines can, in fact, be "new starting points that bring into play untapped possibilities for bonding, community building and empowerment" (Braidotti, 2013: 54). A posthuman affirmative ethics therefore does not dismiss misfortune in lieu of an unrealistic utopian vision of reality, but rather actively works with the misfortune in critical creative fashion. In this way, I believe, design education can capitalise on the productive energy already immanent in post-apartheid South Africa and so contribute to affecting felt change.

Conclusion

It has been argued that critical citizenship education can often stem from a position of inequality (Rancière, 1999) or difference as sameness (Deleuze, 1994). This origin positions critical citizenship as teleological, dependent on dualistic logic and human-centred. In theoretically exploring design and its education from posthuman perspectives, I have demonstrated how embracing monism and relational ontology can challenge and extend the anthropocentric tendencies within the notion of critical citizenship education. I believe that such an extension can hold great value in terms of working towards the kind of change that the notion of critical citizenship hints at, but often fails to affect in tangible, everyday ways. As design educators, I believe that we should work with the restrictive forces offered by the existing structures within which we function. Through embodying active experimentation with *potestas* within the extended context of neoliberal higher education in South Africa, for example, design can provide us with great possibility to explore what our posthuman bodies are capable of doing (Braidotti, 2013). Instead of asking how to educate *for* citizenship, I believe the central question is how we can harness the productive power of ontological design *within* the context of South Africa through its education.[5] Through "creatively identifying what is possible in what is already immanently given, by experimenting with the virtual potential in every actual state of affairs, and by being oriented towards a future that does not merely attempt to 'solve problems'" (Hroch, 2015: 237), I believe more just relations can be enabled. Therefore, to move forward, design and its education in 'post' South African society ...

> ... [should] not [be] the future in itself but participate in its creation through becoming; it [should] not [be] an event in itself but participate in its generation; it [should] not [be] history itself that is designed, but the becoming past of the present. To be a designer [and educator], then, means to occupy the extraordinary space between the world as it is, the world as it could be, and the world that was. It means always to be ready to leap into the unknown. (Brassett & Marenko, 2015: 22)

---

[5] This is also part of what I am practically looking at in research towards my doctoral degree ("Thinking about, with and through design: A cartography for transformation"; forthcoming, 2018).

References

Barad, K. 2003. Posthumanist performativity: Toward an understanding of how matter comes to matter. *Signs: Journal of Women in Culture and Society,* 28(3), 801–831. https://doi.org/10.1086/345321

Barad, K. 2007. *Meeting the universe halfway: Quantum physics and the entanglement of matter and meaning.* Durham: Duke University Press. https://doi.org/10.1215/9780822388128

Belluigi, D.Z. 2014. The paradox of 'teaching' transformation in fine art studio practice: Assessment in the South African context. *International Journal of Education through Art,* 10(3), 349–362. https://doi.org/10.1386/eta.10.3.349_1

Biesta, G. 2010. A new logic of emancipation: The methodology of Jacques Rancière. *Educational Theory,* 60(1), 39–59. https://doi.org/10.1111/j.1741-5446.2009.00345.x

Bonta, M. & Protevi, J. 2004. *Deleuze and geophilosophy: A guide and glossary.* Edinburgh: Edinburgh University Press.

Braidotti, R. 2011. *Nomadic theory: The portable Rosi Braidotti.* [Kindle version.]

Braidotti, R. 2013. *The posthuman.* Cambridge: Polity Press.

Braidotti, R. 2016. *The posthuman glossary.* Utrecht: Utrecht Summer School, University of Utrecht.

Brassett, J. & Marenko, B. (Eds.). 2015. *Deleuze and design.* Edinburgh: Edinburgh University Press.

Buchanan, I. 2015. Historicizing the 'schizo society'. Keynote address delivered at the Deleuze & Guattari & Africa: Southern Responses Conference, 15–16 July, Cape Town.

Buck-Morss, S. 2008. *Theorizing today: The post-Soviet condition.* Cornell University. Available at http://falcon.arts.cornell.edu/sbm5/Documents/theorizing%20today.pdf [Accessed 22 August 2016].

Chakrabarty, D. 2009. The climate of history: Four theses. *Critical Inquiry,* 35, Winter, 197–222. https://doi.org/10.1086/596640

Crawford, H. 2015. Thinking hot: Risk, prehension and sympathy in design. In: J. Brassett & B. Marenko (Eds.). *Deleuze and design.* Edinburgh: Edinburgh University Press, 84–106.

Davis, H. & Turpin, E. (Eds.). 2015. *Art in the Anthropocene: Encounters among aesthetics, politics, environments and epistemologies.* Available at http://openhumanitiespress.org/books/download/Davis-Turpin_2015_Art-in-the-Anthropocene.pdf [Accessed 18 April 2017]. https://doi.org/10.26530/OAPEN_560010

Deleuze, G. 1994. *Difference and repetition.* London: Athlone Press.

Deleuze, G. & Guattari, F. 1987. *A thousand plateaus.* Minneapolis, MN: University of Minnesota Press.

Dolphijn, R. & Van der Tuin, I. 2012. *New materialism: Interviews & cartographies.* London: Open Humanities Press. https://doi.org/10.3998/ohp.11515701.0001.001

Escobar, A. 2012. *Notes on the ontology of design.* Available at http://sawyerseminar.ucdavis.edu/files/2012/12/ESCOBAR_Notes-on-the-Ontology-of-Design-Parts-I-II-_-III.pdf [Accessed 17 April 2017].

Guénoun, S., Kavanagh, J.H. & Lapidus, L. 2000. Jacques Rancière: Literature, politics, aesthetics: Approaches to democratic disagreement (interview). *SubStance,* 29(2), 3–24. https://doi.org/10.2307/3685772

Hroch, P. 2015. Sustainable design activism: Affirmative politics and fruitful futures. In: J. Brassett & B. Marenko (Eds.). *Deleuze and design*. Edinburgh: Edinburgh University Press, 219–245.

jagodzinski, j. 2010. *Visual art and education in an era of designer capitalism: Deconstructing the oral eye*. New York, NY: Palgrave Macmillan.

Johnson, L. & Morris, P. 2010. Towards a framework for critical citizenship education. *The Curriculum Journal*, 21(1), 77–96. https://doi.org/10.1080/09585170903560444

Kasibe, W. 2015. *Social networking* [Facebook], 17 November. Available at http://www.facebook.com/wandile.kasibe [Accessed 17 November 2015].

Latour, B. 2008. A cautious Prometheus? A few steps toward a philosophy of design (with special attention to Peter Sloterdijk). In: J. Glynne, F. Hackney & V. Minton (Eds.). *Networks of design: Proceedings of the 2008 Annual International Conference of the Design History Society* (UK), 3–6 September, University College Falmouth, Penryn. Florida, CA: Universal Publishers. Available at www.bruno-latour.fr/sites/default/files/112-DESIGN-CORNWALL-GB.pdf [Accessed 6 February 2016].

Lewis, T.E. 2013. Jacques Rancière's aesthetic regime and democratic education. *Journal of Aesthetic Education*, 47(2), Summer, 49–70. https://doi.org/10.5406/jaesteduc.47.2.0049

Mbembe, A. 2015. *Decolonizing knowledge and the question of the archive*. Wits Institute for Social and Economic Research. Available at http://wiser.wits.ac.za/system/files/Achille%20Mbembe%20-%20Decolonizing%20Knowledge%20and%20the%20Question%20of%20the%20Archive.pdf [Accessed 18 April 2017].

Moulier Boutang, Y. 2011. *Cognitive capitalism*. Cambridge: Polity.

Murris, K. 2016. #RhodesMustFall: A posthumanist orientation to decolonising higher education institutions. *South African Journal of Higher Education*, 30(3), 274–294. https://doi.org/10.20853/30-3-653

Olivier, B. 2014. *Capitalism: Why we live in a 'schizo society'*. Thought Leader. Available at http://thoughtleader.co.za/bertolivier/2014/07/18/capitalism-why-we-live-in-a-schizo-society/ [Accessed 17 April 2017].

Parr, A. (Ed.). 2010. *The Deleuze Dictionary*. Revised edition. Edinburgh: Edinburgh University Press.

Price, M. & Ally, R. 2016. *The challenge of decolonisation: UCT's transformation journey*. Available at https://www.uct.ac.za/dailynews/?id=9659#.VwVwFliRp1k.email [Accessed 14 May 2017].

Rancière, J. 1995. *On the shores of politics*. London: Verso.

Rancière, J. 1999. *The ignorant schoolmaster*. Stanford: Stanford University Press.

Shay, S. & Peseta, T. 2016. A socially just curriculum reform agenda. *Teaching in Higher Education*, 21(4), 361–366. https://doi.org/10.1080/13562517.2016.1159057

Simanowitz, S. 2015. Designing the rainbow nation: Contemporary design in South Africa. *The Huffington Post*, 5 December. Available at http://www.huffingtonpost.com/stefan-simanowitz/designing-the-rainbow-nation_b_7260008.html [Accessed 11 April 2017].

Stagoll, C. 2010. Difference. In: A. Parr (Ed.). *The Deleuze dictionary*. Edinburgh: Edinburgh University Press, 74–76.

Thiele, K. 2014. Ethos of diffraction: New paradigms for a (post)humanist ethics. *Parallax*, 20(3), 202–216. https://doi.org/10.1080/13534645.2014.927627

Willis, A.M. 2006. Ontological designing: Laying the ground. *Design Philosophy Papers*, 3, 80–98. https://doi.org/10.2752/144871306X13966268131514

www.ingramcontent.com/pod-product-compliance
Lightning Source LLC
Chambersburg PA
CBHW080133270326
41926CB00021B/4460